# EVANGELIZATION AND RELIGIOUS FREEDOM

## *Ad Gentes, Dignitatis Humanae*

# REDISCOVERING VATICAN II

*Series Editor: Christopher M. Bellitto, PhD*

*Rediscovering Vatican II* is an eight-book series in commemoration of the fortieth anniversary of Vatican II. These books place the council in dialogue with today's church and are not just historical expositions. They answer the question: What do today's Catholics need to know?

This series will appeal to readers who have heard much about Vatican II, but who have never sat down to understand certain aspects of the council. Its main objectives are to educate people as to the origins and developments of Vatican II's key documents as well as to introduce them to the documents' major points; to review how the church (at large and in its many parts) since the council's conclusion has accepted and/or rejected and/or revised the documents' points in practical terms; and to take stock of the council's reforms and paradigm shifts, as well as of the directions that the church appears to be heading.

The completed series will comprise these titles:

# Evangelization and Religious Freedom

## *Ad Gentes, Dignitatis Humanae*

Stephen B. Bevans, SVD
and
Jeffrey Gros, FSC

Paulist Press
New York/Mahwah, NJ

Cover design by Amy King
Book design by Celine M. Allen

Library of Congress Cataloging-in-Publication Data

Bevans, Stephen B., 1944–
    Evangelization and religious freedom : Ad gentes, Dignitatis humanae / Stephen B. Bevans and Jeffrey Gros.
        p.   cm.
    Includes bibliographical references and index.
    ISBN 978-0-8091-4202-6 (alk. paper)
    1. Vatican Council (2nd : 1962–1965). Decretum de activitate missionali ecclesiae. 2. Catholic Church—Missions. 3. Vatican Council (2nd : 1962–1965). Declaratio de libertate religiosa. 4. Freedom of religion. 5. Catholic Church—Doctrines. I. Gros, Jeffrey, 1938– II. Title.
    BX8301962.A45 A572 2008
    266'.2—dc22

                                                                            2008025905

Published by Paulist Press
997 Macarthur Boulevard
Mahwah, New Jersey 07430

www.paulistpress.com

Printed and bound in the
United States of America

# CONTENTS

## SECTION I
### DECREE ON THE CHURCH'S MISSIONARY ACTIVITY
### *Ad Gentes*
### Stephen B. Bevans, SVD

## SECTION II
### DECLARATION ON RELIGIOUS FREEDOM
### *Dignitatis Humanae*
### Jeffrey Gros, FSC

# ACKNOWLEDGMENTS

The church and modern society can be grateful especially for the council fathers and their experts who set the largest member of the Christian family on a new pilgrimage of life and advocacy of a free church in a free society, a dialogue begun and a goal to be achieved. Likewise, Catholics can be grateful that, without sacrificing the treasure of the tradition or the truth claims of the gospel, or without sacrificing its own missionary mandate, a host of educators, canonists, theologians, lay leaders in society, and church ministers have begun the long and gradual process of calling the church and civil societies around the world to the conversion that is entailed in making the natural human right to religious freedom in society a basis for the relationship of human beings around the globe.

We can also be grateful to Paulist Press for the vision of recalling to us the riches of Vatican II in this series, and the promises yet to be realized in its reception. In the laborious and gratifying task of providing this new resource for reviving attention to what may have become two of the more taken for granted texts of the council, the contribution of Father Thomas Stransky, CSP, must be singled out. He wanted this volume to be one unified text on mission and freedom, a vision that was shared by a young expert at the council, our present Pope Benedict XVI: "Thus the idea of mission provides the intrinsic basis for the idea of religious liberty, and this liberty is visibly and intrinsically involved in what is most fundamental in the revealed Christian message."* Tom has dedicated his life to implementing the council's work on religious freedom, mission, ecumenism, and interreligious relations. He has pioneered the dialogues with evangelical Christians and solidified the relations of the Catholic Church with the World Council of Churches. That task has been served by the monumental postconciliar work

---

*Joseph Ratzinger, *Theological Highlights of Vatican II* (New York: Paulist Press, 1966), 145.

on religious freedom and Christian mission, work that these two texts made possible.

Jeffrey Gros would also like to offer a very personal word of gratitude to Tom for years of mentorship in the 1980s and careful attention to the review of parts of this volume. His careful eye, Jeff knows, has not saved it from weaknesses that are the author's burden.

Jeff also would like to express appreciation to the hospitality of the De La Salle Christian Brothers at Bethlehem University and the staff at Tantur Ecumenical Institute. Christopher Bellitto has been a careful and generous editor. He is also appreciative to Father Michael Joyce, CM; Drs. John Borelli, David Gides, and Maura Hagarty; Brothers Enrique Garcia and Daniel Casey, FSC; Thomas Quigley; and Fathers John Keane, SA, and Patrick Granfield, OSB, for providing invaluable resources and suggestions. The assistance of Father John Lynch, CSP, with the Stransky archives at St. Paul's College helped unearth some most interesting surprises. Members of the library staff of Memphis Theological Seminary are to be congratulated for their ingenuity in locating some important sources. Finally, Jeff also offers a word of gratitude to Father John Ford, CSC, for an initial invitation to look at the ecumenical reception of *Dignitatis Humanae*, an opportunity that opened up a very rich research opportunity and ecumenical project over many years.

Stephen Bevans would also like to thank Christopher Bellitto for his superb editing skills and for his patience with the writing process, which took considerably more time than had been anticipated. Steve would also like to thank Jeff Gros for his original invitation to join him in this project and for his encouragement all along the way. Thanks are also due to the library staff at Catholic Theological Union, especially library director Mary Ocasek and director emeritus Ken O'Malley, and to Steve's colleagues Roger Schroeder, Gil Ostiek, Barbara Reid, Claude Marie Barbour, James Okoye, and Carmen Nanko-Fernández. Robert Schreiter has also been a friend and colleague, and Steve wants especially to acknowledge how important his thought has been for this writing. Bill Burrows has been a friend and conversation partner for more than forty-five years, as has John Markey over the last twenty-five, and especially during this past year. In so many ways, Steve's section of this book is the work of these wonderful people as well.

# ABBREVIATIONS

## Documents of Vatican II

| | |
|---|---|
| *AA* | *Apostolicam Actuositatem* (Apostolate of the Laity) |
| *AG* | *Ad Gentes* (Missionary Activity) |
| *CD* | *Christus Dominus* (Bishops) |
| *DH* | *Dignitatis Humanae* (Religious Freedom) |
| *DV* | *Dei Verbum* (Revelation) |
| *GE* | *Gravissimum Educationis* (Christian Education) |
| *GS* | *Gaudium et Spes* (The Church in the World of Today) |
| *IM* | *Inter Mirifica* (Means of Social Communication/Mass Media) |
| *LG* | *Lumen Gentium* (The Church) |
| *NA* | *Nostra Aetate* (Non-Christian Religions) |
| *OE* | *Orientalium Ecclesiarum* (Eastern Catholic Churches) |
| *OT* | *Optatam Totius* (Priestly Formation) |
| *PC* | *Perfectae Caritatis* (Religious Life) |
| *PO* | *Presbyterorum Ordinis* (Ministry and Life of Priests) |
| *SC* | *Sacrosanctum Concilium* (Liturgy) |
| *UR* | *Unitatis Redintegratio* (Ecumenism) |

## Other Abbreviations

| | |
|---|---|
| *AAS* | *Acta Apostolicae Sedis* |
| ADA | Antepreparatory Documents |

| | |
|---|---|
| AS | *Acta Synodalia S. Concilii Oecumenici Vaticani II* |
| ASS | *Acta Sanctae Sedis* |
| CC | *Cum in Constitutione* |
| CIC | *Codex Iuris Canonici* (Code of Canon Law) |
| CPC | Central Preparatory Commission |
| DI | *Dominus Iesus* |
| DP | *Dialogue and Proclamation* |
| EiA | *Ecclesia in Asia* |
| EiAf | *Ecclesia in Africa* |
| EN | *Evangelii Nuntiandi* |
| ES | *Ecclesiae Sanctae* |
| IM | *Inter Mirifica* |
| PB | *Pastor Bonus* |
| PCPCU | Pontifical Council for Promoting Christian Unity (SPCU until 1989) |
| PP | *Populorum Progressio* |
| PT | *Pacem in Terris* |
| RM | *Redemptoris Missio* |
| REU | *Regimini Ecclesiae Universae* |
| RSQ | *Responses to Some Questions Regarding Certain Aspects of the Doctrine of the Church* |
| RT | *Relationes in Territoriis* |
| SPCU | Secretariat for Promoting Christian Unity (PCPCU since 1989) |
| UN | United Nations |
| WCC | World Council of Churches |
| WEA | World Evangelical Alliance (Fellowship until 2001) |

# Section I
## Decree on the Church's Missionary Activity

# *Ad Gentes*

Stephen B. Bevans, SVD

PART I

# THE DOCUMENT

### INTRODUCTION: THE DOCUMENT IN CONTEXT

Scholars of the Second Vatican Council point out that it is not enough simply to consult any of its texts that deal directly with a specific theme—e.g., church, revelation, liturgy—in order to understand how that theme was developed by the council. Rather, they say, one needs to see how an individual theme is expressed throughout all the sixteen council documents.[1] This is *particularly* true in terms of the theme in this first section of this book—"evangelization" or "mission"—because in many ways it is a theme that is at the heart of what the council was about. Vatican II was a missionary council. Its central theme was the mystery of the church, both in its interior reality (as sacramental sign) and in its activity in the midst of the world (as instrument of salvation [see *LG*, 1]). It was not a council that had as its main purpose the clarification of a doctrine that had come under debate or the condemnation of a dangerous heresy. Rather, John XXIII's reason for calling the council was to help the church preserve and teach Christian doctrine in a more effective way.[2] Mission is what gave the council its basic direction.[3]

In order to understand the council's decree on missionary activity properly, then, we need to situate it in the context of some of the council's most important documents, and in the context of the style of those documents as well. In the first place, the 1985 Synod of Bishops laid down the principle that interpretation of the council can best be done through its four "constitutions."[4] Each one of these—on the church (*Lumen Gentium*), on the church in the modern world (*Gaudium et Spes*), on the liturgy (*Sacrosanctum Concilium*), and on revelation (*Dei Verbum*)—has dimensions that illumine the nature of the church's evangelizing mission, and it is to these dimensions that the mission decree

3

intentionally aligned itself. Second, documents such as those on other religions (*Nostra Aetate*), and on religious freedom (*Dignitatis Humanae*) are extremely relevant for understanding the scope of the church's task of evangelization, since the council realized that mission today needs to be done in dialogue with the world's religions and with respect for people's freedom of conscience and freedom of choice. Third, in terms of style, the *tone* of the council's documents is meant not so much to *decree* as to *persuade*. The purpose of the sixteen documents, in other words, was an evangelical one.

## The Four Constitutions

The very first paragraph of the Dogmatic Constitution on the Church, *Lumen Gentium*, speaks of the church's mission: "Christ is the light of all nations," and the church gathered in council wishes to shed that light on the world by "proclaiming the Gospel to every creature." The paragraph continues on to speak of the church as a kind of "sacrament" —both a sign and an instrument of the fullness of salvation. Later in the decree, in paragraph 48, the church is called the "universal sacrament of salvation," a phrase that also appears in the very first line of *Ad Gentes*. Paragraphs 2 through 5 then root the reality of the church in the life and saving action of the Trinitarian God, and it is in this way that the church "receives the mission to proclaim and to spread among all peoples the Kingdom of Christ and of God and to be, on earth, the initial budding forth of that kingdom" (*LG*, 5).

Joseph Ratzinger asserts that in *Lumen Gentium* 13 to 17 "one finds the central text of the council on the nature, the task and the way of mission."[5] The evangelizing mission of the church is clearly stated in paragraphs 13 and 17, and other important missionary themes are expressed as well: the goodness of all peoples' customs and cultures that the church can adopt and purify (*LG*, 13 and 17), the importance of ecumenical activity (*LG*, 15), and the possibility of salvation beyond the boundaries of explicit faith in Christ and incorporation into the Catholic Church (*LG*, 16).

We meet a missionary consciousness also in the rediscovered notion of episcopal collegiality, by which individual bishops are charged not only with the care of their own dioceses but also with that of the universal church (*LG*, 23). Such a perspective is echoed in the council's decree that deals specifically with the bishop's pastoral office (*CD*, 6), and provides the theological foundation for one of the most important parts of the decree on missions: its call for a reform of the Congregation for the Propagation of the Faith (*AG*, 29). Finally, the renewed understanding of laity points to the fact that *every* member of the church is called to share in its mission by virtue of baptism—there are no passive Christians because the church *as such* is a communion-in-mission (see *LG*, 31). This finds an echo in the document on the laity, where we read that "the Christian vocation by its very nature is also a vocation to the apostolate" (*AA*, 2), and in *Ad Gentes* 35, where we read that "the work of evangelization is a basic duty of the People of God." However, as we shall see in the course of this section, *Ad Gentes* is not always consistent in this regard.

The council's Pastoral Constitution on the Church in the Modern World serves as a complement to its Dogmatic Constitution on the Church, and explores in more sociological and contemporary ways how Christ, through the church, is indeed the "light to the nations."[6] Its famous first lines—that the joys and hopes, the griefs and anxieties of all peoples, especially the poor, are the same as those of the followers of Christ (*GS*, 1)—sketch in a few broad strokes what the church is supposed to be in the world. One could also say that the constitution lays out concretely what is meant by the phrase, "the pilgrim church is missionary by its very nature" (*AG*, 2—my translation). Christians are a people "led by the Holy Spirit in their journey to the Kingdom of their Father" (*GS*, 1), who interpret the "signs of the times" (*GS*, 4), who are at the service of individuals and humanity and sense God's presence in their world (*GS*, 40–44), who appreciate the wealth found in the world's cultures (*GS*, 53–62), and who are committed to justice and peace (*GS*, chapters 3, 4, and 5).

The other two constitutions of the council—on the liturgy and on revelation—are also marked by a missionary spirit. The first paragraph of *Sacrosanctum Concilium*, for example, speaks of the renewal of the liturgy in the wider context of the council's goal to "strengthen whatever can help to call all humanity into the household of the Church." Paragraphs 37–40 made particularly significant contributions to the development of liturgies that show respect for what *Ad Gentes* calls the "treasures" that "a bountiful God has distributed among the nations of the earth" (*AG*, 11). Johannes Schütte, the superior general of the Society of the Divine Word (SVD), who was largely responsible for the passage of *Ad Gentes* at the council, points out how intensely the bishops from the so-called missionary countries were involved in the development of the Constitution on the Liturgy.[7] And surely the renewal of the liturgy at the council owes much to the urgent needs of local liturgical expression in non-Western contexts.

*Dei Verbum* begins with the words of the first letter of John: "We announce to you the eternal life which was with the Father, and has appeared to us. What we have seen and heard we announce to you, in order that you may have fellowship with us, and that our fellowship may be with the Father, and with his son Jesus Christ (1 John 1:2–3)." God's revelation to humanity is then described in strongly missionary language: in the act of revelation God speaks to women and men "as friends...and lives among them" so that God might invite and take them into communion with Godself (see *DV*, 2). Revelation is ultimately not about the impartation of information; it is the utterance of a Word that is itself "missionary by its very nature" (see *AG*, 2—my translation).

## Other Council Documents

We might point out briefly other elements by which the specific document on mission is clearly influenced. These elements can be found in the Decree on Religious Freedom and the Decree on Non-Christian Religions.

*Dignitatis Humanae* provides an essential perspective to the church's missionary activity in that the conviction of human dignity and the freedom of individual conscience (*DH*, 1) is itself the condition of the possibility for an evangelization worthy of God. There are two aspects to consider here. On the one hand, the commitment to religious liberty challenges nations and peoples who oppose any exercise of mission or possibilities of conversion to acknowledge the freedom of individuals to change their religious allegiance or affiliation. On the other, the conviction of an individual's freedom leads necessarily to a refusal of any proselytism—of attempts to bring about conversion by threat or unworthy means of manipulating a person's decisions. Mission, as Pope

John Paul II would put it a quarter of a century after the publication of *Ad Gentes*, only issues an invitation, it *imposes* nothing (*RM*, 39).

This attitude of respect for the conscience and worldview of others is also central to the council's document on non-Christian religions. The document acknowledges both that within the religions of the world there is reflected "a ray of that Truth which enlightens all women and men" (*NA*, 2—my translation), and that, nevertheless, the church must continue to proclaim Jesus Christ as "the way, the truth and the life" (*NA*, 2, referring to John 14:6). Even though, in other words, the obligation of evangelization still exists, the council emphasizes that there are many things in other religions that find a resonance in Christianity. Because of this it urges "dialogue and collaboration with the followers of other religions," so that all that is good in these religions can be preserved and promoted (*NA*, 2). As Ratzinger puts it succinctly, "it would seem that mission does not exclude dialogue, but actually includes it."[8]

## An Inviting Tone

In an article in the March 2006 issue of *Theological Studies*,[9] eminent church historian John W. O'Malley suggests that besides the fact that many of the documents of Vatican II offered quite a different perspective in terms of *content*—e.g., a new approach to ecumenism, a new encouragement for Catholics to read and study the Bible, a new attitude toward religious freedom—the documents also offered a new *form*, or style, by employing a new and more pastoral literary genre. Up until Vatican II, O'Malley points out, the genre of council documents came much more from the legal and juridical traditions of the Roman Empire, and the implicit model of a council was the Roman Senate. This was a literary style studded with "power-words," words "of threat and intimidation, words of surveillance and punishment, words of a superior speaking to inferiors, or, just as often, to an enemy."[10] We see this style reflected in the drafts of the documents that were presented to the bishops at the first session of the council, and this style was reflected as well in the first draft of the document on the church's missionary activity. What happened in the first session of the council, however, was an across-the-board rejection of documents that were written in a style that was so triumphal, clerical, and juridical, as Bishop Emil de Smedt famously described the first draft of the schema on the church.[11] The new genre was one that was more pastoral, more positive, and more persuasive in tone. It had its roots not in the legal language of the Roman republic but in the language of the Greek and Roman rhetoric that was employed by the early theologians (the so-called "fathers") of the church. O'Malley speaks of this genre as "epideictic": "the epideictic genre is a form of the art of persuasion and thus of reconciliation. While it raises appreciation, it creates or fosters among those it addresses a realization that they all share (or should share) the same ideals and that they need to work together to achieve them."[12]

The use of this new genre is crucial for understanding how the council approached the church's task of evangelization. There is a departure from approaches to mission in the past, not only often in terms of the *content* of what the council said—namely, that the church is missionary by its very nature, that it is rooted in Trinitarian life, that it calls every Christian to gospel witness, that it respects the freedom and religious conviction of those it evangelizes, that it values local cultures and customs—but, just as significantly, in the *very tone* of the documents, which is pastoral and missionary. They are not so much decrees from on high—in this sense the generic word "decree" for the council documents is somewhat ironic—as they are documents of appeal, of persuasion, meant to attract readers, not to intimidate them with the weight of authority. In many ways the turn to this new style of presentation represents the story of the composition of the documents themselves, and certainly represents the stages of composition of *Ad Gentes*. The document on mission started out as a document with a curial, juridical spirit, a spirit that persisted when it was reduced at the council's third session to a set of mere propositions. In the end, however, the Decree on the Church's Missionary Activity is marked by the pastoral and dialogical spirit with which all mission needs to be done, and in which the council's theology of mission needs to be seen. *Ad Gentes* is not written completely in this spirit, but it is the spirit in which the document is most fully understood.[13]

It is to the story of the difficult journey of the development of the mission document, a journey "strewn with ambushes,"[14] that we now turn.

## THE DEVELOPMENT OF THE DOCUMENT

Missions and missionaries, of course, have always accompanied the church throughout its two-thousand-year history. In fact, many scholars would argue today that not only has the church always engaged in missionary activity but that such activity has actually *made* or *constituted* the church. This is what *Ad Gentes* means when it says in its second paragraph that the church is missionary by its very nature. Indeed, mission *precedes* the church, since to be church means to participate in the mission of the triune God (see *AG*, 2).

*Jesus* was a missionary, and—once they were endowed with the Holy Spirit—his disciples continued his mission of preaching and witnessing to the reign of God. Paul writes in Romans 16 of various women and men—Prisca and Aquila, for example, or Andronicus and Junia, Mary, and Urbanus—who worked with him. Syrian Christians soon moved east to Persia and India, and eventually even to China in the seventh century. Irish monks wandered through Europe preaching the gospel and founding monasteries. Franciscan women and men went guilelessly among Muslims in the thirteenth century. Jesuits protected indigenous peoples in Paraguay and evangelized in the Chinese emperor's court. Thousands of missionaries—male and female—set up schools and hospitals in European and U.S. colonies in the nineteenth and early twentieth centuries.

Because of such a long history of missionary commitment, therefore, it may come as a surprise to some that *Ad Gentes* represents the first time in history that an ecumenical council issued a particular document dedicated to the church's missionary activity.[15] Perhaps even more surprising, though, is the fact that, despite centuries of the *practice* of mission, the development of this document at the council had an "uncommonly turbulent history."[16] What had started out as a rather practical, rather juridical document for the "missions"—"a routine task in which the issue was a few organizational improvements,"[17] was at one point almost marginalized by being reduced to a number of mere propositions as pressures mounted to end the council with the third session. There were, on the one hand, practically irreconcilable tensions among members of the commission working on the document, both before and during the council. One group, mostly canonists, was in favor only of an approach to mission that basically preserved the traditional territorial understanding of "missions." The other, of a more theological bent, argued for a more inclusive understanding of mission as being rooted in God's overflowing, triune nature. The first group was also in favor of maintaining the status quo of the Congregation for the Propagation of the Faith (Propaganda Fide); the second group pushed strongly for the congregation's reform. And, if this internal tension did not make things turbulent enough, the document was beset by obstacles ("ambushes") outside the commission as well. A first draft had been reduced from seven to two chapters, but didn't even make it to the council floor. A second draft was not approved by the Coordinating Commission, and revision of this draft reduced it to a number of propositions that ended up being rejected by the bishops in debate in the *aula* (council hall). Only at the fourth session did a genuine schema on the missions finally come before the council fathers. But it had to travel a long way to get there.[18]

## Antepreparatory Phase: May 1959 to April 1960
### *A Few Canonical Adjustments*

On January 25, 1959, much to the surprise—and chagrin—of many, Pope John XXIII announced that an ecumenical council would be held. Subsequently, on Pentecost Sunday, May 17 of that year, the pope announced the formation of an Antepreparatory Commission that was to receive suggestions for the agenda of the council from the church's bishops, abbots, and superiors general, and from the faculties of Catholic universities and pontifical colleges. In addition, each curial congregation was to set up study groups to review relevant suggestions and to submit their own suggestions to the commission as well. In November 1959 such a study group was set up at the Congregation for the Propagation of the Faith. Group members met in February 1960 to discuss responses from the leaders of the church that the president of the Antepreparatory Commission, Cardinal Domenico Tardini, had forwarded to the group. What the group members sent back to the commission was a text containing twenty-three propositions, all of which were "very practical and juridical,"[19] that treated areas in ecclesial discipline concerning mission territories. All but one of the propositions—

"which urged that no new dogmas be proclaimed by the council"—
dealt with legal questions.[20]

## Preparatory Phase: May 1960 to September 1962
### *From Seven Chapters to Two*

A practical and juridical approach to the schema on mission was
something that marked it through its rather tortuous development,
and it was an approach that was abandoned (at least partially) only at
the very end of the process, during the interval between the third and
fourth sessions of the council, in early 1965.

To a large extent, the non-theological perspective of the draft was
due to the makeup of the Preparatory Commission for the schema on
missionary activity. In June 1960 it was announced that Cardinal
Gregory Peter Agagianian, prefect of the Congregation for the Propagation of the Faith, would serve as president of the commission.
Archbishop D. Mathew, a former Vatican diplomat to East Africa (in
what is now Kenya), was appointed secretary, although the actual work
would mainly be done by Saverio Paventi, an official at the Propaganda
and professor of mission law at the Pontificia Academia Ecclesiastica,[21]
the school in which Vatican diplomats were trained. Although the commission was composed of members from all over the world, forty-one
of its fifty-four members were from Europe; half resided in Rome and
either were members of missionary congregations or taught at one of
the several Roman universities. Almost one-third were members of the
Propaganda Fide.[22]

There were some fine theologians and missiologists on the
commission—people such as Suso Brechter, Thomas Ohm, Domenico
Grasso, and André Seumois—but the majority, it seemed, were mostly
experts in canon law and did not approach the issue of mission from a
theological perspective. Seumois would complain about the commission's overly canonical orientation in a letter to Cardinal Agagianian on
December 19, 1962, when the commission's original schema needed to
undergo revision at the end of the council's first session. Certainly not
the most liberal thinker himself, Seumois complained that the canonists
on the commission were "stuck...in the old canonical schema that the
council could not accept and unable to conceive a new authentically

missionary schema that would really and frankly address the major missionary problems that face the church today...."[23]

The first meeting of the commission took place on October 24, 1960. Five subcommissions were set up to address the five areas the schema on the missions was envisioned to comprise: (1) administration of the sacraments and liturgy, (2) organization of the missions and reform of the Code of Canon Law, (3) the life of the clergy and of the Christian people, (4) reform of the training of clergy and religious, and (5) support for the missions by the faithful.[24] The members of the subcommissions who resided in Rome met regularly, and all the secretaries met together eight times in the period between October 1960 and April 1961. The subcommission that dealt with liturgical questions met several times with the Preparatory Commission on the Liturgy, since some of the issues that the Preparatory Commission on the Missions was discussing regarding the liturgy would have to be harmonized with questions under discussion in preparation for the schema on the liturgy.

In April 1961, the entire Preparatory Commission working on the mission document came to Rome for a week's plenary session. Brechter (who was there) writes that the various issues "were candidly and thoroughly discussed,"[25] and while a number of questions could be resolved and disposed of, a good number had to be sent back to the smaller subcommissions for further discussion. The second plenary session, held from November 20 to 30, 1961, approved all of the subcommissions' work, which formed a schema of seven chapters for the consideration of the Central Preparatory Commission (CPC). The chapters were as follows:

1. The Governance of the Missions

2. The Formation of the Clergy

3. Religious

4. The Sacraments and the Sacred Liturgy

5. The Formation of the Christian People

6. Seminary Studies

7. Missionary Cooperation

The schema, unfortunately but not surprisingly given the makeup of the Preparatory Commission working on it, was strongly juridical in tone, and took into little account the suggestions sent to the Antepreparatory Commission by bishops from Asia and Africa— suggestions that had amounted to 1,242 printed pages![26] Like other schemas at this stage of preparation for the council, the proposed document on mission was a product of Roman curial thinking.

What was not immediately approved by the second plenary was a *proemium*, or preface. It was hotly debated and a special commission was set up to redraft it. In its final version, it sketched a brief history of missionary work, describing it as "wholly spiritual and not political or temporal work," and quickly pointing out "hopeful and difficult aspects facing it."[27] The preface contained no real theological content. There was, for example, no reference to the "lively and interesting"[28] debate about the nature of mission that had taken place throughout the first half of the twentieth century as to whether the purpose of mission was primarily the salvation of souls or the implantation of the church. The commission, says Komonchak, seems to have considered such theological issues as having already been resolved, and Cardinal Agagianian even remarked at a session of the CPC that "the work of evangelization posed no special doctrinal problems since recent Popes had clarified the basis and purposes of missionary work."[29] There was also no reference in the schema as to whether "mission" referred only to "non-Christian" territories or to "de-Christianized" areas as well. This latter idea had been proposed, with much controversy, in a small book published in 1943 entitled *France: A Mission Country?*[30] The idea that would become so prominent in the final version of the schema on mission—that the church's various missionary efforts are rooted in the mission of the triune God as such—was completely absent.

Because so much of the content of the proposed schema (e.g., liturgical matters, questions about religious, seminary education) was included in the agenda of other preparatory commissions, the editorial subcommission of the CPC decided that other schemata might deal with such overlapping material. In this way, it suggested, missionary issues could be addressed across the board, and not just confined to a particular schema. What was left, then, of the seven chapters that the Preparatory Commission on the Missions had proposed were only two: the first on governance of the missions and the seventh on missionary cooperation. The latter, the CPC directed, was to include material from the proposed schema on the apostolate of the laity.

For many, this move to include missionary issues in other schemata was seen as a real gain, especially when many of the liturgical issues were designated for inclusion in the document on the liturgy. These and many other truly urgent questions would thus be brought "from the periphery as it were into the centre of the Church's life."[31] There were, in fact, a number of theologically astute bishops who seriously considered the possibility of having no document on missionary activity at all, thinking that the church's missionary commitment could be better served by having a missionary theology woven throughout the document on the church. In any case, the CPC decided otherwise, and what was submitted to the council for its deliberation was a schema that consisted of only a preface that was somewhat out of touch with contemporary theological and political trends, and two chapters that were largely juridical and practical in nature.

### First Session and Intersession: October 1962 to September 1963
*An Undiscussed Schema*

The schema on missionary activity, however, was not discussed in the council hall during the first session of the council, and it soon became clear that, had it been, it would have been rejected outright. This was because other curia-dominated schemata, such as those on the church, on Mary, and on revelation, had come under a barrage of criticism from a number of bishops. Many of these were missionary bishops, who made up nearly one-third of the council members and whose voices were heard in this first session much more than in subsequent ones.[32] The juridical spirit in which these first schemata were written (excluding, of course, that on the liturgy) provoked strong attacks against both the curia in general and the Propaganda Fide (the Roman congregation immediately in charge of the church's missionary activity) in particular. Against the latter, Saverio Paventi reports, some francophile African bishops actually circulated a proposition that the Propaganda should be deprived of power and reduced to a fund-raising body.[33] In fact, the reform of the Propaganda would become a major issue in the eventual schema on missionary activity. The missionary bishops demanded and eventually received a "deliberative vote" in the congregation's decisions. Nevertheless, the first session of the council ended with the rejection of three out of the four schemata discussed, and so it was evident that any document on mission would need to be reformulated and rethought during the months before the council resumed for its second session the following September.

At the outset of the council, the work of the Preparatory Commission on the Missions was complete and that commission was disbanded. An official conciliar commission was then appointed, this time much more representative of the worldwide episcopacy. On the newly established commission were, for example, bishops from China, Tanzania, Vietnam, Ivory Coast, the Philippines, and Guatemala. Also on the commission was Bishop Fulton J. Sheen, the famous radio and television personality, who served as the director of the Society of the Propagation of the Faith in the United States. The commission did not meet at all during the council's first session—a sign perhaps of the inadequacy of the schema that the Preparatory Commission had submitted.

Immediately after the close of the first session, however, the commission's vice president, Bishop V. Sartre, and the secretary, Saverio Paventi, met together with a number of the commission's theological consultors (*periti*) to draft a new schema. The group met some seven times through January and February 1963, but no agreement was reached on a new draft. Once more, as André Seumois's letter to Cardinal Agagianian in December 1962 attests, there was bitter disagreement between the canon lawyers and the theologians.[34] When the entire commission was called together in late March, the ensuing discussions over nine days were "unprofitable and uninspiring," and "opinions and standpoints were so divergent that the . . . Commission never in any phase of its existence formed a unity or became an effective working team."[35] No doubt the issue in contention was whether the schema should have a more theological orientation or should remain the more canonical document that had been presented previously. In the end, a schema entitled *De Missionibus* (On the Missions) was prepared. Written by an editorial commission, and probably not fully acceptable to anyone, it consisted of a preface and two parts (basically the contents of the two chapters of the earlier draft), with three chapters in each part.

This text was submitted to the council's Coordinating Commission in June 1963, but it was sent back to the Commission on Mission with very unfavorable comments. In the judgment of Coordinating Commission members Cardinals Liénart, Döpfner, and Suenens, the document was not yet ready for full discussion on the council floor, and so the Commission on Mission had to work on revisions of the schema during the second session of the council, with the hope that the document would come up for debate in the third session.

## Second Session and Intersession: October 1963 to September 1964
### *A Set of Propositions*

The work of revision was carried out in ten stormy sessions between October 23 and December 3, 1963. It became clear that the previous schema needed to be totally revamped, but what the revision should look like was in contention on every side, with "unbridged and un-bridgeable differences."[36] The result of these ten difficult meetings, a schema approved on December 3, consisted of four chapters in twenty-three pages dealing with

1. Doctrinal Principles

2. General Reasons for the Church's Missionary Apostolate

3. Missionary Formation

4. Missionary Cooperation[37]

Unfortunately, however, this "hard-won draft"[38] was not to reach the council floor. It had been approved at last by the Coordinating Commission and sent out to the world's bishops for their comments. But in April 1964 it was announced that, in the interests of time, all schemata not yet discussed in the council hall were to be reduced to a few proposals to be put to a vote without discussion. It seems that those directing the council were getting impatient for its closing and were attempting to make sure that the upcoming third session would be the last. So, once more, the schema encountered an obstacle or "ambush" on its way toward approval.

The Commission on Mission then began the task of compressing their work into a set of relatively short topics and statements. This they did in May 1964, at which time they also changed the title of their draft to "On Missionary Activity," both because the former title—"On the Missions"—now seemed a bit pretentious, and also because a number of bishops had observed that the council had been speaking of the mission of the church in a wider sense. "Missionary Activity" was a single aspect of that one mission. The resulting document, consisting of six printed pages, contained a preface and thirteen (eventually fourteen) short propositions.[39] Compared to the previous, longer schema, it "was even more feeble from the standpoint of theology and as a reading of the historical moment: decolonization, the globalizing of problems, and poverty remained outside its scope, as did the ecclesiological criteria recognized in the schema on the Church."[40]

Of particular note, however, was proposition 4, which proposed creating within the Congregation for the Propagation of the Faith a "Central Council for Evangelization." The congregation had been established in 1622 by Pope Gregory XV. One of its chief aims was to assert the rights of the church over against the more nationalistic interests of Spain and Portugal, and it was for centuries the final ecclesiastical authority in mission countries—that is, where the church had not been formally established with a hierarchy. That situation had changed over the years. The congregation had been reformed in 1909 and was certainly due for reform now with the establishment of hierarchies in many mission churches.[41] This changed situation was reflected in the lively debate in the first session, during which some parties even proposed the congregation's suppression. Proposition 4 in this abbreviated document reflects a solution that would keep the congregation in existence, but at the same time give missionary bishops a greater role in the governance of their particular churches. This idea, at least in its germ, would eventually be retained in the council's final mission document.

During the council's second session the Commission on Mission had been expanded to include more African, Asian, and North American participation.[42] The new member who would make the most difference, however, was German: Fr. Johannes Schütte, superior general of the Society of the Divine Word. In the intersession between the third and fourth sessions of the council, a more adequate schema would be developed under his leadership—and as a result of both a virtual rejection of the schema of propositions and the insistence by many on the council floor that the church's missionary activity deserved more ample treatment. But at this point there was still a long way to travel on the "difficult path" that lay ahead.

## Third Session: October to December 1964
### *The Council Wants More*

On November 5, 1964, it was announced that the presentation and discussion of the schema on the church's missionary activity would begin the next day (the decision that the schemata reduced to propositions would simply be voted on without discussion had been modified to allow for limited discussion).[43] It was also announced, to applause by the assembly, that Pope Paul VI would attend the session and address the assembly before discussion on the mission schema began.

That the pope had chosen to attend a working session of the council was quite extraordinary. This was to be not only the first—and, as it turned out, the only—working session that either he or John XXIII attended; it was the first working session of an ecumenical council that a pope had attended since the Middle Ages.[44] Why the pope chose this particular session to make an appearance is open to some speculation. He himself said in his short address that it was because of the importance of the theme to be discussed. He had recently indicated his interest in the missions by canonizing the Ugandan martyrs just a few weeks earlier (on October 18), and had announced in his sermon on that occasion his intention to travel to India to attend the national Eucharistic Congress. The distinguished historian Norman Tanner wonders, however, why, by his presence, the pope showed his support for a schema that was finding very little support among the assembly, and probably had no real hope of being accepted by the council.[45] It is possible that the pope was showing his support for Agagianian, whose congregation was coming under so much vitriolic criticism and who was very much in favor of the schema and thought it would be passed with little difficulty. It is also possible that the pope's presence was a subtle way of asserting his authority and control over the council. He may have felt that being present for what was supposed to be a short discussion on the mission schema would be less "dangerous" than being present for a full-fledged conciliar debate.[46] The pope himself highly recommended the schema, and while he acknowledged the possibility of improvement, he seemed confident of the schema's passage. This is why what happened subsequently must have caused him some embarrassment—the pope was "extremely mortified by the rejection of the schema on the missions," theologian and council *peritus* Gerard Philips observed in a conversation with Yves Congar.[47]

The pope had been present for the Mass at the start of the session—a eucharistic celebration in the Ethiopic rite with drums and clapping. Then he delivered his brief address, warmly commending the schema, expressing his appreciation for the members of the council who worked in mission lands, and giving them his apostolic blessing. Cardinal Agagianian thanked the pope for his presence and read an introduction to the schema. Then the secretary general announced that the pope would give his blessing to all the council fathers and to the faithful committed to their care, as well as to any devotional objects that the fathers had brought with them. Following this, the pope left the basilica.

Bishop Stanislaus Lokuang of Tainan, Taiwan, a member of the Commission on Mission, read the *relatio* or preliminary commentary on the text. This was followed by twenty-eight addresses over the course of three days—the remaining time on Friday, November 6, then the entire session on the following day and the first part of the session on Monday, November 9.[48] These speeches, says Tanner, were well prepared, and there seemed to have been considerable coordination among the speakers. A good number of the speakers represented large groups of council members, especially from Africa.

Brechter reports that the first day of discussion was "fairly calm," since the schema was considered to be possibly acceptable. African Cardinal Rugambwa spoke in its favor. Cardinal Paul Léger spoke to the fourth proposition, which, as noted above, called for a Central Council for Evangelization. He recommended that, rather than serving as an advisory body, it be integrated into the Propaganda and given the authority to make decisions on issues pertaining to churches in mission lands. Cardinal Tatsuo Doi of Tokyo called for a definition of mission that would restrict it to the proclamation of the gospel among non-Christians. Cardinal Augustine Bea of the Secretariat for Christian Unity, speaking in the name of all the bishops of Africa and many of Asia, asked that there be a rethinking of the theology of mission from a more biblical basis. The final speech of the day was by Martin Legarra Tellechea of Panama, who appealed to the council for a fair share of financial help for prelatures, even if they were not officially called "missions."

But the next day—again in Brechter's words—the powerful speech of Cardinal Frings of Cologne that opened the meeting burst the dikes "and the waters swallowed up the helpless schema." The problem of the missions, Frings said, was so important today that there was no way it could be solved with the few propositions with which the council had been presented. On the contrary, a more ample schema devoted to the church's missionary activity would have to be developed and presented for discussion at the fourth session.[49] Bishop Daniel Lamont of Southern Rhodesia (now Zimbabwe) described the propositions in terms of Ezekiel's vision of the dry bones (Ezek 37). The propositions needed to be given the nerves and flesh of a full schema, so that under the inspiration of a new Pentecost, the great deeds of God could be proclaimed once more to the four corners of the globe. Bishop Cornelius Geise of Bogor, Indonesia, also called for a "normal schema." With a flourish of rhetoric, Geise quoted a dictum of Horace: "*Parturiunt montes, nascitur ridiculus mus!*" ("The mountains give birth and there is born a ridiculous mouse!") The propositions in the schema under debate, he said, were not ridiculous; they were actually good—but they were too few and not exhaustive of the material with which they dealt.

Speaker after speaker said the same thing, to the extent that at one point (after Lamont's speech), the moderator had to caution about repetition. Other issues revolved around the need to develop a more adequate theological basis for the missionary document, various practical matters—chief of which were proposals to restructure the Propaganda—and issues relating to missionary "adaptation."

In his opening report, Bishop Lokuang had admitted that, because of the brevity of the schema, because of the fact that the topic of mission was included in the document on the church, and because the members of the commission were divided in their opinions, the underlying theology of mission had been largely undeveloped. The reason the commission was so divided, said Bishop Jucundo Grotti from the prelature of Acre and Purùs, Brazil, was both amazing and absurd—let those scholars who disagree be sent to the missions to find out! Bishop Riobé of Orléans, a member of the commission, urged that the schema be brought into line with other relevant teachings of the council, particularly with those having to do with the missionary nature of the entire church. Bishops Xavier Geeraerts and Melchite Bishop Elias Zoghby both spoke of the importance of a Trinitarian foundation for mission. Zoghby was particularly insightful: "The gospel message, coming to a land not yet evangelized, sows the seed of the word of God in souls that are not far from the Word of God and, indeed, have long been prepared by the Holy Spirit."

While many of the speakers were appreciative of the work of the Propaganda Fide, they were also uncomfortable with the fact that what were considered "missions" were only those territories under the congregation's jurisdiction. Other areas—such as dioceses and prelatures in Latin America—were not regarded technically as missionary territories, but they were in dire need of the financial assistance that the Propaganda provided. Bishop Legarra Tellechea had argued this point on the first day, and Bishop Grotti also pointed out this anomaly. Like Cardinal Léger, Cardinal Frings too addressed the issue of the proposed Central Council for Evangelization and urged that it have a greater role within the context of the Congregation.

Cardinal Doi of Tokyo spoke of the need for the church to value and respect local cultures. Cardinal Rugambwa pointed out that where missions flourished was where missionaries had appreciated local culture and had, as it were, baptized its values. Mission, he said, is to continue Christ's incarnation. Léger commended the schema for its encouragement of dialogue with non-Christian *cultures*, but noted that, in the light of the recently published encyclical *Ecclesiam Suam*, the schema should include encouragement as well for dialogue with both other Christians and with non-Christian religions.

Things obviously were not going well for the shortened schema, and so, in what Brechter calls "a masterpiece of skill and elegance," Cardinal Agagianian attempted to stave off a full rejection of the schema on the council floor. Before the final vote on the schema on Monday, November 9, Bishop Lokuang addressed the council, offering appreciation for what had been said during the discussion. He suggested that, should the fathers agree, the Commission on Mission would rework the schema and take their wisdom into account. When he had finished speaking, he received enthusiastic applause—to which the secretary general, Cardinal Felici, responded by reminding the body that "applause says nothing juridically." What was put before the body, then, was not a vote to accept or reject the schema of propositions, but a resolution that read: "Do the fathers wish the schema on the Missionary Activity of the Church to be revised by the competent

Commission?" Felici asked all those who were at the coffee bars right outside the nave of the basilica to return for the vote, and of the 1,914 present, 1,601 voted affirmatively, 311 negatively, and 2 abstained.

The Commission on Mission now had the task of drafting a new schema from scratch during the rest of the third session and especially during the months of the intersession. The de facto leadership would now pass to that "tireless German,"[50] SVD superior general Johannes Schütte. Under his leadership, what seemed like a disaster would actually be turned into a windfall for the document on mission. Now that the bishops in the *aula* had been heard, there was an opportunity for a new schema that would open up some new frontiers in missionary thinking. Obstacles to this still existed, but the momentum was changing.

## Preparing for the Fourth Session: December 1964 to September 1965 Ad Gentes *Begins to Take Shape*

Even with the third session still in progress, the Commission on Mission began to meet to develop an adequate schema for discussion at the fourth session the following fall.[51] The mandate to revise the schema had been given on November 9; only seven days later, on November 16, the commission held a plenary session at which it decided to develop a schema that would take into account the speeches and written observations of the council members. The schema would also be written in the light of the theological principles (e.g., collegiality, a Trinitarian perspective, the importance of the local church) already worked out by the council. To accomplish this an editorial committee was formed, consisting of Bishop Riobé, Bishop Lokuang, Bishop Zoa of Yaoundè, Cameroon, Bishop Lecuona of the Spanish National Seminary for Foreign Missions in Burgos, Spain, and Fr. Schütte. As *periti* who would assist in the writing of the text, the commission chose Yves Congar, Xavier Seumois (the brother of André), Domenico Grasso, Josef Neuner, and Joseph Ratzinger. At first, Cardinal Agagianian balked at accepting Congar into the commission, but he was eventually persuaded.[52] The cardinal was nevertheless very much opposed to a totally new schema, and continued to insist that it should address mission in the strict sense as those territories under the Propaganda. Others on the commission, however, believed strongly in speaking about mission more generally and theologically as rooted in God's Trinitarian life. This tension would never quite be resolved in the schema or the final document, even though the latter idea would find clear expression in the text. Oppositions between canonists and theologians still persisted.

In December 1964 and January 1965, Congar, Riobé, and Xavier Seumois met in Paris and Strasbourg and started drafting a new schema. Congar began to prepare the theological part, while Seumois dealt with more pastoral aspects of missionary activity. The entire group of editors—minus Ratzinger, who had sent some notes on the theological foundation for the missions—met at the Tertiate house of the Society of the Divine Word at Nemi, south of Rome in the Alban Hills, at the invitation of Fr. Schütte. In this lovely setting, overlooking the jewel-like Lake Nemi immediately below with the Mediterranean Sea in the distance, the editorial committee began its work on the new schema by sorting through a number of drafts that had been proposed by various *periti* and members of the commission. The immediate task was to present an adequate concept of mission itself. For the theological chapter of the schema, Congar's work, "a 'broad' understanding of mission, which was described as one of the proper characteristics of all the Church's activity" was chosen. Theologically, then—in a real change in the commission's understanding—mission was understood in a general way, belonging to the nature of the church as such. Focus was not on a geographical or juridical perspective, but on human beings for whom and to whom the gospel was to be preached and witnessed to.

The editorial committee worked at Nemi from January 12 to 26 and was able to complete a draft of a schema. It had a strong theological orientation and was in harmony with the ecclesiology of *Lumen Gentium*, which had been approved at the third session of the council. The idea of mission itself was stated more clearly than before, although no definition was given. The tone of the document was much less juridical than that of its predecessors, and the use of more biblical, patristic, pastoral, and ecumenical language was evident. The draft did not mention the Propaganda explicitly, but it emphasized the importance of having a single body to direct and coordinate missionary work. The draft schema had five chapters that in many ways incorporated the ideas in the previous schema of fourteen propositions, but it was much more fully developed. Chapter 1 dealt with doctrinal principles, chapter 2 with missionary work, chapter 3 with missionaries, chapter 4 with the organization of missionary activity, and chapter 5 with missionary cooperation.

In February the new schema was sent to the members of the full commission and to some of the *periti* for their opinions. It soon became clear that a number of the latter, more traditional missiologists, such as André Seumois, Alfons Mulders, and Lodewijk Buijs (or Buijk[53]), were not at all happy with it. Many of their objections centered on the more inclusive understanding of mission that Congar had proposed in the text, and the struggle over this (again!) was to be brought as well to the plenary session of the commission that was held at Nemi in March. Congar would be at that meeting. Several days before the plenary session was to begin, he wrote in his journal: "It seems that the certified missiologists have prepared for an attack at the meeting in Nemi. They are fixated on a territorial and juridical conception of mission, whereas the conciliar ecclesiology calls for a dynamic conception: looking not so much at territories and organizations as at the vital goals and situations and the tasks these require."[54] The entries in Congar's journal during the meeting at Nemi are full of criticism of the "certified missiologists." On March 30, for example, Congar wrote: "I realize that the Preparatory Commission has been entirely under the influence of Fr. Buijk. He teaches canon law and particularly mission law. . . . In his critiques of my text, which according to him is entirely to be rejected, he says that the missions have no relation with the trinitarian processions!!! . . . And Frs. Seumois (A.) and Reuter have the same tendency as Buijk. And this morning Msgr. Paventi as well: for him, the "real" (his expression) begins with the juridical. Otherwise, it is only spirituality or poetry."[55]

Cardinal Agagianian was present on the first day of the plenary session, and he delivered an address that also took a more juridical approach to missionary activity. The commission, he said, was not to focus on mission in general, but on those territories that come under the jurisdiction of the Congregation for the Propagation of the Faith. However, since the cardinal immediately left the meeting, his remarks were not taken all that seriously, although André Seumois and Buijs sharply insisted on the cardinal's position. Burigana and Turbanti report that Congar offered a solution that tried to combine both positions in the text, and this seemed to carry the day. This "double-mindedness" (in the words of Burigana and Turbanti) resulted in the theological part of the schema being quite different in tone from the more practical part—something that would persist into the final document itself. But at least—at last—some rapprochement had been achieved between the two opposing positions.

Another point of contention had to do with the proposed Central Council for Evangelization. Should it be an organization *within* the Propaganda that represented the missionary churches and had real authority, or should it be a *separate* body that was superior to the curial congregation? Because the latter position received little support, the schema went in the direction of the former. The name of the body was dropped from the draft of the schema, but the issue of a significant reform of the Propaganda would continue to be a controversial topic as the schema was discussed on the council floor. Since the group could not agree on a text, Fr. Schütte (who had in the meantime become vice president elect of the commission) was entrusted with writing a draft that would be discussed at the full meeting of the Commission on Mission in September, just before the council was to convene for its final session.

In early April the revised schema was submitted to the Coordinating Commission, and although there were concerns about the schema's length, it was finally approved and sent to the members of the council in mid-June for their comments. There was not much response to the schema from the council fathers, and so on September 18 the Commission on Mission met for one last time to prepare the final draft of the schema for the council hall. Although Fr. Schütte was confirmed as vice president at this session, the text that he had prepared about the reform of the Propaganda Fide was not accepted. He was given the task of re-editing the section in the light of the commission's discussions. Behind the scenes, however, Cardinal F. Roberti strongly opposed the formulation and insisted that another version—one that was more general and weaker—appear in the schema to be presented to the council.[56] But because the Commission on Mission had received so many communications against Roberti's version, in his *relatio* before the debate on the council floor, Fr. Schütte presented the Commission on Mission's (original) version as an amendment. But even this original version was not strong enough for the bishops. As we will report below, it had to be further revised for the final vote on December 7.[57]

## Fourth Session: October to December 1965
*Finally, a Document on Mission*

At the fourth session, discussion on the schema—very much the work of Congar, and approved by Ratzinger, Neuner, and even Karl Rahner[58] —began on October 7, and continued through October 8, 11, 12, and 13.[59] Cardinal Agagianian briefly introduced the text, and then Fr. Schütte read a long report in which he showed how the present schema reflected the comments of the council fathers, particularly those made in the debate the previous year on the ill-fated propositions. Schütte concluded with the hope that the document on mission would become the "Magna Carta" for the church's missionary activity and that it "would shape the universal church into a truly missionary church."[60]

Immediately after Schütte's *relatio*, formal discussion began. Interestingly, Brechter states the opinion that the speeches were "very uneven in quality and extremely mixed," with an evident fatigue spreading over the assembly. Peter Hünermann, on the other hand, judges that the discussion "was carried on at a very high level," and that the missionary bishops spoke with "great openness and deep awareness of the problems." However the various addresses are judged, it is clear that the speakers were basically in favor of the schema even though they raised many points of critique. But there was neither the urgency nor the rhetoric (e.g., of Lamont, Grotti, and Geise) that had marked the debate on the propositions presented at the third session.

Over the course of the five days, forty-nine speeches were given, and more than a hundred applications to speak had to be denied. The remarks of these fathers had to be submitted in writing. To highlight some of the addresses: Cardinal Bernard Alfrink of Utrecht, Holland critiqued the schema's understanding of mission as too hierarchical. Mission according to *Lumen Gentium* is the task of the entire people of God, he insisted, not just of the hierarchy. This critique was echoed by Bishops Gonçalves da Costa of Mozambique, McGrath of Panama, and Corboy of Zambia. Bishop Legarra Tellechea of Bocas del Toro, Panama, encouraged genuine collaboration between the missionary orders and the bishops in whose dioceses these orders minister. Similar ideas were voiced by Bishop Joseph Sibomana of Ruhengeri, Rwanda. Cardinal König of Vienna stressed the necessity of interreligious dialogue in missionary situations. Indian Bishop Joseph Attipetty was quite strong in his defense of the Congregation of the Propagation of the Faith, and found the proposed reform of the congregation an attempt to force the pope to put into practice the doctrine of collegiality. Cardinal Paul Zoungrana of Upper Volta (now Burkina Faso) emphatically insisted that the missionary congregations are and remain the principal means for evangelizing the world. Speaking in the name of the bishops of Rwanda and Burundi and several bishops of East Africa and Nigeria, Bishop Michael Ntuyahaga also praised the work of the missionary congregations. He noted, however, that in today's circumstances of growing indigenous churches and indigenous clergy the missionary congregations should "take on the task of collaborating and serving, not of directing."

At the end of the session of October 12, the day's moderator, Cardinal Felici, asked whether the schema was acceptable after further revision in the light of the comments made by the speakers of the last days. The result—made public the following day—was overwhelming in favor of the document, with 2,070 participants in favor and only 15 against. Addresses by speakers who had collected at least seventy names in support of their speaking continued on October 13, but the schema had made it safely through the debate.

The next weeks, however, would involve huge amounts of work, as the Commission on Mission would attempt to incorporate the seemingly countless observations into the text (193 spoken and written interventions—about 555 pages of text, according to Brechter). Just two days after the end of the discussion on the schema, the Commission on Mission met to begin the process of revision, again under the chairmanship of Fr. Schütte. The commission was divided into five subcommittees, one for each chapter of the schema, and two *periti*—among whom were Congar, Ratzinger, Xavier Seumois, and Neuner—were assigned to each group. The work was tedious, but it was done thoroughly, and as many observations of the council fathers as possible were included in the text. More emphasis was given to ecumenism, to the laity, and to the work of the local clergy. A new chapter on particular churches was added as chapter 3, and (in Brechter's words) the "ticklish question" of the relationship between the local bishop and missionary congregations, "the autonomous right of the bishops' conferences and of the missionary institutes mutually to regulate their mutual relations by agreement without special approbation of the Holy See" was kept as it appeared in the draft. Also retained, although it had been strongly criticized in the interventions on the council floor, was the idea that the missionary mandate is in the first place the task of the bishops, even though it is true that it is also the work of the entire people of God. Finally, as previously observed, because of a groundswell of opinion against it in the written interventions, the amendment limiting the reform of the Propaganda Fide was not accepted by the Commission on Mission, and wording closer to Schütte's original draft had been substituted.

On November 9 the revised schema was put to a vote and all the chapters were approved with the exception of chapter 5. This chapter on the organization of missionary activity received 712 votes with reservations (votes *juxta modum*), and so failed to receive the needed two-thirds majority.[61] The schema was then returned to the Commission on Mission for a final revision. At the request of 461 fathers, the paragraph on reform of the Propaganda was further strengthened with the addition of the idea that bishops who serve as representatives in the congregation should have a "deliberative vote."[62]

A few days before the schema was to be brought to the council for a final vote, Paventi reports, Bishop Pellegrino, who had recently been named bishop of Turin but who had been a professor at the university in that city, pointed out that the citations of the fathers in the schema did not always reference texts from a critical edition. Joseph Ratzinger was then asked, at this late hour, to make the necessary changes. The final obstacle on the schema's long journey was thus overcome, and the schema was submitted for a final vote by the council on December 7. It was the last document the council approved, but it was approved nevertheless, by 2,394 votes in favor, and only 5 against—the highest number of "yes" votes for any of the documents issued by the council.

Peter Hünermann's history of the final weeks of the council sums up the long and difficult journey that the document on mission had taken through all four sessions:

> If we survey the uncommonly turbulent history of this document, we may well be struck by the stubbornness and determination of many Council fathers about rethinking and

strengthening the missionary activity of the Church as an expression of its nature and mission in changed social, political, and even ecclesial conditions. At the beginning, the whole enterprise seemed a routine task in which the issue was a few organizational improvements. The crisis over its acceptance during the third period, despite the personal involvement of Paul VI, then led to a radical revision. There was great theological competence among the bishops and theologians to whom the work of drafting was entrusted, but the contribution of the Council fathers themselves was unusually extensive at both the theological and pastoral levels.[63]

Part II will help us see the richness—as well as some of the weaknesses —in this document, a text that still has enormous significance for the church today.

PART II

# MAJOR POINTS

The structure, headings, and article numbers of the Decree on the Missionary Activity of the Church (*Ad Gentes*) are as follows:

Preface (1)

Chapter 1: Principles of Doctrine (2–9)

Chapter 2: Mission Work Itself (10–18)
    Article 1: Christian Witness (11–12)
    Article 2: Preaching the Gospel and Gathering the People of God (13–14)
    Article 3: Forming a Christian Community (15–18)

Chapter 3: Particular Churches (19–22)

Chapter 4: Missionaries (23–27)

Chapter 5: Planning Missionary Activity (28–34)

Chapter 6: Cooperation (35–41)

Conclusion (42)

## TITLE AND PREFACE

The decree's title, "Decree on the Missionary Activity of the Church," was first given to the short schema of fourteen propositions discussed—and basically rejected—at the council's third session. In the earliest versions of the schema, the title was simply *De Missionibus* or "On the Missions," but the title of the shorter schema was retained in the version brought before the fourth session. As was pointed out in the previous section (note 4), a "decree" is considered to have a bit less authority and importance than a "constitution," but a bit more than a "declaration." Even though *Ad Gentes* includes a substantial doctrinal and theological section (chapter 1), the focus of the decree on missionary *activity* is still appropriate, since even the theology of mission focuses on what the church *does*.

The first two or three Latin words in church documents are also used as the title of documents, and the words *"Ad Gentes"*—to the nations (or to all the nations) are particularly appropriate for the council's document on mission. The church's mission is a world mission; no one is excluded as a potential recipient of the good news of God's universal love. Mission to all nations and cultures is constitutive of the church, which began to realize its true identity as it crossed the boundaries of Judaism and began to include Gentiles. Its living of its identity is ongoing as the Spirit continues to lead it across new boundaries today.[1]

The decree's preface makes three points as an introduction to the rest of the document: (1) The church has always been called to the entire world to be for it "a universal sacrament of salvation," to preach God's word and proclaim and establish the reign of God throughout the world. (2) This task today is more urgent than ever. (3) Consequently, the council wants to "sketch the principles of missionary activity" and inspire the faithful to continue the church's missionary work.

The very first line of the decree establishes the connection between it and the Dogmatic Constitution on the Church. The church is called to be a *sacrament*, "a universal sacrament of salvation." The phrase is a reference to *Lumen Gentium* 48, but it is important to recall that *Lumen Gentium*'s first paragraph as well refers to the church as a sacrament—as both *sign* and *instrument* of unity between God and humanity, and unity as well among all the peoples of the world. The church, in other words, is called to effect what it signifies, and so is essentially missionary. Quoting St. Augustine ("The Apostles...'preached the word of truth and begot churches'"), the text indicates the double task of mission: to preach the gospel and establish churches (note the plural), a task that is therefore both Christological and ecclesial in nature.[2]

## CHAPTER 1: PRINCIPLES OF DOCTRINE

Chapter 1 presents a rich, concentrated theology of mission. It roots the church's specific cross-cultural and boundary-crossing missionary activity within the context of the church's essential missionary identity. As such, it provides the theological foundation for the entire decree. It is the longest of the six chapters and contains the largest number of references, many of which are references to the Bible and the fathers of the church. Paragraphs 2–4 present mission as having its origin in the self-diffusive life of the Trinity; paragraph 5 speaks of mission as being continued in history by the church. Paragraph 6 discusses mission in the more narrow sense (the "missions of the church"), and paragraph 7 speaks of the necessity of these missions. The last two paragraphs (*AG*, 8 and 9) speak of the eschatological nature of missionary activity.

## Trinitarian Origins

Paragraph 2 begins with what mission theologian William R. Burrows believes is "the most memorable line" of the document, and the line which "the decree's promoters wanted etched in the minds both of the council fathers and of the church at large": this is the lapidary phrase "The pilgrim church is missionary by its very nature" (my translation). Besides being memorable, the phrase may be one of the most important statements of the council, and one that has perhaps not yet been fully appreciated. It points to the fact that mission—in both its general sense and in the more specific sense to be developed in the decree—is not just *one* thing among others in which the church is engaged. It is what makes the church the church. Should mission cease to exist, so would the church.

The chapter expresses the motive for mission in various ways, such as a response to the command of Christ (e.g., in Mark 16:15 and Matt 28:18–20 [*AG*, 5]) or the glorification of God (*AG*, 1, 7). The most fundamental motive, however, is expressed here as being rooted in the very life of God, who exists as an overflowing communion of love and calls humanity to a participation in that communion. The church is "missionary by its very nature" because "it is from the mission of the Son and the mission of the Holy Spirit that it draws its origin, in accordance with the decree of God the Father" (my translation). The church is missionary, in other words, because God in God's deepest reality is missionary. In the words of British missiologist Anthony Gittins, being missionary is simply who and what God is—it is God's "job description."[3]

The source of God's active, saving presence in creation's history is the "fount-like love" of the unoriginate Father, the "principle without principle" (*AG*, 2). This means ultimately that the source of God's mission to reconcile, save, and unify humanity and all of creation resides in Mystery, as sheer grace. By sheer grace as well is the fact that God calls humanity to share the divine life not as individuals, but as a communion, a community, a people. This call can be discerned in the depths of human experience, or even in the religious yearnings of humankind. Human experience and even human philosophies and religions can serve as "leading strings" or a "preparation for the Gospel," but they always need to be "enlightened and healed" (*AG*, 3). This is the motive for the Incarnation. God's son is sent among women and men, fully identifying with them, bringing good news to the poor, healing the broken-hearted, proclaiming release to captives and sight to the blind (Luke 4:18), seeking and saving what was lost (Luke 19:10), giving his life as a ransom for all (Mark 10:45), reconciling women and men to God and to one another (2 Cor 5:19).

In order to make available for all people everywhere and in all times what Jesus accomplished in history—in a particular place and at a particular time—the Holy Spirit was sent to form the disciples who believed in Jesus into a community that would both spread the good news of God's forgiveness and love to the ends of the earth and be itself a sign of a new humanity united to one another and to God. Paragraph 4 points out that the Spirit was already at work in the world before Christ was glorified—it was the Spirit, indeed, who prepared women and men in their cultures and religions for the coming of the gospel—but the task of the Spirit now was to call the church to its identity as the community that was to continue Jesus' work of solidarity, liberation, and reconciliation. In a phrase in which the hand of the chapter's principal author, Yves Congar, is particularly evident, we read how the Spirit is lavished upon the Jesus community just as the Spirit anointed Jesus at the beginning of his ministry, and came upon Mary to effect the Incarnation.[4]

In his commentary on this first chapter of *Ad Gentes*, Congar briefly sets the document's Trinitarian perspective in the context of the history of theology and of missiological thinking current at the time. The approach taken here, he says, goes back to Augustine's theology of the missions of the Trinity, and was shared as well by the great scholastics of the thirteenth century—Alexander of Hales, Bonaventure, Albert the Great, and Thomas Aquinas. The rooting of mission in the life of the Trinity appears also in the theology of Cardinal Pierre de Bérulle of the seventeenth century French School of Spirituality. Intriguing, however, is Congar's remark that one finds here "at least in a general form" the influence of contemporary Protestant thought.[5] He gives as a reference a work by the great twentieth century missiologist and ecumenical figure Lesslie Newbigin, but reference could be made as well to the document issued by the 1952 conference of the International Missionary Council at Willingen, Germany, where the idea of mission as rooted in the *Missio Dei*—the mission of God as Trinity—was developed. The idea is a rich one, but it has its dangers: in the 1960s it was used by some theologians as a way to denigrate the mission of the church. Since mission is about participating in God's mission, it is *God*—not the church—who sets the agenda for mission by divine action in world.[6] *Ad Gentes* clearly does not go in this dangerous direction, and it is to be commended for tapping into the best mission theology of the time—and a theology that is very much in tune with the revival of Trinitarian theology in our own day.

## Missionary Church

Moving back to consider Jesus' earthly ministry, paragraph 5 locates the origin of the church's missionary mandate in Jesus' establishment of the Twelve. After his death and resurrection, Jesus sent these Twelve as the Father had sent him (John 20:21) and commanded them to go into the whole world to preach the gospel and make disciples (Matt 28:19; Mark 16:15–16). While the text can be read as a summons to the entire church—clergy and laity—to be missionary, it came under severe criticism on the council floor by a number of bishops for not being in line with *Lumen Gentium*, which speaks of the entire church, the people of God, before it deals specifically with any particular function or state. Nevertheless, the text remained unchanged from the draft presented. In his basically positive evaluation of *Ad Gentes*, Peter Hünermann cites this more hierarchical approach to mission as one of his two main criticisms of the text, and remarks that, given the makeup of the drafting commission—bishops like Lokuang, Zoa, and Riobé, and *periti* like Congar, Ratzinger, and Neuner—the fact that the critiques from the council floor were unheeded is even harder to understand.[7]

The mission of the church is described here, in any case, in very broad terms as that activity which makes it "fully present to all women and men or nations" (*AG*, 5—my translation), so that by its witness, its preaching and its celebration of the sacraments, it will lead them "to the faith, the freedom and the peace of Christ," and so open to them a "full participation in the mystery of Christ." The church is called to "walk in the same path on which Christ walked" (*AG*, 5), which is one of poverty, obedience, service, and self-sacrifice. The general mission of the church is thus presented a bit abstractly here, but the image is one of great beauty.

## Mission in the Strict Sense

From a general reflection on the missionary nature of the church, the document takes a crucial turn in paragraph 6, which focuses on mission in the strict sense as "preaching the Gospel and planting the Church among peoples or groups who do not yet believe in Christ." In describing mission or "missions" in this way, the council chose a middle path between two opposing positions that had developed in Catholic missiology since its formal beginning in the early twentieth century.[8] One position, championed particularly by the pioneer German Catholic missiologist at Münster, Josef Schmidlin, emphasized the importance of preaching the gospel and individual conversion. The other position, proposed especially by Louvain missiologist Pierre Charles, focused more on the activity of planting the church—establishing the hierarchy, developing parishes, educating clergy. The council takes a step forward in accepting both ideas.

Another important aspect of the view of mission put forth here is that mission is not understood in a territorial way, but as an outreach to persons. The territorial understanding of mission is not absent from the document completely—in fact, as the document progresses the territorial understanding becomes more and more pronounced—but the text tried to be sensitive to a number of calls from council fathers to move away from a notion that spoke of mission in only juridical, territorial terms. The reader of the decree will realize that this success was only partial. The decree still reflects the persistent argument of the more juridically inclined members of the Commission on Mission during the preparation of the document.

While the church has the duty always to be missionary in this stricter sense of the word, the document points out that mission always has to be carried out with sensitivity to particular circumstances in which the church finds itself. There are times when, because of certain circumstances, the gospel cannot be openly and directly preached—the council may have had in mind the situation in the "Iron Curtain" countries of Eastern Europe or behind the "Bamboo Curtain" in places like China or North Korea; today we may think especially of countries (such as Indonesia and India) where conversion to Christianity continues to be against the law. But even here, "missionaries can and must at least bear witness to Christ by charity and by works of mercy, with all patience, prudence and great confidence" (*AG*, 6). In another circumstance, mission involves a kind of re-evangelization of people in places where the gospel had once flourished but does so no longer. Today, for instance, Europe is more and more being understood as a place where mission in the strict sense of the word needs to be carried out.[9] During his pontificate, John Paul II spoke of this aspect of mission as the "new evangelization" (see, e.g., *RM*, 33).

Missionary activity in the sense in which *Ad Gentes* describes it here in paragraph 6, and the way in which mission will be understood in the rest of the document, is to be distinguished both from pastoral activity among those Christians already evangelized and from ecumenical activity among Christians. Both of these activities, of course, are closely connected with mission in the strict sense: pastoral activity is carried on within communities located among peoples where the gospel has not fully taken root (e.g., in Japan), and work for Christian unity is urgently needed because the scandal of disunity among Christians is certainly one of the stumbling blocks toward a truly credible preaching of the gospel. But the distinction that the document makes is nevertheless necessary and helpful.

## The Necessity of Mission

The main reason why Christians undertake mission, as pointed out above, is that they have been incorporated into God's very life by means of their baptism and so are drawn into the Trinitarian activity of calling all creation into communion. Paragraph 7, however, lays down three other reasons that are closely connected to this principal one. First, God *wills* all women and men to be saved and come to the knowledge of the truth. The text says— echoing *Lumen Gentium* 16 and *Gaudium et Spes* 22—that God has ways of leading to the faith people who do not know Christ explicitly, but, as *Lumen Gentium* 14 also says, salvation would be impossible for someone who, "aware that God, through Jesus Christ founded the Church as something necessary," still does not "wish to enter it, or to persevere in it" (*AG*, 7). Because of this, the church has the "sacred duty to preach the Gospel" (*AG*, 7). The second additional reason for the necessity of mission is that Christians will naturally want to share their love of God and the benefits of salvation with as many people as possible. The gospel is simply good news—or, as Protestant missiologist D. T. Niles famously put it, mission is simply "one beggar telling another where to find food."[10] Finally, the church must preach the gospel because only in that way can God be fully glorified. This full glory of God can come about only when all humanity forms one people of God and shares the harmony that "corresponds with the inmost wishes of all women and men" (*AG*, 7—my translation).

## Mission and Eschatology

The point of paragraphs 8 and 9, despite some repetition of things already stated in previous paragraphs, is the eschatological nature of Christian mission. Every understanding of mission requires an eschatology, since an understanding of the world's and humankind's future determines the urgency of the message. Is salvation an individual matter having to do with a reward in heaven or a punishment in hell? Or is it about the end of history and the recovery of cosmic wholeness? Is the coming of the "new heavens and new earth" (Rev 21:1) imminent? Or is it in a relatively far distant future? Will the end mean the dissolution of this world? Or will it be its fulfillment?

The eschatology presented in *Ad Gentes* is clearly concerned with human beings in their communal, historical, and material existence. There is not much, however, in terms of a more ecological consciousness of *cosmic* fulfillment. Such consciousness will only grow gradually in missiological thinking and will be the subject of part of our reflections in Part 4. What is expected, rather, at the end of history is the fulfillment of human longings, and a fulfillment of the promise of liberty, communion, and peace. "Not without cause is Christ hailed by the faithful as 'the expected of the nations, and their Savior'" (*AG*, 8, quoting the "O" Antiphon for December 23). It is this time between Jesus' first coming in the flesh and his second coming in glory that the church understands to be the time of mission. "For the Gospel must be preached to all nations before the Lord shall come (cf. Mark 13:10)" (*AG*, 9). Drawing on the insights of Melchite Bishop Elias Zoghby's speech during the debate about the fourteen propositions at the third session, the text speaks of mission in this time of "now and not yet" as "nothing else and nothing less than an epiphany" (*AG*, 9) of God's will in world history. As God's will is more and more manifest with history moving closer and closer to its goal, human culture is not only preserved, but "healed, uplifted, and perfected for the glory of God, the shame of the demon, and the bliss of women and men" (*AG*, 9—my translation). What is revealed in the eschatological fullness is that there has always been a "sort of secret presence" (*AG*, 9) of God among all nations, which has worked to free them and their cultures from all evil and restores them to Christ.

With this theological foundation clearly laid, *Ad Gentes* moves to a number of practical issues in the next five chapters.

### CHAPTER 2: MISSION WORK ITSELF

In this chapter the work of the church's mission is described under three aspects, each of which is carried out in a diversity of contexts: among adherents to the world's great religions, among people of complete religious ignorance, among atheists, and even among anti-theists (here the council is no doubt thinking of Communists). Paragraphs 11–12 speak of mission as witness; paragraphs 13–14 reflect on preaching the gospel; and paragraphs 15–18 deal with the dynamics of forming the Christian community.

## Christian Witness

To Francis of Assisi is often attributed the saying, "Preach the gospel always; if necessary use words." Whether he actually said it is debatable, but the point is powerfully made: mission is, in the first place, witness.

Wherever Christians live, says the text, all are bound to demonstrate by their example and by their words that faith in Christ brings true human fulfillment. Christians do this specifically by forging real solidarity with the people among whom they live. Christians are not to live apart and aloof from society; they are to immerse themselves in it. They should be involved in cultural and social activities; they should be "familiar with their national and religious traditions" (*AG*, 11). In this kind of serious involvement, they can discover "the seeds of the Word" that lie hidden in their cultural heritage.

This last phrase, a quotation from Justin Martyr, emphasizes the goodness of the cultures and societies in which mission is carried out. For missionaries in the past, such an attitude was not always evident, and the policy followed was often one of destroying or disparaging local cultures. Rather than providing witness to the fullness that faith in Christ brings, such attitudes provided a counterwitness to what the gospel was really about. But, as the previous chapter insisted as well, local customs and cultures provide a "preparation for the gospel" (*AG*, 3); there is among all women and men a "secret presence of God" (*AG*, 9). The way of missionary witness is a way of respect and appreciation, for as Christians live in solidarity with their neighbors, they will "learn by sincere and patient dialogue what treasures a generous God has distributed among the nations of the earth" (*AG*, 11). This phrase is followed by a reminder that these "treasures" are not perfect, and need to be "baptized." But surely it is one of the great phrases of the document, and even of the entire council.

The text continues to call Christians to active collaboration and solidarity with those among whom they live in the areas of social and economic life, education, justice, health care, and peacemaking. They should do this even in collaboration with people of non-Christian religions—a radical recommendation in light of past Christian attitudes of suspicion and separation from those who did not share the Christian faith, and one that reflected the new attitude of the church expressed in *Nostra Aetate*.[11] At the same time, it is important to note that the church itself does not want to intrude into politics in a way that would compromise the church's religious and spiritual task. The purpose of involvement in the world is not to attain power for the church, but to witness to the wholeness of salvation in Christ. Involvement in the world is the way to preach the gospel at all times, even when Christians can't use words.

## Preaching the Gospel and Gathering Together the People of God

Witness is important, but missionary work must include—when it is opportune—the explicit preaching of the gospel. As Paul VI would put it in *Evangelii Nuntiandi* on the tenth anniversary of *Ad Gentes*, "there is no true evangelization if the name, the teaching, the life, the promises, the kingdom and the mystery of Jesus of Nazareth, the Son of God are not proclaimed" (*EN*, 22). To be noted, however, is that the text says that the mystery of Christ is to be proclaimed "wherever God opens a door of speech" (*AG*, 13). As mentioned above, there may be circumstances where only witness is possible, or when the time is not yet ripe for a clear presentation of the gospel message.

The aim of proclamation is conversion, but several caveats are expressed in the text, evidencing a sensitivity to the seriousness and delicacy of the conversion process. First, conversion to Christ is understood not as a once-for-all event, but as a journey that a person undertakes, passing from the "old humanity" to the "new humanity" in Christ. The text—perhaps too glibly—acknowledges that "the convert often experiences an abrupt breaking off of human ties," but that the joy he or she experiences more than makes up for this. Second, there is to be no undue pressure to convert to Christianity. Conversion by definition is a free act, and it cannot be forced. One recognizes the influence of *Dignitatis Humanae* here, and in the insistence in the next sentence that, on the other hand, no one should be frightened away from conversion. A third caveat is that the motives for conversion should be closely examined and, if need be, purified.

In a way that dovetails with the Constitution on the Sacred Liturgy (*SC*, 64 and 109), paragraph 14 focuses on the liturgical aspects of conversion. *Sacrosanctum Concilium* 64 called for a restoration of the catechumenate, and this prolonged introduction to the Christian faith is briefly elaborated on here. It should be not just "a mere expounding of doctrines and precepts, but a training period in the whole Christian life," and the catechumens should be "introduced into the life of faith, of liturgy, and of love, which is led by the People of God" (*AG*, 14). The connection between the catechumenate as a journey toward baptism and the Christian celebration of the season of Lent is also made clear, as is the recognition that the process of initiation is not just a matter for catechists or priests, but for "the entire community of the faithful."

This section on proclamation and conversion ends with a statement that, in the new Code of Canon Law—the revision of which was announced together with the announcement of the council by John XXIII on January 25, 1959[12]—the juridic status of catechumens should be defined, in accord with *Lumen Gentium* 14, to make clear that they are already joined to the church. All of these provisions in *Ad Gentes* 14 would be developed in the Rite of Christian Initiation of Adults, published in 1972.

### Forming a Christian Community

This rather lengthy section deals with the formation of a community of faith that actively exercises "the priestly, prophetic, and royal office [with] which God has entrusted" it (*AG*, 15). The Christian community is to be nothing less than "a sign of God's presence in the world" (*AG*, 15). The missionary task is not over, in other words, when women and men are incorporated into the church. The community must in turn become missionary, bearing witness to Christ as it is nourished on the word of God, walking in charity and imbued with the apostolic spirit. Witness is never enough; when possible, Christians of every kind should find ways to proclaim the gospel.

The text insists that the newly formed church needs to be deeply engaged in the life of the people from whom it takes its origin. Here is another example of the strong cultural sensitivity that is evident throughout the document: the Christian community needs to be one that continues to be part of the culture, not set apart from it. This cultural connection has long been a part of Catholic mission theory, even though it has often been ignored. In 1659, for example, the newly established Congregation for the Propagation of the Faith wrote to the bishops of China saying that they should not bring France, Spain or Italy to the people, but only the faith.[13] Another area of engagement is that of ecumenism—between Catholic rites and with other Christians—and a third area is engagement in civic life: "As good citizens, they should be true and effective patriots, altogether avoiding racial prejudice and hypernationalism...." (*AG*, 15).

The importance of the laity is briefly mentioned—it is seen as "a leaven working on the temporal order from within" (*AG*, 15)—but paragraphs 16 to 18 are concerned with those having specific ministries in the community—priests, catechists, deacons, and male and female religious. In accord with the strong instructions of the five mission encyclicals that were written in the first half of the twentieth century between 1919 and 1959,[14] *Ad Gentes* emphasizes the importance of training a local clergy. The students should receive an intellectual, spiritual, and pastoral formation of the first order, and this formation should be conducted with openness to the cultural and pastoral context of the place in which they will serve. In addition, "suitable priests should be chosen, after a little pastoral practice, to pursue higher studies" (*AG*, 16), especially in Rome. We see these directives bearing fruit today in the vibrant local episcopate and clergy of Asia, Africa, Latin America, and Oceania.

*Lumen Gentium* 29 restored the diaconate to a "proper and permanent rank in the hierarchy," and, to a great extent, this was a result of the influence of many of the missionary bishops present at the council.[15] The last lines of paragraph 16 call for the institution of the permanent diaconate in the newly established churches. As the missionary bishops had pointed out, many men had faithfully carried out the function of deacons for years as catechists, leading scattered Christian communities and being involved in the works of charity. *Ad Gentes* says here that it is only right that they be ordained, so that their ministry can be carried out "more effectively because of the sacramental grace of the diaconate" (*AG*, 16).

A good bit of space is then given to the ministry of catechists within the Christian community. They are commended for their work, and it is recommended that they be provided with better training and adequate financial support, with funds for this coming from a new office at the Propaganda Fide. Fully trained catechists should receive a formal *missio canonica*, an official recognition of their competence and authority that should be celebrated with a liturgical rite. Finally, the council calls for the establishment of communities of religious, again adding that these should preserve the traditions of the individual congregations "according to the nature and genius of each nation" (*AG*, 18). Remarkably, the text suggests that elements of the ascetic and contemplative life "planted by God in ancient cultures" (*AG*, 18) be incorporated into the communities' practices.

## CHAPTER 3: PARTICULAR CHURCHES

This chapter was added to the document during the revision of the schema that had been presented at the beginning of the fourth session (October 7, 1965). It deals with the local churches that are still "missionary" in that they are not quite ready to stand on their own in terms of numbers of Christians, local clergy, or material resources. Nevertheless, the members of the council insisted, these are *churches* in their own right, and should be treated as such. William R. Burrows makes two observations that are worth noting at the outset as we survey the main points of this chapter. First, while there is evidence of the openness and sensitivity to culture and context that mark the decree in general, the churches described in paragraphs 19 to 22 are ultimately meant to be very similar to the churches of Europe and North America that founded them. Second, while many churches in Africa, Asia, and Oceania are accurately described as "young churches" or "new churches," this is perhaps not the most felicitous term to describe many other churches that are nevertheless still in a "missionary" situation. Burrows singles out in particular the churches of Latin America, which at the time of the decree's publication were almost five hundred years old. But we could also say the same about many churches in Asia (e.g., the Indian church or the Japanese church) and Africa (the church in Egypt and Ethiopia), where Christianity flourished centuries before it arrived, for example, in Britain, let alone North America. A third observation that can also be made is that in this chapter the term "missionary church" is understood wholly as a church in a particular territory; the wider sense of the missionary nature of every particular church is rather eclipsed here, as is the idea that mission in the stricter sense is a matter of the church's presence to a particular people.

## Local and Universal

When a local church becomes rooted in a particular locality, is "somewhat conformed to the local culture" (*AG*, 19) and begins to develop a local clergy, and has the presence of religious congregations and a growing number of lay Christians, it has reached "a certain goal" (*AG*, 19). As it becomes more and more mature as a church, however, it always needs to keep in close communion with the entire church—it needs to be truly "catholic" by keeping the local in balance with the universal. In other words, while there is emphasis on achieving a certain amount of independence in terms of finances, personnel, and missionary outreach to non-Christians within the diocese, this needs to be done within the context of universal communion.

## A Missionary Bishop and Clergy

Paragraph 20 speaks first of the role of the local bishop, who "should be first and foremost a herald of the Faith" (*AG*, 20) and should have a clear grasp of the context in which he leads the church. The priests of the diocese should not only be engaged in pastoral work; they should also be willing to do missionary work among other peoples and cultures, or in neglected places in their own dioceses. In fact, sending missionaries abroad, even cases where there is a shortage of clergy, is seen as a real priority. The rest of the church—both religious and lay—needs to "show the same fervent zeal toward the women and men in their country, especially the poor" (*AG*, 20—my translation).

## A Vibrant Laity

The next paragraph deals somewhat extensively with the laity in these particular churches. The text is insistent on the fact that "the church has not been really founded, and is not yet fully alive, nor is it a perfect sign of Christ among humanity, unless there is a laity worthy of the name working along with the hierarchy" (*AG*, 21—my translation). Their main task is to bear witness by their daily lives, in their professions, and in the context of their cultures. There is special emphasis here on the connection of lay life with the particular culture in which people practice their Christianity. Again, the emphasis is on a Christian life that is not removed from culture or society but is immersed in it. Implicit here is a concern that Christianity not be regarded as a Western or foreign religion, but as one that has taken deep root in local soil. A person can be a genuine African, Asian, Papua New Guinean, Mexican, or Lakota and still be an authentic Christian.[16]

## Culture and Theology

The final paragraph of the chapter is devoted to the encouragement of local, contextual, or inculturated theologies, although the text does not use those terms (such terminology would be developed in the decade or so after the decree was published; the term used here is "adaptation"). In one of the most eloquent phrases of the document, and echoing a phrase often used in the liturgy, these particular churches are encouraged to "take to themselves in a wonderful exchange all the riches of the nations which were given to Christ as an inheritance (cf. Ps 2:8) (*AG*, 22).[17] It is "necessary," therefore that theological speculation should be encouraged "in each major socio-cultural area" (*AG*, 22). This should be done, of course, in the light of the tradition of the entire church, but in a way that submits it to a new scrutiny. In this way "it will be more clearly seen in what ways faith may seek for understanding" (*AG*, 22) in the context of the philosophy, the wisdom, the customs, and the worldviews of local peoples.

### CHAPTER 4: MISSIONARIES

In William R. Burrows's words, this "is an excellent, balanced and far-sighted chapter designed to help prepare future missionaries"— whether they are priests, brothers, women religious, or lay people, and whether they are foreign or indigenous. The council recognized that missionaries could no longer be classified as only priests or religious, nor could they be classified as only *foreign* missionaries. Once again the text implicitly acknowledges that missionary activity is based not on geography but on particular peoples and their needs.

## The Missionary Vocation

Being a missionary is a vocation, a charism bestowed by the Holy Spirit. As in the case of all charisms, however, the Spirit works within the parameters of both natural ability and ecclesial context: missionaries have certain natural abilities—good health, the capability to learn languages, and the capability to adapt to another culture—and missionaries are sent by the authority of the church and are not "Lone Rangers." The missionary vocation is rooted in a particular spirituality, based especially on the example of Jesus himself, who "emptied himself" (Phil 2:7). Although some council fathers objected to the idea, the text indicates that a large part of this missionary self-emptying involves a lifetime commitment to missionary service. Part-time service is taken up in the chapter at a later point (i.e., *AG*, 26), but here the ideal missionary is described as one who has pledged her or his whole life to becoming "all things to all" (1 Cor 9:22).

**Missionary Formation**

Preparation for missionaries is to be extensive and demanding, marked by both spiritual and moral training. Missionaries must have both initiative and perseverance, being "patient and strong of heart in bearing with solitude, fatigue, and fruitless labor" (*AG*, 25). They need an "open mind and a wide heart…a noble spirit" (*AG*, 25) to adapt to different ways of doing things and to constantly changing situations. Needless to say, missionaries should be women and men of prayer, for this is the only way they can develop a constant spirit of zeal, of love, of prudence, and of patience. Theological training is necessary too—and it should be training that "takes in the universality of the Church and the diversity of the world's nations" (*AG*, 26). In addition, studies in anthropology, world religions, linguistics, and missiology should be provided. An understanding of missiology would include knowledge of the norms of the church concerning missionary activity, mission history, current trends in mission situations, and missionary methods. To cite a phrase of Suso Brechter in his important commentary on *Ad Gentes*, this is "a formidable catalogue of virtues" indeed.

**Religious Congregations**

The council paints an ideal picture of the missionary, it admits, but this is because the entire missionary task is not something that can be carried out by individuals alone. This points to the importance of missionary institutes, which can accomplish corporately more than individuals can on their own. In the light of *Lumen Gentium*'s teaching on bishops,[18] the work of these missionary communities is carried out "under the direction of the hierarchy" (*AG*, 27), but it is clear that for centuries these communities have "borne the burden of the day" (*AG*, 27). In the context of a growing uncertainty about the role of foreign missionaries (an uncertainty that would increase to immense proportions in the years immediately after the council), *Ad Gentes* emphasizes the fact that the missionary congregations still have a vital and "extremely necessary" role to play in the work of world evangelization.

### CHAPTER 5: PLANNING MISSIONARY ACTIVITY

Chapter 5 deals with "planning" or "organizing" of missionary work (the Latin title is "De Ordinatione Activitatis Missionalis"). It was the only chapter of the schema that failed to achieve the needed two-thirds majority in the vote that was held on November 9 at the council's fourth session. Many of the *modi* that the members of the council had submitted dealt with the reform of the Congregation of the Propagation of the Faith, and so the final draft of the schema was even stronger on this point.

The directives for the reform of the Propaganda are placed in the context of a theologically based understanding of the direction of the church's mission. Paragraph 28 begins the chapter by stating that all the Christian faithful, according to the gifts bestowed on them, are called to participate in the church's mission. In this way *Ad Gentes* is once more echoing the grand theme of the fundamental equality of the people of God found in *Lumen Gentium*'s chapter 2 (especially parargraph 32).

But, the text insists, this missionary activity of all the faithful needs to have direction, so that (quoting 1 Cor 14:40) "all may be done in order." That direction is provided primarily by the body of bishops, as *Lumen Gentium* 23 teaches. And so, as a way of exercising that collegial responsibility, the council directs that the "stable Council of bishops for the entire Church," what Paul VI named the "Synod of Bishops," should give special consideration to the church's missionary activity.[19]

### Reform of the Propaganda Fide

The Congregation for the Propagation of the Faith, therefore, directs and coordinates the church's missionary work as the "one competent office" (*AG*, 29) empowered to do so—but only as the agent of the entire church's responsibility, and as the agent as well of the college of bishops united with the pope. The text outlines what the direction of the congregation is to be. It should promote missionary vocations and spirituality, zeal and prayer for the missions; it should offer adequate reports, issue directives, and provide financial support. The congregation is seen, in short, as the institutional "incarnation" of missionary work. In an extraordinary phrase, however, the text relativizes the official work of church leadership, admitting that the Holy Spirit is also at work in missionary situations, both arousing the spirit of mission in the church and "oft times" even anticipating "the action of those whose task it is to rule the life of the Church" (*AG*, 29).

Brechter explains that behind the phrase "one competent office" lies the fact that previously there had been particular territories not under the Propaganda's jurisdiction. On account of Portugal's right of patronage, the colonies of Angola and Mozambique in Africa and Goa, Macao, and East Timor were under the Congregation for Extraordinary Affairs. In addition, the Consistorial Congregation was responsible for apostolic vicariates and prefectures in Latin America. The one exception to the streamlining that took place here is that of the missionary work directed by what is now called the Congregation for the Oriental Churches.[20] Brechter suggests that, despite the rather fierce attack to which the Propaganda was subjected during the council, it "actually emerged from this obstinate and emotionally charged struggle considerably increased in power." Not only was its history affirmed; the reform proposed was meant to equip it for the future by increasing and extending its authority. The apostolic constitution *Regimini Ecclesiae* of August 15, 1967, changed the name of the Congregation to "Congregation for the Evangelization of Peoples or 'Propagation of the Faith.'" We will have more to say about this change in Part 3 where we will discuss the implementation of *Ad Gentes*.

At the end of paragraph 29 we read in its final form the passage that went through such a critical revision in the course of the council. As part of the direction of the congregation, there should be a group of representatives of the world's bishops, moderators of the pontifical institutes that support missionary work (e.g., the Propagation of the Faith, the Society of St. Peter for indigenous clergy, the Missionary Union of the Clergy, and the Holy Childhood Association), missionary congregations of men and women, and lay organizations. While they are not referred to as "members" of the congregation (as the original draft had put it), this group should play an active role in the congregation, and should have a deliberative vote in the congregation's decision-making process. The group would be assisted by consultors "of proven knowledge and experience."

Although we will focus on the development of this new group within the Propaganda in Part 3, it must be noted here that this crucial directive of *Ad Gentes* was never fully put into practice. Over the years, through a series of documents, the role of this group of bishops and other missionary leaders was gradually lessened to the point where, in *Redemptoris Missio*, John Paul II only invites "Episcopal Conferences...the Major Superiors of Orders, Congregations and Institutes, as well as lay organizations...to cooperate fully with this Dicastery" (*RM*, 75). Ultimately, as missiologist Josef Glazik has written, practically nothing has changed from what the congregation was before the council.[21]

## The Role of the Bishop

The next paragraph once more deals with the implications of *Lumen Gentium* 23 and *Christus Dominus* 6 (also articulated in *AG*, 5 and 29), that each diocesan ordinary is in some way responsible, as part of the episcopal college, for the evangelization of the entire world. In his own diocese, therefore, the bishop's task is one of promoting missionary activity both within and beyond diocesan boundaries, "in such a way that the zeal and spontaneity of those who share in the work may be preserved and fostered" (*AG*, 30). Within a bishop's diocese, the text says, all missionaries—even exempt religious—are subject to his authority. To better coordinate the pastoral and missionary activity in the diocese, the bishop should set up a pastoral council in which "clergy, Religious, and laity may have a part, through the medium of selected delegates" (*AG*, 30). Collaboration is encouraged within and among episcopal conferences, so that resources might be used more creatively in terms of seminaries, universities, pastoral and liturgical centers, and instruments of social communication. A fine example of such cooperation *among* bishops' conferences would be the Federation of Asian Bishops' Conferences (FABC), founded in 1974. In the words of Thomas C. Fox and Jonathan Y. Tan, the FABC has provided a "new way of being church" and a "new paradigm" in mission theology.[22]

## Bishops and Religious Congregations

Having laid down the role of bishops as the leaders of the work of evangelization in particular churches, the document turns next to the delicate issue of the relationship between bishops and the missionary communities (of men) who work in their dioceses. Until this point in time, missionary congregations (called "institutes" in the text) had worked in missionary territories as a result of contracts between themselves and the Propaganda. These contracts were drawn up under what was called the *jus commisionis*, roughly translated as the system of the "right of entrustment." Under this system, the Holy See (through the agency of the Propaganda) gave charge to particular religious orders and congregations certain specific mission territories. While this system had its advantages in that the territory could be assured of a continual supply of personnel and finances, it also presented a number of difficulties. In the first place, it gave the impression that the responsibility for mission was not with the entire church, but only with the missionary congregations. Second, it took away the missionary responsibility of the local bishop and the particular church. Finally, it gave rise—understandably—to a number of tensions between local bishop and the superiors of the missionary congregations to whom the territory had been entrusted. This was particularly the case as the local church began to grow in numbers and there was an increase in diocesan clergy. What *Ad Gentes* is laying down here, therefore, is a new policy regarding relations between local ordinaries and religious orders, one that harmonizes with the theological principles that the entire church is missionary (*AG*, 2) and that, as we have seen above, it is the *bishop* who has authority over all works of evangelization in his diocese (*AG*, 30; see also *AG*, 32).

Within this new perspective, the text calls for contracts to be drawn up between local bishops and superiors of religious congregations. When the old contract between the missionary congregation and the Propaganda expires—that is, when the hierarchy is established in a mission territory with local bishops rather than vicars or prefects apostolic —"a new state of affairs begins" (*AG*, 32).[23] The *jus commissionis*, in other words, would eventually cease to exist as a principle of mission law in many places, and a new legal principle, the *jus mandati*, would eventually begin to take effect (although it would not necessarily ever cease to exist).[24] The new principle calls for a contract between a religious congregation and a local bishop that will "mandate" certain tasks within a diocese, to be carried out under the bishop's authority for a stipulated length of time. The text states that "it will be the role of the Holy See to outline the general principles according to which regional and even particular contracts are to be drawn up" (*AG*, 32). These would be provided in the instruction *Relationes in Territoriis* in 1969 and in canon 790.1.2 of the 1983 Code of Canon Law. We will speak in greater detail about the implementation of the *jus mandati* in Part 3.[25]

The discussion in *Ad Gentes* of this issue of the relationship between religious and local ordinaries concludes with words of encouragement for collaboration and cooperation across the board. As the local clergy in a diocese begin to grow numerous, the religious congregation should remain faithful to the diocese. When there are several congregations working in a diocese, means should be found to coordinate their work. Conferences of religious men and religious women should be established, and these should be in close communication with episcopal conferences. In "home lands" (we see how the decree easily falls into the old pattern of "sending" and "receiving" churches) religious should work together in areas of formation, courses for missionaries, and connections with government and international organizations.

## Collaboration for Missionary Training

The chapter concludes with a further call for collaboration among "scientific institutes which specialize in missiology and in other arts and disciplines useful for the missions," such as anthropology, linguistics, history of religions, and sociology. Such collaboration will ensure that missionaries are adequately trained for their ministry, "especially for dialogue with non-Christian religions and cultures" (*AG*, 34).

### CHAPTER 6: COOPERATION

The decree's final chapter, on missionary cooperation—or on how various Christians contribute to the missionary activity of the church—begins with the council once more affirming that "the whole Church is missionary, and the work of evangelization is a basic duty of the People of God" (*AG*, 35). Because of this, all Christians are invited to "a deep interior renewal" so that "they may do their share in missionary work among the nations" (*AG*, 35). The text then speaks about how individual Christians—ordained, religious and lay—contribute to evangelization (*AG*, 36) and continues by addressing the role of the Christian community (*AG*, 37), of bishops and priests (*AG*, 38–39), of the various types of religious (*AG*, 40), and then of the laity (*AG*, 41). There is a great distance between this chapter and the strong statement about the missionary nature of the local church in chapter 2, with that chapter's effort to move away from the more traditional "territorial" concept of mission. Here "missions" basically means "foreign missions"; there are "home countries" and "mission countries."

Paragraph 36 makes the point that the very sacramental life of Christians propels them toward participation in the church's mission: baptism, confirmation, and Eucharist in particular are missionary sacraments. Ultimately these sacraments lead Christians to *act*, but most fundamentally they call Christians to *be*—to live lives that are witnesses to the power of the gospel in their own lives. From such lives, prayer and works of penance will naturally result, and from this will come a blessing on missionaries' work throughout the world, new missionary vocations, and generous financial support for the church's work throughout the world. Very subtly but significantly, the text adds that such "testimony of a good life" (*AG*, 36) will be more effective if it is practiced in union with members of other Christian communities; this is one aspect of what has come to be called "common witness."[26]

Individual Christian witness, however, is not enough. Christianity is essentially a life together, and so witness must be given as parish and diocesan communities. One way of doing this is for each community to have a global consciousness, and devote the same "care to those afar off as it does to those who are its own members" (*AG*, 37). A community presumably would do this by praying for the needs of other churches when its members are gathered together, by raising its consciousness of issues in other parts of the world, and by financial aid. Another way that the text suggests is by keeping "in contact with missionaries who are from one's own community, or with some parish or diocese in the missions" (*AG*, 37). This last idea—sometimes known as "twinning"—was recommended by a good number of bishops at the council. Brechter points out that the Propaganda always looked at this practice with some suspicion, not wanting there to be "poor and rich missionaries, needy and well-to-do missions," depending on which parish or diocese supported them. An earlier version of the decree had a stronger recommendation for this practice, but the final version mentions it here only as a possibility, "provided the universal scope of mission work is not thereby neglected" (*AG*, 37).

The chapter moves on now to a rather long treatment of the role of bishops in world evangelization. Repeating once more one of the "major themes of the decree,"[27] that bishops are responsible not just for one diocese but for the entire world, it insists that the gospel mandate "primarily and immediately concerns them, with Peter and under Peter" (*AG*, 38). The bishop of a particular diocese has to see to it that it becomes missionary. He does this by urging his people—"especially the sick and those oppressed by hardship" (*AG*, 38)—to offer prayers and penance for the success of evangelization. He will encourage vocations to missionary congregations and not keep them all for the work in his own diocese. He will promote organizations that foster missionary awareness—such as the Society for the Propagation of the Faith and the Holy Childhood Association. He will send his own priests to help in dioceses that lack clergy, at least for a time. This last idea builds on Pius XII's 1957 encyclical *Fidei Donum*, in which the pope asked bishops to release priests of their diocese for work in Africa. *Ad Gentes* extends this appeal, Brechter points out, to the rest of the world, on the basis of episcopal collegiality and bishops' co-responsibility for the work of the universal church.

On the territorial level, the text urges episcopal conferences to supply priests as well, and to institute a kind of tax for missionary work. They might also work to help—and even found—missionary congregations, and assist in ensuring that diocesan priests and those of missionary congregations work more closely together. Episcopal conferences should also provide pastoral care for migrants from mission lands, and recognize the opportunity to witness to the gospel and preach it to non-Christian migrants in Christian lands.

Paragraph 39 offers several reflections on the intrinsic missionary dimension of the priesthood. Because they are collaborators with the bishop's ministry, priests, like the bishops, are in some way responsible for the worldwide mission of the church. An intrinsic part of their ministry, therefore, involves raising missionary awareness among the women and men to whom they minister, fostering missionary vocations, praying regularly for the missions, and not being ashamed to ask for alms for the church's missionary work. The last part of the paragraph calls for professors in seminaries to develop a missionary dimension to the courses that they teach, and so form a missionary awareness in seminarians.

The document next turns to the role of religious, both "active" and "contemplative." It is often thought that missionary work is the work of only active congregations—evangelizers, teachers, nurses, community organizers—but the council turns first to a brief reflection on contemplative communities and their indispensable role in evangelization. Because it is *God* who ultimately opens the hearts of women and men to accept the gospel, the prayers, sufferings, and acts of penance offered by groups of contemplative men and women contribute immensely to the conversion of non-Christians. The text goes on to recommend to such communities that they found houses in mission lands so that "living out their lives in a way accommodated to the truly religious traditions of the people, they can bear excellent witness among non-Christians to the majesty and love of God, as well as to our union in Christ" (*AG*, 40). The council then poses a number of probing questions to active congregations: whether or not they were originally founded as missionary congregations, could they extend their missionary commitment—even changing their constitutions if necessary? Could they leave some of their ministries to others in order to send personnel to the missions? Are they as culturally adapted as possible to local circumstances? A final short word is said about secular institutes, the growth of which the council acknowledges here: they might consider missionary work as "a sign of complete dedication to the evangelization of the world" (*AG*, 40).

The final paragraph of this chapter (*AG*, 41) focuses specifically on the laity. As in several other significant places in the council documents (*LG*, 31; *AA*, 2) the lay vocation is understood in itself as a direct participation in the church's mission. In Christian lands, the laity do this by being themselves conscious of missionary work, and by helping others to come to the same awareness. They also participate in the work of the missions by encouraging missionary vocations in schools, in Christian associations, and in their own families; and of course they assist with their financial support. In missionary contexts, however, the document urges lay men and women to be active in ministry: to teach in schools, administer finances in parishes and dioceses, and organize and develop various forms of the lay apostolate. Proper training for the laity is strongly recommended, so that they will not be "stumbling blocks" (1 Cor 10:32–33) to the gospel for the people among whom they work. A word is said about lay scholars who engage in studies of non-Christian religions, because in this way they help missionaries prepare for dialogue with people of other faiths.

### CONCLUSION

The decree concludes with a salutation to all missionaries, especially those who are suffering persecution. The council fathers and the pope assert once more that they are firmly committed to preaching the gospel, but that they know that, in the end, the church's mission is the work of God. In this spirit they pray for the conversion of the world to the gospel, through the intercession of Mary, Queen of Apostles. The date of the approval of the decree is December 7, 1965, and there follows an announcement entitled "A Suspension of the Law," declaring that any changes in the law of the church provided for in the decree will take effect on June 29, 1966. In the meantime, the pope will issue norms for the implementation of these laws. It is to this implementation that we turn in Part 3.

# IMPLEMENTATION

## INTRODUCTION

*Ad Gentes* is a document that is both profoundly theological and eminently practical. Any adequate treatment of the implementation of the decree, therefore, needs to reflect on the implementation or reception of its more theological dimension as well as on the various official moves of implementation mandated in subsequent papal and curial documents issued over the last four decades. Accordingly, the first section of this third part will be devoted to tracing the understanding of mission as it has developed since the council up to our own day. What we will consider here, in other words, is how the theology of mission articulated in *Ad Gentes* was implemented in the church—and among missionaries in particular—in the years following the council. A second section—considerably longer—will focus on how the recommendations, exhortations, and directives in *Ad Gentes* have been implemented through a rather large number of documents issued by the pope, by the Congregation for the Evangelization of Peoples (known until 1967 as the Congregation for the Propagation of the Faith, or the Propaganda), by other Roman congregations, and by the 1983 Code of Canon Law.

## MISSION AFTER THE COUNCIL: RECEPTION AND DEVELOPMENT

The century and a half prior to Vatican II had seen a period of immense missionary effort, with phenomenal growth of both men's and women's missionary congregations and an expansion of the church's missionary presence all over the world. It was, as Robert Schreiter characterizes it, a "period of certainty"[1] about the value of missionary activity and world evangelization.

This missionary presence was often in league with the extraordinary development of the exploitative colonialism of the Western powers in the latter part of the nineteenth century, although many missionaries raised prophetic voices against colonialism's excesses.[2] Mission was supported, but it was also critiqued and challenged by the five papal mission encyclicals that were published throughout the twentieth century up until the eve of Vatican II (from 1919 until 1959). While these encyclicals paid scant attention to the *theological* foundations of missionary work, they placed particular emphasis on the development of an indigenous clergy, and some emphasis as well on the need to value local cultures. In the new field of missiology (the first Catholic chair of missiology, held by Josef Schmidlin, was established at Münster in 1911), the issue was not so much the *nature* of mission but rather its *goal*. The debate had to do with whether the purpose of mission was the conversion of individuals or the establishment of the church, with German scholars tending to defend the former, and French and Belgian scholars tending to defend the latter.[3] Any discussion with regard to the *why* of mission—its theological foundations—tended to be grounded on Jesus' commands to "make disciples of all nations" (Matt 28:19) or on God's universal salvific will. Throughout the twentieth century missionary vocations flourished, particularly in North America, in Holland, Germany, Ireland, and France.

## A Time of Ferment

*Ad Gentes* was promulgated at the end of this "period of certainty," and at the beginning of a period of intense ferment and epochal change, both within the world at large and within the world of mission. During the years after World War II, the period of European and U.S. American colonialism gradually came to an end. In 1946 the Philippines achieved independence from the United States; in 1947 India and Pakistan became independent from Great Britain; in 1949 The Netherlands recognized Indonesia's independence; and in 1957 Ghana in West Africa became the first of many African states to achieve independence throughout the decade of the 1960s. Through the 1960s and

1970s other nations in Asia, Oceania, and the Caribbean would achieve sovereignty as well.

The outspoken nationalism of the time was matched by both a revival of local cultures and a renewed appreciation of local religions. In the nineteenth century there had been no doubt about the preeminence of European culture over all others, with evolutionary theory being interpreted in a way that gave a certain inevitability to the advancement of Western "progress." Similarly, the great world's religions were regarded as moribund and the triumph of Christianity in the twentieth century was hailed as absolutely inevitable.[4] With the demise of colonialism and the rise of nationalism, however, the importance of local cultures and cultural identity increased, and local religions took on new vigor. At the same time, the 1960s were marked by a strong optimism in terms of the possibility of economic progress for the entire world. Nations that were considered "mission territories" in Asia, Africa, and Latin America were described as "developing countries," and it was believed by the "developed" West and North that their achieving economic stability would only be a matter of time.[5]

## Mission in Crisis

When the movements of nationalism, cultural identity, and religious revival connected with the openness of the church at Vatican II to the "modern world," the effect on the church's understanding and practice of mission was "seismic."[6] We have seen in our summary of the main points of *Ad Gentes* how the document is open to the autonomy of the newly evangelized churches (e.g., chapter 3 of the decree), to the "treasures a bountiful God has distributed among the nations of the earth" (*AG*, 11), and to the "leading strings" toward God, those aspects of local religious systems which serve as a "preparation for the gospel" (*AG*, 3). This openness changed the understanding of mission profoundly. While paragaraph 6 clearly stated that the goal of mission was both the witness and preaching of the gospel and the establishment of the church, the recognition of the *ecclesial* nature of the newly evangelized churches and the appreciation of their cultural and religious traditions moved mission away from the idea that it was only about expanding a basically Western institution and saving women and men from certain damnation. Rather than being viewed as "extending the perimeters of the church," says Robert Schreiter, mission "was to be something motivating the very heart of the church, not because some command had been laid upon the faithful, but because by being missionary the church was drawn into the life of the Trinity itself." Schreiter goes on to say that this shift of theological foundation brought a change in the metaphors used for missionary activity—from military metaphors of commission and conquest to metaphors of "invitation, dialogue, and sharing."[7]

Such a profound change in the theology and recommended practice of mission was welcomed by many bishops and missionaries alike. It was something that had been brewing in mission situations, in missiology, and in theology in general for a long time.[8] However, the change that *Ad Gentes* indicated also served to precipitate a serious crisis in missionary thinking and motivation, and it was this crisis that marked the first years after the council and the promultation of the decree. Gone was any certainty of the superiority of the more firmly established "sending churches," and gone was the certainty of the superiority of Western culture. What was seen as more and more important was to allow the churches once regarded as moving toward the ideal model of the churches of Europe and North America to develop instead their own autonomy as churches in their own right, and with their own cultural resources. Foreign personnel, rather than helping this process, were often in the way, and might serve the local church better by returning home. And, perhaps more radically, with Vatican II's acknowledgment of the possibility of salvation outside of explicit faith in Christ and membership in the church (*LG*, 16 and 9; *NA*, 2 *AG*, 9 and 11), many Catholics—including missionaries—no longer saw missionary activity as an urgent need. If people could be saved by following their own consciences in the context of their own religions, why try to convert them? How could the traditional understanding of evangelization be harmonized with the new emphasis on invitation and dialogue?

Schreiter reports that in the first years after the council the number of missionaries throughout the world continued to rise. After 1968, however, "the numbers moved into a steady and often precipitous decline." Some of this decline, he says, could be attributed to the massive numbers of priests and religious in general who left the ministry in the years after the council. "But the growing insecurity about what was the exact nature of mission in a post–Vatican II church surely fueled this development as well."[9] Among Protestants and Catholics alike, the very idea of missionary activity—and foreign missionary activity in particular—was being called into question. In 1967, prominent American churchman Monsignor Ivan Illich called for a withdrawal of U.S. American missionaries from Latin America so that they could work at home against the forces that were keeping Latin Americans in structures of poverty. In that same year, Catholic missiologist Ronan Hoffman shocked his audience at a meeting of U.S. mission sending societies by announcing that the era of foreign missionary activity was over, and that the structures that supported foreign mission work should now be dismantled. In 1971 Protestant church leaders John Gatu of Kenya and Emerito Nacpil of the Philippines called for a "moratorium" on foreign missionaries so that the funds used for that purpose could be directed toward the development of the poorer churches of Africa and Asia.[10]

For the moment, it would seem, Fr. Johannes Schütte's claim, when he presented the mission schema to the council, that *Ad Gentes* represented the Magna Charta of the church's missionary activity, and that it would inspire the entire church to become missionary, was hardly being positively received on many fronts.[11]

## A New Vision Begins To Unfold

Despite these problems of reception, however, there was a movement stirring throughout the church that would contribute to the reception and implementation of *Ad Gentes* in ways that the bishops at Vatican II perhaps could not have imagined. This movement began from one quarter with the recognition of the close connection between the church's mission and the church's witness to justice—the latter a major strand in Catholic tradition since Leo XIII's 1891 encyclical *Rerum Novarum*. It began from another quarter with the recognition of the wisdom in Paul VI's first encyclical *Ecclesiam Suam* (1964), in which he called for an attitude of dialogue as the best way that the church could engage the world to which it is sent. This movement of renewal in understanding the nature of mission was further developed in Paul VI's apostolic exhortation *Evangelii Nuntiandi* (1975) and John Paul II's encyclical *Redemptoris Missio* (1990), both of which recognize that the church's mission is not confined to witnessing to and proclaiming the gospel message, but is lived out in all its "richness, complexity and dynamism" (*EN*, 17) as a "single but complex reality" (*RM*, 41.) Mission, in other words, as it is articulated by further papal teaching, consists of a number of constitutive elements (although proclamation continues to hold a certain "permanent priority" [*RM*, 44]).

What we will sketch out here are the broad outlines of this development. More detailed reflection on the various constitutive elements of mission will be done in Part 4, where we will discuss the state of the questions surrounding mission today.

## Mission and Justice

Reading *Ad Gentes* today one is struck by the fact that very little emphasis is placed on a topic or theme that has become a major element of mission today: justice and peace. There are some hints in paragraph 12 that—in language evocative of *Gaudium et Spes* 1—the church shares in people's "joys and sorrows, knows their longings and problems, suffers with them..." and brings them the "peace and light of the gospel." A bit further on Christians are urged to engage in "waging war on famine, ignorance and disease," and to work with people who are "struggling to better their way of life and to secure peace in the world"—while not getting involved in "the government of the earthly city." By and large, however, the issues of justice, economic development, and peacemaking were dealt with at the council not in the document on the missions but in the Constitution on the Church in the Modern World—a document closely aligned with the decree on missionary activity but one not specifically connected to *mission*.

What becomes significant, however, is how the issues dealt with in *Gaudium et Spes* become closely connected with missionary concerns in the years after the council. There are three significant moments when the relatively small hints at the connection between justice and peace in *Ad Gentes* become explicitly connected with mission: the meeting of the Conference of Latin American Bishops (CELAM) at Medellín, Colombia, in 1968, the Synod of Bishops' document on justice in the world in 1971, and the inclusion of justice and peace in a broader understanding of mission in Pope Paul VI's apostolic exhortation *Evangelii Nuntiandi* in 1975. It was with this third document that, according to Schreiter, the missionary movement, battered by crisis in the late 1960s and early 1970s, came to a new understanding and a new birth.

In August, 1968 some 130 bishops, representing all the bishops of Latin America (more than 600), met in Medellín, Colombia, for the purpose of reflecting on the church's task in Latin America in the light of Vatican II.[12] This was the second meeting of CELAM, the first having taken place in Rio de Janeiro in Brazil in 1955. In the sixteen documents of conclusions from the meeting, *Ad Gentes* is quoted only four times, while *Gaudium et Spes*—overwhelmingly the most quoted Vatican II document—is quoted forty-four times, and yet the documents very clearly deal with the mission of the church in a frontier or missionary situation. Several address the same topics treated by the council—there are documents on liturgy, priesthood, religious, formation of the clergy, mass media, and education. But the most significant documents—the ones for which Medellín is remembered as marking a new era in the Latin American church—are those that reflect on the mission of the church in the Latin American context. These are the documents on justice, on peace, on pastoral care of the masses, and on the poverty of the church. The documents are filled with phrases that in the decades to come would become the standard coinage of the language of mission, and they critique the rather naive notion of inevitable development or economic progress that was present in the West during these years. Medellín denounced "institutionalized violence," which it spoke of as a "situation of sin." It called for a "consciousness-raising evangelization," and in several places referred to *comunidades de base* or "base communities" as small communities of Christians that were ordinarily led by lay women or men. It spoke, finally, about liberation, and linked the process of liberation in today's oppressed Latin American situation with the biblical event of the exodus.[13]

What Medellín did was to link issues of justice, peace, development, and liberation to the evangelizing mission of the church. This was not done explicitly, but such an explicit connection would be made a few years later at the 1971 Synod of Bishops. In its document, entitled *Justice in the World*, the synod famously proclaimed that "Action on behalf of justice and participation in the transformation of the world fully appear to us as a constitutive dimension of the preaching of the Gospel, or, in other words, of the Church's mission for the redemption of the human race and its liberation from every oppressive situation."[14] The document speaks of the "right to development," the importance for the church itself to be a community of justice ("...everyone who ventures to speak to people about justice must first be just in their eyes"), and the need to pursue ways of peacemaking among nations. And, again, this is because the church "has a proper and specific responsibility which is identified with her mission of giving witness before the world of the need for love and justice contained in the Gospel message...."[15] No stronger or clearer statement could be made about the relationship between issues of justice and peace, barely hinted at in *Ad Gentes*, and Christian mission.

## Mission as Multifaceted

Medellín, following *Gaudium et Spes* and Pope Paul VI's encyclical, *Populorum Progressio*, highlighted the church's commitment to justice as central to its life. The 1971 Synod made the connection between the centrality of justice and the church's evangelizing mission. In 1974, in the midst of the "period of crisis" in regard to the church's missionary activity, the Synod of Bishops met to discuss the theme of evangelization in the contemporary world. Unlike the synod in 1971, however, at this synod the bishops did not produce a final document—they were unable to come to an agreement about an appropriate statement.[16] At the suggestion of Cardinal Karol Wojtyla (the future John Paul II), they asked Paul VI to write a document on the basis of their deliberations. In December 1975, therefore, the pope published what some say is the document that *Ad Gentes* had been intended to be: the apostolic exhortation *Evangelii Nuntiandi*.[17]

The document is a rich and inspiring work, but what is of most concern to us here is its second chapter, entitled "What Is Evangelization?" The pope begins the chapter by cautioning against understanding evangelization in any reductionistic way that would be only "partial and fragmentary" (*EN*, 17).[18] Even the pope's choice of "evangelization" rather than "mission" for the topic of the 1974 synod, and his use of the term here, point to a more comprehensive understanding of mission than was offered in *Ad Gentes*.[19] For Paul VI, the explicit proclamation of Jesus as Lord and Savior is the *sine qua non* of evangelization (*EN*, 22), but essential too is the witness—without which words are empty—of individual Christians and the Christian community (*EN*, 21). "But," the pope adds, "evangelization would not be complete if it did not take account" of the whole life of women and men. This is why there must be an evangelization of human cultures in a way that takes culture with absolute seriousness (*EN*, 20); and this is why, too, evangelization is a message "about life in society, about international life, peace, justice and development—a message especially energetic today about liberation" (*EN*, 29).

*Evangelii Nuntiandi* does not go as far as to say that interreligious dialogue is itself one of the elements of evangelization. This will be the task of later documents such as *Redemptoris Missio* and *Dialogue and Proclamation*, which we will discuss in Part 4. Already in 1974, however, in a document issued in preparation for the 1974 Synod of Bishops of which *Evangelii Nuntiandi* was the fruit, the bishops of Asia spoke for the first time about evangelization in Asia involving inculturation, dialogue with Asia's religions, and dialogue with Asia's poor.[20] It is this perspective that would be strongly advocated in the 1974 Synod of Bishops and that was presumably a strong influence on Pope Paul VI when he composed *Evangelii Nuntiandi*.[21] For the Asian bishops, evangelization is first about building up the local church, and so it involves a "humble and loving dialogue...with all the life-realities of the people in whose midst it has sunk its roots deeply and whose history and life it gladly makes its own." Second, evangelization involves dialogue with Asia's great religions, because only in this way "can we discover in them the seeds of the Word of God" (referencing here *AG*, 9). Finally, because of Asia's overwhelming poverty, the Asian bishops—like the Latin American bishops at Medellín six years earlier and the 1971 Synod of Bishops as well—see mission or evangelization as involving a dialogue with the poor. As the bishops insist, "the search for justice, evangelization and the promotion of true human development and liberation, are not only not opposed, but make up today the integral preaching of the Gospel...."[22]

What *Evangelii Nuntiandi* provided, therefore, was a new space for reflection on the nature of mission, very much building on *Ad Gentes*, but going considerably beyond it. While not retreating one whit from the church's commitment to missionary activity and world evangelization (e.g., *EN*, 5, 53), Paul VI demonstrated the comprehensiveness of the church's evangelizing mission and its continuing relevance in a world not only of newly independent nations, newly appreciated cultures, and newly revived religions, but also of struggle, violence, and institutionalized structures of poverty and oppression. The perspective of *Evangelii Nuntiandi* did not completely solve the crisis of missionary vocations or revive the era of certainty about missionary activity. But it did maintain the church's missionary commitment while at the same time allowing the ideas expressed at the council to be concretized and implemented in the context of a world in the process of rapid and even radical change.

This first section has traced the reception or implementation of the new theology of mission that found expression in *Ad Gentes* in the years following the council. This reception or implementation developed as the church in general and missionaries in particular struggled to make sense of the often unjust world in which the church's mission was being carried out, and of the new theological insights into the local church, local cultures, and the validity of other religious ways. It was articulated by further documents issued by the church's leadership, but validated more indirectly by the entire church's approval and appropriation. We turn now to examining the more direct norms of implementation contained in a number of documents issued in the months and years following the council.

## THE DOCUMENTS OF IMPLEMENTATION

In the conclusion of Part 2 it was noted that appended to the date of approval of *Ad Gentes*, December 7, 1965, was an announcement declaring that any changes in current law would be suspended until June 29, 1966 and that within that span of time the pope would issue norms for the implementation of any new laws or policies. In a first step toward that implementation, Paul VI issued a *motu proprio* on January 3, 1966, setting up a number of postconciliar commissions to ensure that the various council documents would be implemented as quickly as possible. These commissions—on bishops, on religious, on the missions, on Christian education, and on the lay apostolate—would be coordinated by a central commission that would report to the pope.[23] On June 10, 1966, the pope issued another *motu proprio* in which he noted that all the postconciliar commissions had worked diligently and had finished their assignment on time, but because there were so many things to implement, the Coordinating Commission had recommended that the decrees of implementation be published gradually. The pope concurred with this recommendation and accordingly deferred the date of implementation from June 29 until the particular dates indicated in the individual decrees, which the pope promised would be promulgated as soon as possible.[24]

### Ecclesiae Sanctae

There was not long to wait for the first of these. On August 6, 1966, Paul VI issued the *motu proprio Ecclesiae Sanctae* in which the norms for the implementation of the decrees on bishops, presbyters, religious, and the missions were promulgated.[25] The pope made clear, however, that because of the impending revision of canon law, these norms were being promulgated *ad experimentum*. The norms would go into effect on October 11, 1966, the feast of the Maternity of the Blessed Virgin and the fourth anniversary of the opening of the council.

*Ecclesiae Sanctae* consists of three sections: the decrees on bishops and presbyters (*Christus Dominus* and *Presbyterorum Ordinis*) are dealt with in the first, the decree on religious life (*Perfectae Caritatis*) is dealt with in the second, and implementation of *Ad Gentes* is dealt with in the third. This final section is developed in twenty-four relatively short points. A good many of these points are somewhat exhortative in nature. Several, however—such as those dealing with the structure of the Congregation for the Propagation of the Faith and relations between bishops and religious—are more concrete and juridical in character. Most focus on specific issues mentioned in the fifth and sixth chapters of *Ad Gentes*, issues having to do with missionary planning and missionary cooperation.

The document deals with a number of topics, and they are roughly grouped together in the text (though not always). In examining the content of the document, we will summarize what it says about each particular theme. We will treat the reform of the Propaganda and the issue of the relationships between local ordinaries and religious institutes as these appear in the document but, because of significant developments relating to each of these topics in subsequent documents, we address these two topics again at the end of Part 3.

**Mission Theology.** The introductory paragraph and the first point of section 3 deal with the importance for the church at large to understand the missionary nature of the church. To this end, "discourses on the Decree should be given to the clergy and sermons preached to the people in which everyone's responsibility in conscience with regard to missionary activity is pointed out and inculcated" (Introduction).[26] The theme of the church's mission and the church's missionary nature should be evident throughout the whole of theology, and, as *Ad Gentes* 39 suggests, this should be "taken into account" in teaching theology in seminaries and universities (1).

There are some indications that this missionary aspect of theology continued to be emphasized in the years following the council as well. In late September of 1966 a major conference was held in Rome on the theology of the council, and one of the conclusions of this conference notes that the missionary and ecumenical dimension of theology is not just to play a marginal role, but is to be at theology's very center.[27] This same idea also found its way into the 1970 *Ratio Fundamentalis* for priestly formation in several places.[28] In 1970 The Congregation for the Evangelization of Peoples issued a circular letter to the presidents of episcopal conferences throughout the world on the missiological formation of future priests. The concern of the congregation was the formation of a missionary *spirituality*, but the document recognizes that such a spirituality can be fostered only within the context of a theology that takes account of the missiological dimensions of all the theological disciplines. While acknowledging that diocesan seminarians do not need the thorough missiological training that future missionaries need, it points out that it is still important to know about places where mission work is being carried out and about the fundamentals of a missionary theology.[29] Whether this ideal is being implemented universally is hard to say, but it still appears as a requirement, at least, in the latest edition of the *Program of Priestly Formation* in the United States, and in the United States Conference of Catholic Bishops' 2005 statement on world mission, *Teaching the Spirit of* Ad Gentes: *Continuing Pentecost Today*.[30]

Among Protestants there is a growing literature relating to the missiological nature of theology and the importance of a missiological perspective in ministerial training, but this issue has been less extensively explored by Catholics.[31]

**Missionary Spirit.** Points three through five discuss ways in which a "missionary spirit" can be fostered among the Christian people, referring to *Ad Gentes* 36 (3) and 38 (4–5). Point three calls for the encouragement of "daily prayers and sacrifices" so that the annual mission day (this will be mandated by the 1983 Code of Canon Law in canon 791.3) will be a spontaneous celebration. It also calls for either bishops or episcopal conferences to prepare prayers to be added to the Prayer of the Faithful during the celebration of the Eucharist. In order to ensure the development of a missionary spirit, point four calls for a priest to be appointed who will especially promote missionary work. He should also be a member of the diocese's pastoral council. Finally, the document suggests in point 5 that seminarians and youth should have some kind of contact with their counterparts in mission lands, "so that an exchange of knowledge may foster among the Christian people a missionary and ecclesial awareness."

**Missionary Vocations.** Again referring back to *Ad Gentes* 38, the sixth point of this third section of *Ecclesiae Sanctae* calls for bishops to promote missionary vocations both among their own diocesan clergy and among young women and men. Bishops are encouraged to provide the opportunities for missionary congregations to make their diocese aware of the needs of the missions, and to inspire vocations—presumably by allowing them to recruit in their dioceses.

**Monetary Contributions.** Points number seven, eight, and nine take up the directive in *Ad Gentes* 38 that bishops' conferences "should consider how to direct and organize the ways and means by which the missions receive direct help." The pontifical mission societies—the Propagation of the Faith, the Society of St. Peter for indigenous clergy, the Missionary Union of the Clergy, and the Holy Childhood Association—should be promoted in every diocese (7). Each diocese should establish a policy of contributing a certain amount to the missions, while still encouraging individual members of the diocese to contribute as well (8). Point number nine speaks of the need for each episcopal conference to establish an "episcopal commission for the missions" that will work to promote missionary activity, mission awareness, cooperation in missionary matters among dioceses and other episcopal conferences, and developing ways to give adequate and equitable missionary aid. Whether this last point has found universal implementation is probably impossible to determine, but it certainly is the case that the United States Conference of Catholic Bishops has a very active Committee on World Missions.[32]

**Missionary Congregations.** Points ten through twelve address issues in *Ad Gentes* 23, 27, 37, and 38. The term "missionary institutes" is used in *Ecclesiae Sanctae* and refers here to the missionary *congregations*, or missionary *orders*. Point number ten emphasizes that these missionary groups are still "extremely necessary" for the work of evangelization, and that their work helps carry out the missionary duty of the people of God. Repeating what was said in point six, the document calls on bishops to use missionary congregations to inspire the faithful, and to provide ways for these groups to foster missionary vocations in general, recruit for their own communities, and seek monetary contributions. This last activity, however, should always be coordinated with the various pontifical mission societies. Finally, according to point number twelve, each congregation should take steps toward its own renewal, especially in terms of its own methods of missionary work and its internal community life. This last point is a reference to the council's document on religious life, *Perfectae Caritatis* 3.

Point number seventeen also addresses missionary congregations, but in regard to their relation with local bishops. As soon as possible, the text says, the Propaganda should consult with episcopal conferences and then "outline general principles according to which agreements should be made between local Ordinaries and missionary institutes to govern their mutual relations." This responds to *Ad Gentes* 32, which says that the outlining of such general principles governing contracts between communities and ordinaries is the role of the Holy See. The result of the directive here in *Ecclesiae Sanctae* was published as *Relationes in Territoriis*, promulgated by the Congregation for the Evangelization of Peoples in 1969.[33] We will discuss this document in some detail below.

Point number twenty-one refers to the recommendation in *Ad Gentes* 33 that organizations for women and men religious are to be set up in mission territories in which major religious superiors are to participate and by which congregations can coordinate their work.

**The Sacred Congregation for the Propagation of the Faith.** Points number thirteen through sixteen concern the implementation of the directives in *Ad Gentes* 29 on the reform of the Congregation for the Propagation of the Faith. This paragraph was vigorously discussed during the council, and it was dissatisfaction over the reform of the Propaganda in this paragraph that prevented the passage of chapter 5 at the council's fourth session.[34] *Ecclesiae Sanctae* substantially repeats the directive in *Ad Gentes* 29 that there should be one curial office—namely the Propaganda—that deals with issues regarding the church's missionary work. As we noted in our summary of the main points of *Ad Gentes* in Part 2, this changed the current practice, since other congregations were at this time responsible for Portuguese colonial territories and countries in Latin America.[35] Because of this change called for by *Ad Gentes*, and because the reform of the curia had not yet been promulgated, *Ecclesiae Sanctae* states that "since certain missions are for special reasons temporarily still subject to other curial offices, a missionary section should in the meantime be established in these offices which will maintain close relations with the Sacred Congregation for the Propagation of the Faith so as to provide a completely constant and uniform method and norm in the organization and direction of all the missions" (13.1).

The text then repeats from *Ad Gentes* 29 that the four pontifical mission societies (the Propagation of the Faith, the Society of St. Peter for indigenous clergy, the Missionary Union of the Clergy, and the Holy Childhood Association) are under the direction of the Propaganda (13.2). Point number fourteen states that the president of the Secretariat for Christian Unity is automatically to be a member of the Propaganda, and the president of the Propaganda is to be likewise an ex officio member of the Secretariat. This directive makes more concrete the call in *Ad Gentes* 29 for the Propaganda's "coordination" with the Secretariat.

The next two point numbers (15 and 16) take up the reorganization of the Propaganda proposed in *Ad Gentes*, making specific what the council decree only outlined in general. Ordinarily—that is, unless the pope decides otherwise in individual cases—twenty-four representatives "take part in the direction of the Sacred Congregation for the Propagation of the Faith with a deliberative vote" (15). The twenty-four members of this new commission are to be

- twelve missionary bishops,

- four bishops from other regions of the church,

- four (male, one supposes) superiors general, and

- representatives from the pontifical mission societies.

The group will be called together twice a year. Its members will be named for five-year terms, with four or five ("approximately one fifth") rotating out of the group each year. The terms of these representatives, however, could be renewed for another five years. They are all to be chosen by the pope, upon the suggestion of episcopal conferences, religious congregations, and the pontifical mission societies.

Representatives of missionary communities working in mission countries, of regional mission societies, and of lay associations are to be given a consultative vote (16). In this way *Ecclesiae Sanctae* interprets the directive in *Ad Gentes* that these groups be "suitably represented." The implementation document does not say specifically whether these representatives could be either male or female, but it does not preclude the possibility of female representation.

**Episcopal Conferences.** The topic of episcopal conferences is treated at some length. The first reference to such conferences is found early on, in the section on the implementation of *Ad Gentes* (2), and refers to paragraph 29 of the conciliar document, the first section of which charges the newly established Synod of Bishops with giving special attention to missionary activity in its deliberations. Here episcopal conferences are invited to propose to the Holy See any questions dealing with missionary issues that can be dealt with at the first meeting of the synod. This may have in fact been done. In fact, however, the synod, held the following year, in 1967, did not deal with any particularly missionary topics, but with more general issues, such as the preservation of the faith, mixed marriages, and the revision of the Code of Canon Law.

Point number eighteen takes up the topic again, particularly in a number of sub-points. The text begins by calling on the Propaganda to ensure that episcopal conferences in "so-called socio-cultural areas" are well coordinated. Then the function of conferences is laid out. They are to explore new methods by which Christians—religious and lay—"incorporate themselves into peoples or groups with whom they live or to whom they are sent" (18.1). Anthropologists call this "acculturation." Second, in a way intended to implement *Ad Gentes* 19 and 22, episcopal conferences are also to "establish study groups" to investigate local ways of understanding the world—what would eventually be called "inculturation." This should lead to appropriate ways of preaching the gospel, celebrating the liturgy, living religious life, and legislating for the church. Any proposed liturgical innovations, however, should be submitted to the post-conciliar council for the implementation of the Constitution on the Sacred Liturgy. With a reference to *Ad Gentes* 18, caution is voiced lest more attention be given to external forms such as gestures, dress, and the arts than to work for real religious conversion in the context of a particular cultural situation. This same directive will find an echo in a famous line of *Evangelii Nuntiandi*, which calls for an evangelization of cultures that is done "not in a purely decorative way as it were by applying a thin veneer, but in a vital way, in depth and right to their very roots" (*EN*, 20).

Third, episcopal conferences are to promote meetings of seminary teachers to adapt study programs and exchange information. In this way, and by conferring with the study groups mentioned previously, they can better prepare men for ordination. This is an effort to implement *Ad Gentes* 16. In the fourth place, says the document, episcopal conferences should investigate a better method of distributing priests and catechists, so that there can be more personnel in more densely populated areas. Finally, in response to *Ad Gentes* 17 and 29, money should be set aside each year for the training and support of local clergy and the training of catechists. Records of this should be submitted to the Propaganda (19).

Point number twenty deals more with individual dioceses than with conferences, but it might be appended here. We read of how a pastoral council should be established—presumably in every diocese—to "investigate pastoral works, to weigh them and to formulate practical conclusions regarding them," as *Christus Dominus* 27 directs. Such a pastoral council should prepare for a diocesan synod and see to it that its decisions are properly implemented.

**Scientific Institutes, Migrants, and Lay Missionaries.** The last three implementation directives in this third section of *Ecclesiae Sanctae* deal very briefly with scientific institutes, migrants, and lay missionaries. Scientific institutes are encouraged in mission countries, according to *Ad Gentes* 34, but they should cooperate among themselves and not duplicate each other's work. In the years since the council, most likely in response to this directive, institutes like Ishvani Kendra in Pune, India; the Melanesian Institute in Goroka, Papua New Guinea; the Lumko Institute in Johannesburg, South Africa; and the Institute for Aymaran Studies in Puno, Peru can be seen as examples of the kind of scientific (and pastoral) institutes that both *Ad Gentes* and *Ecclesiae Sanctae* had in mind.

Point number twenty-three speaks briefly of the need for bishops in more traditionally Christian countries in Europe, North America, Australia, and New Zealand to cooperate with missionary bishops from whose countries many immigrants have come. For all sorts of reasons, migration has only increased in the decades since the close of the council, and the need for such cooperation for the sake of proper pastoral care for migrants has correspondingly become more urgent.

The final point, number twenty-four, makes four statements regarding lay missionaries in an effort to implement *Ad Gentes* 41. First, what is to be urged among lay missionaries is sincere intention, maturity, suitable preparation, professional specialization, and sufficient time in missionary work. Second, lay missionary organizations are to be coordinated properly. Third, local bishops should be concerned about the welfare of lay missionaries. And finally, lay missionaries are to receive some kind of "social security."

### *Regimini Ecclesiae Universae* to *Pastor Bonus*
### The Sacred Congregation for the Evangelization of Peoples

*Regimini Ecclesiae Universae.* On August 15, 1967, Pope Paul VI published the apostolic constitution *Regimini Ecclesiae Universae*, which laid down norms for the reform of the Roman curia in the light of Vatican II. In chapter 9 of the third part of the document (which deals with the sacred congregations) the reform of the Congregation for the Propagation of the Faith is treated, and in this way *Ad Gentes* is further implemented.[36]

The first paragraph (81) states that what has up until now been called the "Sacred Congregation for the Propagation of the Faith" will in the future be named the "Sacred Congregation for the Evangelization of Peoples or for the Propagation of the Faith." Over the next twenty years this is how the congregation is referred to in official documents; in other circles it increasingly is called only the "Sacred Congregation for the Evangelization of Peoples." In 1988, in another reform of the curia under Pope John Paul II, the name of the congregation is designated officially with this shorter name, as we will see below.

Paragraph 83 discusses the important reform that was supposed to bring into the congregation bishops and others who would represent the mission churches. This had been proposed in *Ad Gentes* 29 and implemented in *Ecclesiae Sanctae* 15 and 16, as discussed above. According to *Regimini Ecclesiae Universae*, members of the congregation, besides the cardinals assigned to it by the pope, were now to include the presidents of the secretariats for Christian unity, for non-Christians, and for non-believers (83.1). The presidents of the last two secretariats mentioned were an addition from what had been stipulated in *Ecclesiae Sanctae*, which had required only that the president of the Secretariat for Christian Unity be a member. Besides these, and in order to deal with issues of major importance, bishops from the missions, representatives of superiors general of missionary congregations, as well as representatives of the pontifical mission societies were to participate in plenary sessions of the congregation as full members (*tamquam earundum Membra*) and—if it pleased the pope—to be given a deliberative vote (83.2). This directive is slightly different from that in *Ecclesiae Sanctae* 15 and *Ad Gentes* 29, where the deliberative vote is given unless the pope decides otherwise. *Regimini Ecclesiae Universae* does, however, refer to *Ecclesiae Sanctae* in regard to the number of the representatives (twenty-four) from the wider church (83.3).

Paragraph 90 speaks about consultors to the congregation, but in a way that differs from that in *Ad Gentes* 29 and *Ecclesiae Sanctae* 16. While consultors are delineated in paragraph 90 (they are experts, secretaries of the three secretariats mentioned above, directors of the pontifical mission societies, and representatives from international societies of lay persons), nothing is said of representatives of male or female religious, or whether the consultors have a consultative vote. Rather, the group of consultors "gathers useful information about the local situation of the various regions, the mentality of diverse groups of peoples, and in regard to the methods of evangelization to adopt; then it proposes scientifically valid conclusions for missionary work and missionary cooperation."

*Regimini Ecclesiae Universae* outlines in paragraphs 84–91 the rather vast responsibilities and powers of the newly renamed congregation—responsibilities and powers even vaster than those it had before the council. The congregation is now responsible for the missionary activity in territories assigned to it; it promotes missionary spirituality and missionary vocations; it offers prayer for the missions and furnishes accurate and timely information about them. It has responsibility for the education of youth and the formation of clerics, and it makes sure that synods are celebrated and bishops' conferences are organized. It makes visitations at predetermined times and, through the pontifical mission societies, sees to it that financial help is distributed. It has under its jurisdiction all religious congregations founded in the missions or working there, as well as the seminaries that are founded for the purpose of sending forth foreign missionaries (85 and 86). These responsibilities and powers are limited only in those areas that would conflict with responsibilities and powers of other congregations, such as the Congregation for Religious, or for Catholic Education, or for the Doctrine of the Faith, or for the Discipline of the Sacraments. In this way *Regimini Ecclesiae Universae* confirms Suso Brechter's remark in his commentary (quoted in Part 2) that the congregation, despite much opposition on the council floor and many calls for reform, actually emerged from the council "considerably increased in power." Brechter notes that the congregation's "historical achievement was acknowledged and confirmed," adding that "for the future it is to be renewed, better equipped and its powers are even to be increased and extended."[37]

**Cum in Constitutione.** *Regimini Ecclesiae Universae* 83.3 mentions that, in regard to the number of the additional members of plenary sessions of the congregation, the directives of *Ecclesiae Sanctae* should be kept in mind, as well as "the special instruction that will be published by the Sacred Congregation." This instruction, *Cum in Constitutione*, was published several months after the apostolic constitution on curial reform, in February 1968, and concerned itself with both the "adjunct members" (as the document calls them) and the consultors.[38]

The first section deals with the "adjunct members," who are listed exactly as in *Ecclesiae Sanctae* 15—twelve missionary bishops, four bishops from other regions, four superiors general, and four representatives of the pontifical mission societies. However, rather than saying that they "take part in the direction...with a deliberative vote" (*ES*, 15), the text says only that they have an "active part" (*CC*, I.1). These twenty-four adjunct members are appointed by the pope, but are proposed by the cardinal prefect of the congregation upon the recommendation of episcopal conferences, the Roman union of superiors general, and the heads of the pontifical mission societies.

The sixteen bishops chosen by the pope (twelve from missionary countries, four from other regions) enjoy full membership (*pleno jure sunt Membra*) in the congregation and therefore participate in the plenary assemblies that deal with themes of major importance and basic principles of missionary theology and missionary work. If any of these prelates happen to be in Rome, they can also be present in ordinary assemblies—although the text does not specify whether they have a vote in these. The four superiors general and the representatives of the pontifical mission societies chosen by the pope also participate as members (*tamquam Membra*) of the plenary assemblies where themes of major importance and general principle are discussed. They have "the same rights and obligations as the cardinals and the bishops" (*CC*, I.7 and .9), although nothing is said about their right to attend the ordinary assemblies. As in *Ecclesiae Sanctae*, all of the "adjunct members" are appointed for a renewable term of five years, and approximately one-fifth of the membership rotates out of the group each year. At the death of the pope, all have to be reconfirmed by the new pope three months after his election (*CC*, I.10).

The consultors are also chosen by the pope after nomination by the congregation and also serve for a renewable term of five years (*CC*, II.1). They can be bishops, religious or diocesan priests, lay women or lay men; the only requirement is that they be truly experts in missionary thinking and experienced in missionary work (*CC*, II.2). They can serve in a number of ways: they can be asked to send their thoughts to Rome in writing or they can be invited by the cardinal prefect to Rome or to another location. They can even be invited to the plenary assembly when this seems necessary. In every case, the consultors have a consultative vote (*CC*, II.5).

The first plenary assembly of the congregation under these new directives took place in Rome from June 25 to 28, 1968, and resulted in the instructions *Quo Aptius*, which dealt with the organization of the pontifical mission societies and with certain matters of mission law, and *Relationes in Territoriis*, which dealt with the relations between missionary congregations and local ordinaries.[39] Plenary assemblies have been held regularly in the forty years since this initial assembly, and have dealt with a variety of issues, including catechists (1992), missionary cooperation (1996), and formation (2003).

***Pastor Bonus.*** A little more than twenty years after the publication of *Regimini Ecclesiae Universae*, John Paul II published on June 28, 1988, the document that further reformed and reorganized the Roman curia: *Pastor Bonus*. In the introduction, John Paul points out that Paul VI had ordered that the norms of *Regimini Ecclesiae Universae* be "examined more deeply" five years after its proclamation (*PB*, 5). Consequently, in 1972 an extensive study and revision of the curia's structures was initiated. The study was to continue through the remaining six years of Paul VI's pontificate and the first ten years of John Paul II's. In light of the revision of the Code of Canon Law in 1983 and discussions held at the 1985 and 1987 Synods of Bishops, the pope was now able to present the church with a more definitive reform.

The new document has a lot in common with *Regimini Ecclesiae Universae*, but the one major innovation is that the category of secretariats (except that of state) in the earlier document is replaced by that of councils. Now the curia's dicasteries consist of the Secretariat of State, nine congregations, three tribunals, twelve pontifical councils, and three offices.

As mentioned above, *Pastor Bonus* shortens the name of the congregation for mission to simply the "Sacred Congregation for the Evangelization of Peoples." This is done without any comment. Other changes in the structure of the congregation, however, are even more subtle. *Regimini Ecclesiae Universae* and *Cum in Constitutione* had spoken of the twenty-four non-cardinal representatives from among missionary bishops, other bishops, superiors general, and members of the pontifical mission societies as members of the congregation when in plenary session. *Pastor Bonus* does not speak of this group of twenty-four at all, but states in I.3.3 that only the cardinals and bishops are members of the congregation strictly speaking. Although superiors general and members of the pontifical mission societies are not mentioned specifically in the text, it would seem that they still have representation in these plenary assemblies, since they are called "members" in the profile of the Congregation on the Vatican website.[40] Plenary sessions are now to take place solely once a year—and this only "as far as possible"—in contrast to the directive in *Ecclesiae Sanctae* that they be held twice annually (I.11.2). The document also speaks about consultors for the congregations, individuals who can be bishops, priests, male or female religious, or lay men or women, but it does not use the term "consultative vote"; rather, consultors study and present their considered opinion on particular issues, usually in writing, although they can also be called together for deliberation in common (I.12).

*Ad Gentes* had called for a reform of the Propaganda to include members of the wider church as having an integral part in determining the direction of the congregation. It provided that "representatives of all those who cooperate in missionary work" be "called together at stated times" to "exercise supreme control of all missionary work under the authority of the Supreme Pontiff" (*AG*, 29). A close reading of the documents of implementation summarized here, however, shows that this major change in the organization of the congregation was not really put into effect. *Ecclesiae Sanctae*, by limiting the "stated times" of the meetings to twice a year—in what *Regimini Ecclesiae Universae* calls plenary assemblies—does not allow for the representatives' participation in the "ordinary" sessions of the congregation. It is in these "ordinary" sessions that the major work of the congregation is carried out, and so the representatives meeting twice yearly could hardly "exercise supreme control." The limitation of such exercise is also expressed by the hesitation to call the representative group "members" of the congregation and to give them a clear deliberative vote. Although they are called members on the Vatican website profile, *Pastor Bonus* says that only the cardinals and the bishops are members in the strict sense; the superiors general and national directors of the pontifical mission societies are to be invited only to the plenary assemblies, held as far as possible only once a year. The implementation of *Ad Gentes* 29 has certainly provided for a wider representation of those with firsthand experience of local churches that are still under the direction of the congregation. But this does not seem to be exactly what the council had in mind in this particular paragraph.

Perhaps, however, the council was a bit too ambitious in this regard. Suso Brechter suggests in his commentary that when the council called for "selected representatives" to "exercise supreme control" (*AG*, 29), it "obviously took a false step."[41] To exercise the kind of oversight envisioned by the council, the representatives from the wider church would have had to meet much more than the once a year directed by *Pastor Bonus*—or even more than the twice yearly prescribed by *Ecclesiae Sanctae*—and this would certainly have interfered with the ordinary duties of the local bishops, religious superiors, and national directors. Although the judgment was made forty years ago, canon lawyer and future bishop Viktor Dammertz's conclusion, quoted by Brechter, is still valid: the congregation "will therefore remain in the future a congregation of cardinals in which the cardinals have the decisive influence and it is probably more than chance that the ambiguous sentence is not repeated in the Instructions for implementing the Missionary Decree."[42]

Still, it is unfortunate that the vision of Fr. Schütte and of many bishops at the council for more participation in the Congregation for the Evangelization of Peoples (at it is now known) has not been more fully realized, even while acknowledging the overambitious nature of the structure called for by *Ad Gentes*. In a commentary on the decree published in 2005, that is, forty years after the council, German theologian Peter Hünermann traces the gradual lessening of wider participation in the decisions of the congregation from papal hesitation in *Ecclesiae Sanctae* regarding the deliberative vote of the representatives, through bestowal of "quasi-membership" in the congregation in *Regimini Ecclesiae Universae*, to the determination of the representatives' participation only in matters of greater importance and general principle in the 1968 congregational instruction *Quo Aptius*.[43] He notes, finally, how John Paul II in *Redemptoris Missio* 75 refers to *Ad Gentes* 29 in regard to the congregation's overall direction of missionary activity, but not to the participation of representatives of the wider church. Instead, the pope invites "Episcopal Conferences and their various bodies, the Major Superiors of Orders, Congregations and Institutes, as well as lay organizations involved in missionary activity, to cooperate faithfully with this Dicastery, which has the authority necessary to plan and direct missionary activity and cooperation worldwide."[44]

### *Relationes in Territoriis*: Bishops and Missionary Congregations

*Ad Gentes* 32 dealt with the relations between bishops in dioceses that were still under the jurisdiction of the Propaganda Fide and the religious institutes to whom that territory had been entrusted under the system known as the *jus commissionis*. This was a system whereby the Holy See through the Propaganda entrusted a particular mission territory to the care of a specific missionary congregation; this territory was led by a vicar or prefect apostolic, who cared for the church there not as an ordinary bishop but as a prelate directly responsible to the pope. The regulations for the *jus commissionis* had developed over the years, but had been collected in an instruction issued by the Propaganda in 1929 entitled *Quum Huic*.[45]

What *Ad Gentes* recognized, however, was that in the last several decades a number of factors had made it necessary to revise this 1929 instruction. First of all, in the forty intervening years since *Quum Huic* had been issued, the number of ordinary dioceses that had been erected in mission lands had multiplied. In 1927 (two years before *Quum Huic*) there were 402 territories directly overseen by the pope in the person of vicars and prefects apostolics, and only 95 of these (23 percent) were fully constituted as dioceses; by 1969 the total number of mission territories had increased to 827 and the number of regular dioceses to 675 (82 percent).[46] In addition to this change in the overall complexion of the worldwide church was the fact that a growing number of dioceses had developed their own local clergy, so that the pastoral care and the work of evangelization in the diocese was more and more being carried out by those who were native to the place, who knew the local languages from birth, and who were subjects of the local culture. This did not mean that foreign missionaries had become unnecessary, but it did mean that the leadership of the local church was becoming more and more the responsibility of its indigenous members. Finally, Vatican II had laid down the theological principles that "all bishops are consecrated not just for some one diocese, but for the salvation of the entire world" (*AG*, 38; see also *AG*, 29 and *LG*, 33) and that local bishops are responsible for the mission of the church in their individual dioceses (*AG*, 38). And so, with more and more territories becoming full-fledged dioceses, the immediate responsibility for evangelization in them was moving from the missionary congregation to the local ordinary. This is the background for understanding the directives in paragraph 32 of *Ad Gentes* and how the instruction *Relationes in Territoriis*, issued by the Congregation for the Evangelization of Peoples on February 24, 1969, is meant to implement them.[47]

The instruction begins by recalling the circumstances (summarized above) that led to its composition, and then it lays down a number of principles. The first of these is that the *jus commissionis* remains in force in places where dioceses have not yet been established, but it is abrogated in all dioceses in mission territories (i.e., where there is a local ordinary, but where there are still few indigenous clergy, a small group of active and educated laity, and where the diocese is still dependent on the larger church for financial assistance).[48] The system that replaces the *jus commissionis* ("commission") is called the *jus mandati*, ("mandate") and it is the form of a special collaboration of a missionary congregation with a local bishop (2).

Principles three to seven describe this *mandatum* or mandate. It is, first of all, a charge that is given by the supreme authority of the church (the Holy See through the Congregation of the Evangelization of Peoples), on the request of a bishop and accepted by the Holy See, for the sake of collaboration in a missionary diocese with the bishop and under his authority, according to a particular contract (3). The mandate is given only when a missionary congregation takes on within the diocese the care of a specific territory or a specific ministry (4). While those who were eligible for the commission were only communities of male religious, the mandate can be received by lay or clerical institutes, or congregations of men or of women (6).

Principles eight to twelve speak about how the mandate is given. Before requesting a mandate from the congregation, a local bishop must ask the opinion of the bishops' conference of which he is a part, and must inform the congregation of this opinion in writing (8–9). Once the request is made, it is up to the congregation to issue the mandate (9), which can be revoked only by the congregation—although the congregation must consult with the local bishop before doing this (10). A local bishop can also admit other congregations into his diocese, with or without the formal mandate. If a congregation works in a diocese without the mandate, the congregation does not "assume the special responsibility deriving from the concession of the mandate" (11).

The instruction then goes on to determine the rights and obligations of the local bishops. While the bishops have a certain "proper, ordinary and immediate" authority in their dioceses (13; see *LG*, 32), they
nevertheless hold this power in communion with the pope. Papal authority in the case of the missionary dioceses is exercised directly by the
Congregation for the Evangelization of Peoples. But the bishop, as a
true ordinary, is the head and center of the diocesan apostolate and
therefore promotes, directs, and coordinates missionary activity within
his diocese. Nevertheless, this is done in collaboration with the missionary institutes working in his diocese.

The missionary congregations therefore have their own rights and
obligations, which are laid out in principle fourteen. They are to be recognized as valuable assets for the church's mission in the dioceses in
which they have received the mandate. Because of this they should not
be restricted in exercising their own spirituality and autonomy, or in establishing communities or recruiting members. This being said, however, the instruction reminds congregations that they are under the
bishop's authority and must collaborate with him. Both parties are
urged to make clear contracts with one another as to the exact nature of
the work that the congregations will do, the number of missionaries involved, how they are to be appointed to various offices, and the manner
of their transfer, removal, and substitution.

The fifteenth principle deals with the relations between bishops
and congregations regarding temporal goods and their administration,
and only a few principles are presented. Property that belongs to the
diocese should be administered according to canon law (*ad normam iuris
communis*); property belonging to religious congregations should be administered according to canon law, or according to the constitutions of
the congregation or the norms of mission law (*iuxta Statuta pro
Missionibus*). With regard to alms given to the missions, it is important
to respect the will—explicit or implicit—of the donor. Donations received for a particular project or for a particular congregation must be
used for that particular purpose. Donations given to missionaries belong to the missionary her- or himself, or to the congregation, depending on the rules of the individual community.

The final principle (number 16) states that all that is presented in
the instruction should be considered the basis for the contracts to be
written between local ordinaries and the various congregations who re-

ceive the mandate. These contracts are to be drawn up within a year of the promulgation of the decree—that is, by February 24, 1970.

In many ways, *Relationes in Territoriis* (the substance of which is repeated in the 1983 Code of Canon Law)[49] opens a new era in the missionary life of the church. For so many years mission was almost totally in the hands of the foreign missionary, and up until our own day that has meant persons from the more affluent and often arrogant West and North. While the day of the foreign missionary is a long way from being over (indeed, the title of *Redemptoris Missio* 30 will state that missionary activity is only beginning!), and while still in many places the *jus commissionis* remains very much in force, in most of the Catholic world it can be said that "the responsibility of running the Local Church, of determining diocesan policy should be in the hands of the local bishop and his local clergy. The missionary should offer himself to the Local Church to serve where he is needed. Only in this way can the Local Church begin to stand on its own feet and gradually come of age."[50] With this instruction the vision of *Ad Gentes* in this regard, and the vision of the missionary bishops at the council, has basically been fulfilled, despite any flaws in the way it may be carried out in practice.

### THE 1983 CODE OF CANON LAW

Before ending this section on the implementation of *Ad Gentes* it is necessary to speak briefly about how the decree is implemented in the 1983 revision of the Code of Canon Law (canons 781–792). The canons on mission, "The Missionary Action of the Church," appear in the third book of the code, entitled "The Teaching Function of the Church," and they are relatively few. The eleven canons need to be read in light of the longer documents of implementation that have been summarized here, and also in light of the documents of the council, especially *Ad Gentes* and the constitutions *Sacrosanctum Concilium*, *Lumen Gentium*, and *Gaudium et Spes*.

Canon 781 alludes to *Ad Gentes* 2 when it says that, because of the essential missionary nature of the church, evangelization is the task of the entire people of God. As missionary canon lawyer Amand Reuter points out in this regard, this is a change from the former conception that the responsibility for mission is primarily that of the pope.[51] The pope's role now, together with the entire college of bishops, is that of "supreme direction" (782.1), with individual bishops having the task of "initiating, fostering, and sustaining" missionary work in their own particular churches (782.2). It should be noted that the role of the Congregation for the Evangelization of Peoples is not mentioned here, and this is because its task, as a congregation of the Roman curia, is to be an arm of the pope as he carries out his Petrine ministry within the church. Canon 783 speaks briefly about the obligation of religious congregations to take up missionary work, and canon 784 again reflects the new missionary situation envisioned by *Ad Gentes* when it acknowledges that missionaries are not just foreign personnel, but any persons who have been designated as such by "competent ecclesiastical authority." While this does not completely eliminate the overall impression of a territorial understanding of mission, it does imply that mission is more than this. Canon 785.1 and .2 echo the concern in *Ad Gentes* 17 for the important role of catechists.

Canon 786 reprises the definition of mission stated in *Ad Gentes* 6, amending it slightly to emphasize just a bit more the aspect of preaching the gospel over the implantation of the church. The next canon, however, highlights the necessity for missionaries to engage in "sincere dialogue" with non-Christians, and calls for genuine sensitivity to their cultures. Canon 788 takes up the topic of catechumens which was treated in *Ad Gentes* 14. This text had called for their juridical status to be "clearly defined in the new code of canon law." Canon 788.1 directs that catechumens be admitted to the catechumenate in liturgical ceremonies and that their names be inscribed in a book reserved for the names of catechumens; canon 788.3 leaves it up to the conference of bishops to regulate the prerogatives and obligations of catechumens. Canon 789 calls for post-baptismal instruction to be given to the newly baptized.

Canons 790 and 791 focus on missionary activity in individual dioceses. The diocesan bishop of a missionary diocese is to "promote, direct, and coordinate" (see *AG*, 30) the church's missionary activity within his diocese (c. 790.1.1), and to enter into formal agreements with missionary congregations (c. 790.1.2; see *AG*, 32; *ES*, 17; and *RT*). As *Ad Gentes* 30 and *Relationes in Territoriis* prescribed, all missionaries, and especially religious, are subject to the local bishops (c. 790.2). In every diocese throughout the world, missionary vocations are to be promoted, a priest is to be designated to promote missionary causes, an annual mission day is to be celebrated, and an offering for the missions is to be sent yearly to the Holy See (see *AG*, 38; *ES*, 4).

The final canon in this section calls upon bishops' conferences to be hospitable to and pastorally solicitous for women and men who come into their territories from mission lands (*AG*, 38). This canon would take on growing importance in the years to come.


### CONCLUSION

*Ad Gentes* was promulgated at a time when the theological foundations of the church's mission were undergoing a profound reinterpretation and transformation. On the one hand, Christians welcomed the idea that the church in its every aspect was missionary, and that its task was to be present to and caring for "the joys, the hopes, the griefs and anxieties" of the women and men of the entire world" (*GS*, 1). On the other hand, the idea of mission as restricted to witness to and preaching of the gospel and establishment of the hierarchical church was coming under more and more criticism in the light of the demise of colonialism with its denigration of human cultures and economic exploitation, the renaissance of the world's religions, and a more positive attitude toward salvation outside the boundaries of explicit Christian faith. The implementation of the theology of mission presented in *Ad Gentes*, therefore, could be accomplished only as Christians in general and the church's teaching office in particular began to widen the concept of mission to include not only witness, proclamation, and the implantation of the church (*AG*, 6), but also commitment to all aspects of social justice, to elements that included the respect for people's cultures, and to respect and dialogue with peoples' religions. The contemporary understanding of mission includes all these elements, and even more. We will take up a reflection on these in Part 4 when we survey the state of the questions raised by mission today.

From the beginning of the preparation of the document on mission, it was clear that it was to be one that addressed certain practical issues that needed change or reform in a world that had been transformed in the course of the previous century. Among these issues, the reform of the Congregation for the Propagation of the Faith and the formal relationships between bishops and missionary congregations in mission territories were considered most significant, and the implementation of *Ad Gentes* has addressed both in significant ways. If the reform of the Propaganda was not all that the bishops at the council might have wished for, there have indeed been important changes introduced into its structure and ways of operation. The rapid changes in the demography of Christians in the last century have brought about radical changes in the ways that foreign missionaries operate within mission territories, many of which are genuine local churches, and the implementation of *Ad Gentes* has addressed this situation in a very adequate way.

On balance, *Ad Gentes* has been well implemented, although perhaps in ways that might surprise its authors and those who approved it.

# PART IV

# The State of the Questions

## INTRODUCTION

Appraising the significance of *Ad Gentes*, German theologian Peter Hünermann judges that "even after an interval of about forty years it is surprising to see the extent to which the council fathers imagined and fostered perspectives that would have a future but were just emerging then."[1] *Ad Gentes* rooted the church's mission in the overflowing life of the Trinity. It advanced the understanding of mission beyond the debates between the German and French schools of missiology, and it sowed the seeds of an even wider understanding of mission that included sensitivity to culture and context, to the truth found in other religious ways, and to issues of justice and peacemaking. It acknowledged that missionary churches, even though they were not completely self-sufficient, were nevertheless *churches* in the full and proper sense. It spoke of mission as the duty and privilege of the entire people of God, and in so doing placed special emphasis on the laity. It did all this with a sensitivity to ecumenical issues and recognized that a commitment to ecumenical dialogue was a *sine qua non* of the faithful preaching of the gospel. The two great papal missionary documents of the postconciliar years—*Evangelii Nuntiandi* and *Redemptoris Missio*—as well as the powerful documents of the Latin American, African, Asian, and North American episcopates have all developed understandings of mission far beyond *Ad Gentes* in terms of the scope of the church's missionary activity. At the same time, however, there has been an amazing continuity. *Ad Gentes* did what a good document should do: it provided a basis for a deepening and broadening of the major questions with which it wrestled.

The task of this fourth part is to examine the state of those major questions. We have alluded to several of them in the previous paragraph, but it might be important to state them even more clearly. First, we need to look at the nature of contemporary missionary activity, its basic purpose and scope. Second, we need to examine the search for an adequate theology of mission today. Third, we need to see how mission is currently understood as a many-faceted, "single but complex reality" (*RM*, 41) and is constituted by a number of distinct yet interrelated elements. These elements include a more classical emphasis on direct proclamation and witness, but also elements such as liturgical action, commitment to justice, engagement in a culturally sensitive communication of the gospel, and participation in dialogue with women and men of other faiths. Fourth, we need to inquire about the present role of the laity in missionary work.[2]

At the same time, the questions dealt with in *Ad Gentes* have given rise to other questions that make up an integral part of understanding mission today. No discussion of contemporary understandings of mission would be complete without a reference to the phenomenon of globalization. Similarly, in the forty years since the promulgation of *Ad Gentes*, the importance of ecological responsibility and ecojustice has emerged as a growing concern for the church's missionary vision. And, particularly in the years since the demise of Communism and the end of the Cold War, the care of migrants and the ministry of reconciliation have become major concerns of mission in this "new world order" of racial, ethnic, and religious violence and conflict. In all of this development, with the advent of the "second wave" of the feminist movement in the late 1960s, women's role in mission—always a major one—has now been more clearly highlighted, particularly in the history of mission.

In sum, the understanding and practice of mission have changed dramatically since the close of Vatican II and the promulgation of its decree on missionary activity. The issues the decree dealt with have continued to grow in importance and urgency, and they have in turn generated other issues that need to be taken into account in missiological reflection today.

## THE NATURE OF MISSIONARY ACTIVITY

One of the major struggles in the development of *Ad Gentes* was to balance the fact that the entire church, in everything that it is and does, is "missionary by its very nature" (*AG*, 2) with the fact that mission has the specific task of witnessing to and proclaiming the good news of the gospel to women and men who do not yet know it. In working out this balance, the decree made a real effort—though it was not always successful—to avoid thinking about mission in terms of geographical territories and to think rather in terms of people in need of evangelization. In this way, mission could go on anywhere—among people in Asia or Africa in predominantly non-Christian cultures, among unchurched workers in traditionally Christian countries such as France or the United States, among women and men in Latin America who still suffer from a shortage of clergy, or among migrants or refugees who find themselves in new cultural surroundings and are in need of pastoral care. Even though missionary activity in the strict sense is distinguished in *Ad Gentes* 6 from pastoral activity among the faithful and ecumenical activity among Christians of various ecclesial allegiances, it still "wells up from the Church's inner nature." It is not, in other words, just one activity among others, but, as in the words of Roger Haight, it is the basic *symbol* by which the church is to be understood.[3] In the much-used but still excellent phrase, the church does not so much have a mission as the mission has a church.

## "Missionary Activity Proper"

In *Redemptoris Missio*, John Paul II insists nevertheless that "to say the whole church is missionary does not preclude the existence of a specific mission *ad gentes*...." (*RM*, 32). He goes on to say that this mission *ad gentes*, or mission among those who have not yet fully heard the gospel, is actually "missionary activity proper" (*RM*, 34) and needs to be distinguished from pastoral activity and what he calls the "new evangelization" (*RM*, 33). On the other hand, he insists that the boundaries between these three activities of the church cannot be drawn too clearly, for each in its own way embodies the church's essential ex-centric, missionary nature. In fact, in *Redemptoris Missio* 37 John Paul broadens the notion of mission *ad gentes* to "new worlds and new social phenomena." Today, says the pope, the frontiers of mission are in the world's rapidly growing urban areas, among the world's youth, and among the millions of migrants and refugees (about whom we will reflect below). He also speaks about mission in particular "cultural sectors," like the "world of communication," the "safeguarding [of] the created world," and scientific research. And so, even "missionary activity proper" is expressed in ways at which *Ad Gentes* had only hinted.

## Pastoral Work and "New Evangelization"

In much of today's missiological—and indeed *ecclesiological*—thinking, this blurring of boundaries between mission in the strict sense and intra-church pastoral ministry and "new evangelization" has become significant as the church recognizes it missionary nature at every level of its existence. There is certainly a role for the day-to-day pastoral activity of the church in terms of sacramental ministry, continued nourishment through retreats, workshops, and preaching, various kinds of counseling, and community-building activities in parishes. However, there has also been thinking about pastoral work that understands it in a more centrifugal, outward-reaching way. In this way of thinking, one of the major tasks of pastoral work is to equip women and men for witness and ministry *outside* the boundaries of the local parish community. This may be in terms of training people for more direct evangelization in the world, organizing projects that focus on issues of social justice or ecological activity, or simply celebrating the sacraments in a way that is attentive to visitors and perhaps even curious inquirers.[4]

In what might be called a "hallmark of his pontificate," Pope John Paul II spoke "regularly and vigorously"[5] of a "new evangelization"— one that is new in ardor, methods, and expression.[6] In a way, this naming of mission stands between both pastoral work on the one hand and "missionary activity proper" on the other—it is "more" than pastoral work among Christians, but "less" than the preaching of the gospel for the first time. In *Redemptoris Missio* 34 John Paul speaks of this "new evangelization" or "re-evangelization" taking place in countries where the church has been long established, but where people, although baptized, "have lost a living sense of the faith, or even no longer consider themselves members of the Church, and live a life far removed from Christ and his Gospel." Such is the case especially in the highly secularized countries of Europe, but also in North America, Australia, and New Zealand and even in some quarters in Latin America. What we see in these places is a relatively numerous influx of missionaries from Africa and Asia, and a sense that these are certainly places in which missionary activity in its proper sense needs to be engaged in. In these contexts of "new evangelization," the church—and particularly the local churches, the parishes—need to be communities of clear witness to the truth and power of the gospel, and there need to be ways in which Christian communities can be open and available to those who have become "unchurched." At the same time, we have to begin to imagine new ways of demonstrating the richness of gospel living to the men and women of our day—perhaps through movements like the Sant'Egidio community or Folcolare, or through retreat ministry, or through organizing youth for "mission trips" to places like Appalachia, Guatemala, or Kenya.[7]

## Ecumenical Activity

In *Ad Gentes* 6, "missionary activity among the nations" is distinguished from "pastoral activity" and from "undertakings aimed at restoring unity among Christians." *Ad Gentes* in fact highlights ecumenical activity in a particularly strong way as "most closely connected" with missionary activity, and this is the result of a promise made by Fr. Johannes Schütte to give greater emphasis to the ecumenical movement in the final draft of the decree, after it had been tentatively approved by the council on October 12, 1965.

Such commitment to the unity of Christians is the subject of a long and rather eloquent paragraph in *Evangelii Nuntiandi*, in which Paul VI signals approval for "collaboration marked by greater commitment with the Christian brethren with whom we are not yet united in perfect unity...." The pope goes on to say that "by doing this we can already give a greater common witness to Christ before the world in the very work of evangelization. Christ's command urges us to do this; the duty of preaching and of giving witness to the Gospel requires this" (*EN*, 77). In 1980 a Joint Working Group of members of the World Council of Churches (WCC) and the Roman Catholic Church issued a powerful statement entitled "Christian Witness—Common Witness," which revised an earlier 1970 statement in the light of WCC statements, *Evangelii Nuntiandi*, and the important gathering of Evangelical

Christians in 1974 at Lausanne, Switzerland. This document outlined a number of concrete possibilities for ecumenical cooperation and common witness to the gospel in mission.[8]

"Christian Witness—Common Witness" certainly acknowledged the difficulties involved in ecumenical cooperation in mission, especially in the light of the practice of some groups to proselytize (use high-pressure conversion tactics) rather than evangelize (proclaim the gospel, but allow for a free response), yet the tone of the document was basically positive. By 1990, however, John Paul II had some rather harsh words for proselytizing groups in paragraph 50 of *Redemptoris Missio*. While he acknowledged some progress in "ecumenical activity and harmonious witness to Jesus Christ," he stressed that such working together was now all the more urgent because "Christian and para-Christian sects are sowing confusion by their activity." While there are tensions in this regard all over the world today, they seem to be particularly severe in Latin America, where many Catholics are leaving the church to join Evangelical and Pentecostal groups, and so ecumenical activity is not looked on at all favorably by the hierarchy there. This issue was also addressed during the 2007 visit to Aparecida, Brazil, by Pope Benedict XVI. Using the negative term "sects" to refer to these groups, the pope called for the Latin American church to be "more missionary" by communicating the gospel more dynamically and attending to the needs of the poor.[9]

As Cardinal Edward Cassidy points out in his estimation of the state of the question of ecumenism in the church today in the first volume of this series, while there are many signs of progress in the long and tedious journey toward Christian unity, "there are also signs of a certain reluctance on the part of the churches to want to make the sacrifice of unity."[10] The massive loss of Catholics in Latin America, proselytizing pressures in places like the Philippines in Asia and in Africa, the ordination of women, and increasing acceptance of homosexuality in many of the more liberal churches are certainly obstacles to Roman Catholics. On the other hand, documents like *Dominus Iesus* (2000) and *Responses to Some Questions Regarding Certain Aspects of the Doctrine of the Church* (2007), both of which deny the designation of "churches" to Protestant groups and speaks of them as suffering "from defects" (*DI*, 17; *RSQ*, Third Question) have certainly angered many on the Protestant side.

While a commitment to ecumenism is still highly regarded in the church, and is clearly seen as part of the church's life, the strong bond between ecumenism and *mission* seems to have faded.[11] On the other hand, pastoral activity has assumed a new missionary perspective, and the "new evangelization" has emerged as a fresh way to understand the church's task in increasingly secularized contexts. These newer ways of understanding mission, however, take as their paradigm mission in the stricter sense of moving beyond one's own culture and "comfort zone" to witness to the gospel among those who have not yet accepted Christ. In this way, mission even in its stricter sense has moved closer to the center of the church's life. To be missionary is the way the church should be in every aspect of its existence.

### SEEKING AN ADEQUATE THEOLOGY OF MISSION

*Ad Gentes* explained the essential missionary nature of the church by situating mission within the life of God as such. It proposed a Trinitarian motivation for missionary activity, much in line with current Protestant thinking at the time, but, as Yves Congar pointed out, in line with a certain thread in Catholic thought as well.[12] In the years that followed the council, however, this Trinitarian motivation became less prominent, as is evident in the two major documents on mission issued by the Roman magisterium: *Evangelii Nuntiandi* (1975) and *Redemptoris Missio* (1990), each of which approaches the theological basis of mission from a different perspective. My own sense is that these three perspectives represent the three understandings of mission that were struggling for predominance in the years after the council as Christians sought an adequate theology of mission. All three theologies of mission represent a genuine strand of truth, and I believe that what is emerging in the theology of mission is a synthesis of the three.[13]

### *Evangelii Nuntiandi* and Mission as Service of the Reign of God

*Evangelii Nuntiandi* was written on the tenth anniversary of the close of the council as a follow up to the 1974 Synod of Bishops. Rather than starting with the grand doctrine of the Trinity, however, Paul VI begins with the very concrete ministry of Jesus, who proclaims the reign or kingdom of God. Jesus called together a community that, after his resurrection from the dead and his ascension to his Father, gradually began to realize that its task was to continue Jesus' work of proclaiming the reign of God until the end of time. As the church began to realize its identity, therefore, it recognized as well its inseparable link to the work of evangelization. To be church was to be in mission, and to be in mission was to be church. Evangelization, in fact, is the church's "deepest identity" (*EN*, 14); it exists "in order to evangelize, that is to say in order to preach and teach, to be the channel of the gift of grace, to reconcile sinners with God, and to perpetuate Christ's sacrifice in the Mass, which is the memorial of his death and glorious Resurrection" (*EN*, 14). The church "prolongs and continues" (*EN*, 15) Jesus' presence in the world, for "it is his condition of being an evangelizer that she is called upon to continue" (*EN*, 15).

*Evangelii Nuntiandi* speaks eloquently of the primary importance of witness in the work of evangelization. In an often-quoted phrase, the pope points out that the women and men of today listen more willingly to witnesses than to teachers, and that if they listen to teachers it is because they are first of all witnesses (see *EN*, 41). In addition, and in a way that trumps even witness, the pope insists strongly on the need for explicit proclamation: "There is no true evangelization if the name, the teaching, the life, the promises, the Kingdom and the mystery of Jesus of Nazareth, the Son of God, is not proclaimed" (*EN*, 22). But, as we have already seen in Part 3, the pope expands evangelization to include the "evangelization of cultures" (*EN*, 20) and, in the wake of his 1967 encyclical *Populorum Progressio* and the 1971 Synod of Bishops' document on justice, work for justice and liberation as well.

Here the emphasis on justice and liberation (with this being the first time the word "liberation" appears in a Roman magisterial document) begins to be linked with *Evangelii Nuntiandi's* connection of evangelization or mission with the proclamation and witnessing to the reign of God. For many mission theologians and mission practitioners alike, mission was to find its raison d'etre in a commitment to working for justice for the sake of the reign of God. This was particularly true in Latin America, in the light of the liberation theology that had already begun to emerge in the wake of the 1968 Medellín Conference, but it was true also in Asia as the Federation of Asian Bishops' Conferences embraced the "threefold dialogue" with Asian religions, Asian cultures, and the Asian poor. In 1984 and again in 1986, the Vatican's

Congregation for the Doctrine of the Faith issued two instructions that expressed caution about a commitment to liberation that was both too Marxist and too focused on material and political liberation, but which still emphasized the centrality of working for justice as part of the evangelizing mission of the church.[14]

## Redemptoris Missio and Mission as Proclamation of Jesus Christ as Universal Savior

In 1990, twenty-five years after the publication of *Ad Gentes*, and fifteen years after Paul VI wrote *Evangelii Nuntiandi*, Pope John Paul II issued *Redemptoris Missio*, his eighth encyclical. The pope certainly acknowledges the Trinitarian basis of mission as proposed by *Ad Gentes* (see *RM*, 1, 7, 22, 23, 32), he devotes an entire chapter to the relationship between the church and the reign of God (see *RM*, 12–20) and he speaks in strong terms of the constitutive nature of justice and peacemaking for mission (see *RM*, 58–59). Nevertheless, another motive for mission surfaces as the primary one in the encyclical: the obligation to proclaim the truth of the newness of life found in Jesus Christ. This is expressed most clearly at the beginning of the first chapter: "The Church's universal mission is born of faith in Jesus Christ" (*RM*, 4). The same idea is expressed in the paragraph that follows: the "fundamental reason why the Church is missionary by her very nature" is that in Jesus is found "the definitive self-revelation of God" (*RM*, 5). And, toward the end of this first chapter, the pope puts it very clearly: "*Why mission?* Because to us, as to St. Paul, 'this grace was given, to preach to the Gentiles the unsearchable riches of Christ' (Eph 3:8)."

In his presentation at the press conference for the publication of the encyclical, Cardinal Josef Tomko, then president of the Congregation for the Evangelization of Peoples, stated that one of the reasons why the encyclical was written was to counteract a Christology developed by a number of theologians that tended to deny the unique mediatorship of Jesus between God and humanity.[15] This motive becomes clearer and clearer as the text of the encyclical unfolds. For John Paul II, the centrality of Christ, and the obligation for Christians to share this truth, is the underlying motive for mission. Mission issues from faith in Christ, and is "an accurate indicator of our faith in Christ and his love for us" (*RM*, 11). And even though there exists truth outside the boundaries of

Christianity, it needs to be recognized that *"the Church is the ordinary means of salvation* and that *she alone* possesses the fullness of the means of salvation" (*RM*, 55—the pope's italics).

## Mission as Prophetic Dialogue

Each of these fundamental theologies of mission—mission rooted in God's trinitarian life (*Ad Gentes*), mission emerging from the church's identity to share and continue Jesus' mission (*Evangelii Nuntiandi*), or mission springing from the conviction of Jesus' universal Lordship (*Redemptoris Missio*)—is, to my mind, both theologically valid and theologically rich. This is why, in a work published in 2004, Roger Schroeder and I have proposed that mission be understood today as "prophetic dialogue."[16] The term is not our own; we borrowed it from the 2000 General Chapter of our religious congregation, the Society of the Divine Word. We have developed it, however, in some ways quite different from those in the official documents of our congregation. As we understand it, mission needs to have both a "prophetic" as well as a "dialogical" dimension, and it is in this dialectic that we see the synthesis happening among the three major theologies of mission proposed in the last four decades after the council.

First and foremost, mission has to be dialogical. Just as God in Godself is a community of dialogue and acts for the salvation of the world in a non-coercive, persuasive manner, so must those baptized into this Trinitarian community act in mission. What this means in concrete terms is that one approaches the people among whom one engages in mission only after having taken off one's shoes, so to speak, because one is already on holy ground.[17] Or, in an image proposed by Roger Schroeder, when we are engaged in mission we need to come to the people "with our glasses half full."[18] Mission, therefore, is first of all about listening, about learning, about forming relationships; it is about learning the local language, digging deeply into a study of the local culture, making friends with the people we have come to serve, not staying behind the walls of our mission compounds. Dialogue is a basic attitude that pervades all we do, a fundamental openness in imitation of the way God works, a self-emptying, a *kenosis*.

But such a dialogical perspective, in this understanding of mission, is not enough. The missionary is also a prophet, that is, one who "speaks forth" the truth of the triune God she or he represents. This prophetic stance is expressed in several ways. First, it is embodied in a community that by its life together witnesses to another way of living than the one that the "world" ordinarily expects. In the words of Gerhard Lohfink, it lives as a "contrast community."[19] Second, it is an unshakeable commitment to human dignity and justice, and so it embraces all the concerns of those who have helped the church see that mission is about the service of God's reign of justice, peace, and—in our day, increasingly important—the integrity of creation. Third, speaking God's truth as a prophetic people in mission means a commitment to witness to the truth of the gospel and the person of Jesus Christ to the world, and, when appropriate, to proclaim one's faith clearly and confidently. To express the prophetic stance is to address all the concerns of *Redemptoris Missio* as well.

To say that mission today is best understood in terms of "prophetic dialogue" is to say the same thing said by the South African missiologist David J. Bosch when he speaks of the need to do mission in "bold humility."[20] Like the Trinitarian God who is manifest in all God's mystery in the humble life of Jesus of Nazareth, so must those be who "prolong and continue" (see *EN*, 15) his ministry. And yet, Christians are convinced that they have something to say to a world caught up in structures of sin and injustice. Jesus Christ is indeed "the way, the truth and the life" (John 14:6), and his gospel needs to be boldly lived and boldly proclaimed.

## MISSION AS MULTIFACETED

In Part 3, when we dealt with the implementation of *Ad Gentes*, we traced the development of a wider understanding of mission in the years after the council. This development is to my mind one of the key developments of postconciliar thinking about mission, and is central in assessing the state of many of the questions dealt with by *Ad Gentes* in today's context. We saw how the understanding of mission was expanded to include issues of justice as a result of the 1968 Medellín Conference and the 1971 Synod of Bishops' document on justice in the world, and how reflections like those of the 1974 Federation of Asian Bishops' Conferences first plenary assembly helped expand understanding further to include questions of inculturation and interreligious dialogue. These developments all influenced Paul VI in the writing of *Evangelii Nuntiandi* in 1975, in which he warned against any "partial and fragmentary definition" of evangelization which would lessen its "richness, complexity and dynamism" (see *EN*, 17).

In the years since *Evangelii Nuntiandi* up to the present there has been some discussion in missiological literature about which particular elements are constitutive of missionary activity. This has not been a discussion in a formal sense, but there has been a growing consensus over the years as to what particular activities make up the "richness, complexity and dynamism" of the missionary task about which *Evangelii Nuntiandi* first spoke. In 1981 the organization sponsored by missionary congregations headquartered in Rome, SEDOS (Service of Documentation and Studies), sponsored an important seminar on the future of mission. In the remarkable document that summarized the seminar's proceedings, four "principal activities" of the church's mission were singled out: proclamation, dialogue, inculturation, and liberation of the poor.[21] These followed rather closely, in an abbreviated way, how *Evangelii Nuntiandi* had described mission six years earlier.

Three years later, in 1984, the Vatican's Secretariat for Non-Christians (as it was then called) issued a document on the relationship between interreligious dialogue and direct proclamation of the gospel in which mission was described as a "single but complex and articulated reality," having as its principal elements five activities: (1) presence and witness, (2) commitment to social development and human liberation, (3) liturgical life, prayer, and contemplation, (4) interreligious dialogue, and (5) proclamation and catechesis.[22] These elements of mission were quoted verbatim in the document *Dialogue and Proclamation*, paragraph 2, but not (perhaps somewhat strangely) by *Redemptoris Missio*, which was issued just a few weeks prior to *Dialogue and Proclamation* and which uses the language of *Dialogue and Proclamation* by speaking of mission as a "single but complex reality" (*RM*, 41). Nevertheless, John Paul II does speak in *Redemptoris Missio* of mission involving witness, proclamation, inculturation, interreligious dialogue, working for development and liberation, and doing deeds of charity (*RM*, 41–60).

In the wider missiological literature, theologians and missiologists have offered a number of variations on these elements proposed by the magisterium. In 1991 in *Transforming Mission*, David Bosch outlined thirteen elements of what he called the "emerging ecumenical missionary paradigm." In 1999 J. Andrew Kirk spoke of seven elements, adding ecological concern to the list of elements for the first time. In 2000 Irish missiologist Donal Dorr offered his own list of seven elements, stressing the overarching importance of dialogue. To mention only two other prominent missiological thinkers, Anthony J. Gittins and Samuel Escobar have offered their own contributions to reflecting on the multidimensional nature of missionary work. In addition, Robert J. Schreiter has proposed the notion of reconciliation as the fundamental activity for mission in today's post-9/11 world.[23]

Several years ago my colleague Eleanor Doidge and I proposed a synthesis of these various elements that tries to take into account both the diversity of the elements proposed and their similarity to one another. What we offered was a list of six elements, all of which are constitutive of the church's missionary activity. They are: (1) witness and proclamation, (2) liturgy, prayer, and contemplation, (3) commitment to justice, peace, and the integrity of creation, (4) the practice of interreligious dialogue, (5) efforts of inculturation, and (6) the ministry of reconciliation.[24] In our book *Constants in Context*, Roger Schroeder and I discuss each one of these in some detail.[25] What follows here is an abbreviated reflection that incorporates some of the other issues that are shaping the state of the questions surrounding mission today.

## Witness and Proclamation

Witness is treated at some length in *Ad Gentes* 11–12, and, as we have already pointed out, figures prominently in *Evangelii Nuntiandi* in several places (e.g., *EN*, 21, 26, and 41). *Redemptoris Missio* 42 and 43 form a section of chapter 5 entitled "The First Form of Evangelization Is Witness," and *Dialogue and Proclamation* 59 briefly alludes to the "witness of deeds" that validates the word of proclamation. Experience today bears out the truth of Paul VI's statement in *Evangelii Nuntiandi* 21 that "above all the Gospel must be proclaimed by witness." Today more than ever, if something is not perceived as authentic, people will pay scant attention. The witness of a Mother Teresa simply being present and serving the dying of Calcutta, or the ailing John Paul II at a World Youth Day Mass has had a powerful impact on people of all faiths and in every part of the world. Here in the United States, the forgiveness of the Amish community in Lancaster,

Pennsylvania, when a gunman shot and killed five children in a schoolhouse in 2006 spoke volumes about the power of the gospel to reconcile and forgive even the most heinous of crimes. Negatively, the revelations in Boston and other U.S. dioceses in 2002 about the cover-ups regarding priests who sexually abused children and minors provided a counterwitness to the gospel that will not easily be undone.

Proclamation as an element of mission is one that is championed by documents of the magisterium as "the permanent priority of mission" (*RM*, 44) and one that remains "central" to the church's missionary activity (*DP*, 75). There is, however, much hesitation among missionaries and mission theologians about such a central role. Particularly among Asians, but certainly among many other Christians today as well, there is a deeply felt aversion to an approach to mission that would focus on communicating a message that does not take people where they are, that would not respect their current religious faith, that would not respect their cultures and customs, and that would threaten them with divine retribution if they do not become Christian.

Because of this hesitation regarding proclamation, a good deal of discussion about it revolves around its relationship to dialogue. Even in statements of the magisterium it is clear that proclamation today has to be much more nuanced than a simple announcement of Jesus' lordship and the message of the gospel. In the landmark joint statement, *Dialogue and Proclamation*, issued in 1991 by the Pontifical Council for Inter-Religious Dialogue and the Congregation for the Evangelization of Peoples, the meaning of both "proclamation" and "dialogue" are spelled out in detail and their relationship is clearly stated. Proclamation is described as "the foundation, center, and summit of evangelization" (*DP*, 10). It is the "communication of the Gospel message," whether "solemn or public . . . , or in a simple private conversation" (*DP*, 10). Dialogue in this document refers specifically to "interreligious dialogue" (about which we will say more below), but it also refers to "an attitude of respect and friendship, which permeates or should permeate all those activities constituting the evangelizing mission of the church" (*DP*, 9). When the document speaks of the "manner of proclamation" in paragraphs 68 to 71, therefore, it states that proclamation of the gospel message must follow "the divine pedagogy," that is "learning from Jesus himself, and observing the times and seasons prompted by the Spirit." And so, in this way, "the Church's proclamation must be both progressive and patient, keeping pace with those who hear the message, respecting their freedom and even their 'slowness to believe' (EN 79)" (*DP*, 69). The document goes on to speak of several other qualities with which the gospel must be proclaimed: it should be confident and faithful, but also humble, respectful, dialogical, and inculturated" (*DP*, 70). In the lapidary phrase of John Paul II in *Redemptoris Missio* 39, "*The Church proposes; she imposes nothing*" (the pope's italics).

In a talk on this intimate connection between dialogue and proclamation, Archbishop Marcello Zago, then the secretary for the Congregation for the Evangelization of Peoples, put it very plainly: "Proclamation presupposes and requires a dialogue method in order to respond to the requirements of those to be evangelized and to enable them to interiorize the message received."[26] And in an article on proclamation and the mission of the church, Vietnamese-American theologian Peter Phan interprets Pope John Paul II's treatment of proclamation in his apostolic exhortation *Ecclesia in Asia*. Phan emphasizes the fact that nowhere in the document does the pope insist on "exclusive use of *words* or *doctrinal formulas* to convey the message that Jesus is the only savior for all humankind," and speaks of the use of "stories, parables, symbols, personal contact, and inculturation," as well as the importance of personal holiness.[27] Proclamation, in sum, must be carried out in the spirit of the prophetic dialogue that we spoke of above: it should be a clear and faithful presentation of the gospel, but done in such a way that it is part of a real conversation between those who proclaim and those who hear. Proclamation, as it is understood today, does not begin—perhaps ironically—with speech. Rather, it begins with listening, and is an effort to respond to people's needs and questions.

## Liturgy, Prayer, and Contemplation

One of the "cutting edge" issues in mission today, I believe, is the role of liturgy, prayer, and contemplation in the church's evangelizing mission. This constellation of elements appeared first in the list of constitutive aspects of mission in the 1984 document on dialogue and mission, and is repeated at the beginning of *Dialogue and Proclamation* (*DP*, 2), but discussion of this topic is relatively rare in missiological literature.[28] The importance of these aspects of mission, however, is certainly signaled by the fact that there are *two* patrons of mission: the tireless preacher Francis Xavier and the contemplative woman of prayer, Thérèse of Lisieux.

Liturgy today is increasingly seen as a missionary act. It is what prepares Christians for mission: they are nourished by the word, strengthened by communion with one another and by the Lord's body and blood, and sent forth to "love and serve the Lord" in mission. As Gregory Augustine Pierce says insightfully, Christians do not so much "come" to Mass, but "come back" to Mass after having been sent forth the last time they were there. There is, as Eastern Christians express it, a "liturgy after the liturgy," and that is mission.[29] To the liturgy as well are brought the needs of the community and the needs of the world, as the community prays for those among them who are sick, those who are struggling, those who need courage—as well as for all people throughout the world who seek peace, who work for justice, who suffer from hunger, poverty, and oppression. The ends of the earth are indeed the parameters of the liturgical assembly. The liturgy, too, is the place where witness and proclamation take place. It is there that the gospel is freely proclaimed and interpreted; it is there that the community experiences the witness of one another's faith; and it is in the liturgical assembly that the community is able to give witness of its love and authenticity to the chance visitor or occasional guest, and where such "outsiders" might hear the good news through the words of the gospel and its proclamation in the homily.

The practice of *contemplation* is today being increasingly connected to mission, particularly as mission is understood more and more as the fruit of genuine dialogue. To see, to appreciate, to listen are all contemplative processes, and they are the *sine qua non* of mission as well. Although we will reflect a bit more on mission as reconciliation, this aspect of mission is intimately connected with contemplation as well. Robert Schreiter emphasizes how important it is for anyone engaged in the "arduous and often unsuccessful work" of reconciliation to cultivate a "contemplative attitude." Schreiter recommends such an attitude because it "allows one at once to acknowledge one's own wounds...and to learn to wait, watch, and listen."[30]

## Justice, Peace, and the Integrity of Creation

In Part 3 we saw how thinking about mission began to move beyond the narrower focus of *Ad Gentes* by speaking of the work for justice as "a constitutive dimension of the preaching of the Gospel."[31] Such work for justice includes efforts of peacemaking, as many official documents—and many missiologists as well—point out.[32] In a famous line, Pope Paul VI linked the two when he proclaimed that "if you want peace, work for justice."[33]

What has begun to emerge today, however, is an increasing linkage between justice and peacemaking and the commitment to the integrity of creation or ecojustice. This development is another "cutting edge" issue in mission, even though there has not been a lot of writing on the subject. But what writing there has been evidences an unequivocal commitment to preaching, serving, and witnessing to the reign of God that embraces not only the future of humanity, but of the whole of creation.[34] Therefore, practices like recycling paper products and aluminum cans, constructing "green" buildings, reducing our use of fossil fuels, and calling for the preservation of the world's natural resources are as much a part of the church's missionary activity as is the proclamation of the gospel to those who do not yet believe.

While it is sometimes argued that a ministry of care for creation is merely a concern for the more affluent "First World" countries that can afford the luxury of protecting their natural resources, it must be said that Christians in Asia, Latin America, and Africa have also recognized the long- and short-term dangers of exploitation of the natural world. The Catholic bishops of these parts of the world have issued important statements in this regard,[35] and committed Evangelical Christians have formed ecological organizations such as World Vision and A Rocha—founded in Portugal but active in other countries such as Brazil, Ghana, India, Kenya, Peru, and South Africa.[36] In a remarkable book, Zimbabwean missiologist and ecological activist Marthinus Daneels tells the moving story of the "war of the trees" waged against the ravaged environment of Zimbabwe in the last several decades in a cooperative effort of indigenous Shona practitioners of traditional religion and a number of local African Independent Churches. Daneels writes movingly and convincingly of how interfaith dialogue combined with environmental activism is a powerful practice of authentic Christian missionary activity.

While much more work needs to be done in this area, the connection between ecology and mission—ecojustice—represents a new frontier for missiological reflection and missionary action, and we can expect significant inroads into this area in the years to come.


## The Practice of Interreligious Dialogue

The importance of dialogue with other religious ways was stressed in several places in *Ad Gentes* (e.g., *AG*, 9 and 11), but it is probably fair to say that the issue of dialogue is one of the flashpoints—if not *the* flashpoint—of controversy in missiological discussion today. It is not the *practice* of dialogue, however, that is the issue. That dialogue with other religions is necessary, despite its possible difficulties, is not in question. Rather, it is the *motive* for dialogue that is the real issue: Are we called to dialogue only out of respect for these other religions as containing "a ray of that Truth which enlightens all peoples" (*NA*, 2—my translation)? Or is dialogue an imperative that results from the recognition of another religion's genuine validity as a way of salvation—a way that is perhaps as valid as Christianity itself? The question of dialogue, in other words, has become the question of the universal significance of Jesus Christ, and presses the question of the importance of mission itself. Is dialogue now the only valid way of doing mission, with no more room for proclamation of the gospel and the invitation to convert to Christianity and become incorporated into the Christian church?

Since the mid-1980s, with the publication of significant, albeit very controversial, works by Alan Race and Paul Knitter,[37] it has become commonplace to speak of the relation of Christianity to the other religions of the world in terms of *exclusive* Christology, *inclusive* Christology, or a *pluralist* Christology. An exclusivist position would understand human salvation only as the result of an explicit faith in Christ, and engagement in interreligious dialogue would either be completely shunned or employed only as a tactic for better conversion techniques. An inclusive Christology would acknowledge goodness and even some validity in other religions, but any such goodness and validity would be because of the "anonymous" presence of Christ. Within this perspective, dialogue would help each party see the other's Truth, and from a Christian perspective would point out the places where Christianity could "fulfill" the valid but imperfect aspects of the non-Christian faith. A pluralist position, in contrast to these first two, would tend to see every religious way as valid in its own right, and as different but genuine paths toward a Truth that is beyond the grasp of each concrete religion. In this case, then, dialogue would be necessary to grasp the truth of the other religions, and perhaps be enriched by these other perspectives.

In the last decades substantial objections have been made as to the adequacy of these three categories. Paul Knitter now speaks of *four* rather than three (the Replacement Model, the Fulfillment Model, the Mutuality Model, and the Acceptance Model). The entire category of "salvation" through other religions has been challenged in a brilliant work by Evangelical theologian S. Mark Heim. But the question of the uniqueness of Christ and the goal of interreligious dialogue remains a vital one that continues to be explored.[38]

As we have pointed out earlier in this fourth part, one of the motivations for the writing of John Paul II's mission encyclical, *Redemptoris Missio*, was the emergence of a Christology—particularly, it seems in Asia—that tended to deny the unique salvific significance of Christ and was more open to a "pluralist" approach. In the first chapter of the encyclical entitled "Jesus Christ, The Only Savior," the pope states his position very clearly: "Although participated forms of mediation of different kinds and degrees are not excluded, they acquire meaning and value only from Christ's own mediation, and they cannot be understood as parallel or complementary to his" (*RM*, 5). Further on, the encyclical points out that "inter-religious dialogue is a part of the Church's evangelizing mission" (*RM*, 55), but it also insists that this does not negate the obligation for Christians to preach salvation coming exclusively through Christ. On the one hand, therefore, "dialogue should be conducted and implemented with the conviction that the Church is the ordinary *means of salvation* and that *it alone* possesses the fullness of the means of salvation." On the other hand, dialogue needs to be done in a spirit of mutuality: "Other religions constitute a positive challenge for the Church: they stimulate it both to discover and acknowledge the signs of Christ's presence and of the working of the Spirit, as well as to examine more deeply its own identity and to bear witness to the fullness of Revelation which it has received for the good of all" (*RM*, 55–56— my translation).

Probably the best treatment of interreligious dialogue by the Roman magisterium appears in the 1991 document *Dialogue and Proclamation*. Although issued just a few weeks after *Redemptoris Missio*, its treatment of dialogue is much more comprehensive and positive, even though it too insists (rightly!) that dialogue does not replace the proclamation of the gospel as "the foundation, center, and summit of evangelization" (*DP*, 10). The document's section on dialogue (*DP*, 14–54) begins with a theology of religions that is unsurpassed in official church documents in terms of depth and breadth (DP, 14–32).[39] Starting from the Old Testament it summarizes church teaching, up to and including the teaching of John Paul II, on the presence of grace in other religions. It recognizes "elements of grace" in them, while at the same time acknowledging their imperfections and contradictions with Christian revelation (*DP*, 31). Because of this double fact, then, dialogue is about learning and being inspired by each other, but also about mutual challenge. "... Christians, too, must allow themselves to be questioned" (*DP*, 32). This first section is followed by a rich section on "The Place of Interreligious Dialogue in the Evangelizing Mission of the Church" that locates the motivation for dialogue in God's own dialogical action in the history of salvation. "In faithfulness to the divine initiative, the Church too must enter into a dialogue of salvation with all men and women" (*DP*, 38). A third part of the "dialogue" section of the document speaks of four forms of dialogue (dialogue of life, of action, of theological exchange, and of religious experience—*DP*, 42). Then there follow sections on the dispositions needed for dialogue ("neither ingenuous nor overly critical, but open and receptive" [*DP*, 46]), and on the obstacles that impede it (e.g., insufficient grounding in knowledge of the faith, insufficient knowledge of the other, burdens of the past, wrong understanding of conversion—see *DP*, 52). In this document not all the current questions about dialogue and its relation to the place of Christ are answered, but we have here a "vademecum" for dialogue which has yet to be surpassed.

No discussion about the "state of the question" regarding interreligious dialogue, however, would be complete without mention of the document *Dominus Iesus*, issued by the Congregation for the Doctrine of the Faith on August 6, 2000.[40] Right at the beginning of this document the connection is made between the church's mission and interreligious dialogue (*DI*, 2). Dialogue is part of the way in which the church does mission in today's world, and though it does not replace "the Church's proclamation of Jesus Christ, 'the way, the truth and the life'" (*DI*, 2), it does indeed accompany such proclamation. Because of this relatively new connection between dialogue and proclamation, "new questions arise that need to be addressed through pursuing new paths of research, advancing proposals, and suggesting ways of acting that call for attentive discernment" (*DI*, 3). This is what the document addresses, particularly aspects of those new questions, proposals, and ways of acting that seem to go against the church's traditional and recent magisterial teaching—especially in the light of modern relativism that calls into question key elements of Christology, soteriology, and ecclesiology. At the heart of *Dominus Iesus* is a strong move on the part of the magisterium to counter ideas that it believes compromise teachings about the divinity of Christ, his unique saving action in history, and the role of the Catholic Church in witnessing to and embodying that salvation. And so, while dialogue is necessary and part of the church's mission, mission cannot be *reduced* to dialogue, since dialogue "is just one of the actions of the Church in her mission *ad gentes*" (*DI*, 22). In an important passage about the nature of dialogue, *Dominus Iesus* insists that "equality, which is a presupposition of inter-religious dialogue, refers to the equal personal diginity of the parties in dialogue, not to doctrinal content, nor even less to the position of Jesus Christ—who is very God made human—in relation to the founders of the other religions" (*DI*, 22—my translation).

Reaction to *Dominus Iesus* was, from many quarters—Catholic, Protestant, and non-Christian—quite negative, especially since the document insists that many Christian bodies were suffering "from defects" and therefore not churches in the proper sense (*DI*, 17)[41] and that "followers of other religions...are in a gravely deficient situation in comparison with those who, in the Church, have the fullness of the means of salvation" (*DI*, 22).[42] A common criticism of the document was not so much that it had backtracked from Catholic teaching or even the teaching of Vatican II, but that it had a negative, juridical tone—very much unlike the epideictic, exhortatory tone that, as noted in Part 1, marked the documents of Vatican II. In a symposium on *Dominus Iesus* at Catholic Theological Union a few weeks after the document was issued, Robert Schreiter suggested that, while everything in the document lined up with current church teaching, what was missing was

equal emphasis on the possibility of salvation outside Christian boundaries and the intrinsic nature of dialogue for Christian mission.
Schreiter likened the content of the document to a stereo sound system
in which only one speaker was functioning and thus the full effect of the
music could not be heard.

The state of the question regarding interreligious dialogue as constitutive of mission, therefore, remains—at least in official Catholic
teaching—a bit ambiguous. *Dominus Iesus* calls for more research and
theological reflection on the topic (*DI*, 3 and 21), and in fact much is
being done. In the last several years, scholars such as Francis X. Clooney
and James Fredericks have been pioneers in a new field called "comparative theology," in which theologians take both the theology of another
religion and Christian theology with equal seriousness, while nevertheless remaining firm in their Christian faith.[43] On the other hand, efforts
of some theologians to probe the issues that surround authentic dialogue
have been met with suspicion—and in some cases even censure—from
official sources.[44] The state of the question regarding interreligious dialogue is that it is still very much an unanswered question.

## Efforts at Inculturation

The decades after Vatican II have seen a steady growth in the church's
awareness of the importance and necessity of inculturation at every
level of church life. This has been in response to a call expressed con-
sistently throughout the council documents to take the contemporary
context and local culture seriously in such areas as liturgical celebration,
theological expression, communication of the gospel, and training for
ministry. In *Sacrosanctum Concilium* 36, for example, even though Latin
remained the official language of the liturgy, local languages were to be
permitted "since the use of the mother tongue . . . may frequently be of
great advantage to the people." And *Sacrosanctum Concilium* 37–40 laid
down norms for "adapting the Liturgy to the genius and traditions of
peoples." In *Gaudium et Spes* 54–62 we find an extended reflection on
culture and its role in Christian life, with emphasis on the fact that
"faithful to its own tradition and at the same time conscious of its universal mission," the church "can enter into communion with various
cultural modes, to its own enrichment and theirs too" (*GS*, 58—my

translation). Not only does the church offer something to society (*GS*, 41–43) but the world in all its variety and richness can help the church in its mission of witnessing and preaching the gospel (*GS*, 44). Indeed, the use of the world's cultures in preaching the word "ought to remain the law of all evangelization" (*GS*, 44). *Ad Gentes* is filled with lines that point to the importance of culture in missionary work and in the training of missionaries. In a particularly important passage about the development of a local theology, *Ad Gentes* 22 puts it eloquently: "From the customs and traditions of their people, from their wisdom and their learning, from their arts and sciences," local churches "borrow all those things which can contribute to the glory of their Creator, the revelation of the Savior's grace, or the proper arrangement of Christian life."

The terms that Vatican II used in speaking of this interaction between faith and culture tended to be words like "adaptation" or "accommodation" (e.g., *AG*, 22; *SC*, 39, 40; *AG*, 22, 40)—what scholars later designated as forms of a "translation model."[45] This is a model of inculturation that presupposes a particular content (a doctrine, practice, or object) that can be translated—albeit sometimes very creatively—into the terminology of another context or culture without losing the basic meaning of that content. This is still the model preferred by the magisterium of the Catholic Church—at least in most cases (e.g., *RM*, 53).

Gradually, however, other ways of engaging in inculturation have been discerned, and so today there exist a number of models *of* and *for* inculturation. Particularly in Asia, but also in Africa and other parts of the world, theologians like Leonardo Mercado of the Philippines practice what has been called an "anthropological model" of inculturation, where the first task is to listen to the cultural context in order to see how it might enrich a local understanding of the gospel. This has been described as "pulling the gospel out of the culture."[46] Other theologians, particularly those in Latin America in the 1970s, but also U.S. black and feminist/womanist/mujersta theologians, insist that a truly inculturated or contextual theology must lead to a new way of acting in response to a very concrete situation. This model has been dubbed the "praxis model," since it starts with a particular action that is honed in the light of analysis and a re-reading of tradition, only to develop a more effective, more faithful action in turn. Still others, such as Filipino José de Mesa or Japanese theologian Kosuke Koyama, try to balance all three in what might be called a "synthetic model," and a feminist theologian like

Elizabeth Johnson or a Latino/a theologian like Justo González might simply try to articulate the Christian tradition out of their own subjectivity as particular Christian and culturally/socially located subjects, thus articulating a "transcendental model." Other theologians (e.g., Stanley Hauerwas), however, look negatively on context and culture but know that it does indeed figure prominently in theological expression and practices of Christian life. Their task, as they see it, is to critique the context in which Christians find themselves immersed, so as to reveal the fresh challenge of the gospel over against human tendencies to domesticate it.

Whatever model or method is used—and any of the methods sketched out above are certainly valid and take their adequacy from a particular context—there is no question that the issue of inculturation is at the forefront of the agenda in any missionary situation. An inculturated African theology was first on the agenda of the African bishops at their 1994 Synod; dialogue with Asian cultures is one of the three integral aspects of evangelization in Asia, and can be applied to every other place and situation where the church is engaged in evangelization. Also, however, as the church has realized its essential missionary nature in every situation—whether in terms of pastoral activity or engaging in the "new evangelization"—it has become clear that inculturation is not an *option* for the church. In the same way that there is no such thing as "theology" but only theology that is inculturated, there is no such thing as a generic "church." There can only be a church of a particular locality, situation, or culture. As Robert Schreiter has put it trenchantly, "there is now a realization that all theologies have contexts, interests, relationships of power, special concerns—and to pretend that this is not the case is to be blind."[47] Asian theologies, Oceanian theologies, Australian theologies, feminist/womanist/mujerista theologies, Latino/a theologies, gay and lesbian theologies, U.S. American theologies, theologies in post-Christian Europe—all these and more are flourishing today.

Official Roman theology, however, may have major hesitations in the midst of so much theological ferment. In his now-famous Regensburg lecture of September 2006, Pope Benedict XVI received much publicity for remarks that were perceived as anti-Muslim. These statements were certainly regrettable, and certainly will impede Christian-Muslim relations in the future. Another set of remarks in the same speech, however, even though they were not reported on so widely, suggest that the pope may not be so open to the radical kinds of inculturation that many Christians—particularly those from the non-Western world—are calling for. For Benedict, there is a real harmony between Greek (and eventually European) thought and the Christian gospel, to such an extent that a thorough "dehellenization" of Christian doctrine would ultimately betray it. Ultimately, there is no way that we can go back to a Christianity that is able to be expressed in any kind of cultural form. As the pope put it: "This thesis is not simply false, but it is coarse and lacking in precision. The New Testament was written in Greek and bears the imprint of the Greek spirit, which had already come to maturity as the Old Testament developed. True, there are elements in the evolution of the early Church which do not have to be integrated into all cultures. Nonetheless, the fundamental decisions made about the relationship between faith and the use of human reason are part of the faith itself; they are developments consonant with the nature of faith itself."[48]

Once again we see a tension within the church around a central issue of the council. This tension bears out the truth of John Paul II's cautions that the process of inculturation is indeed a "lengthy," "difficult and delicate task" (RM, 52; EiAf, 62).

### The Ministry of Reconciliation

The world has changed dramatically since the close of Vatican II in 1965. In 1989, with the tearing down of the Berlin wall, we witnessed the beginning of the demise of Communism in Russia and Eastern Europe, and hopes were expressed for a "New World Order" of peace and prosperity. What has developed instead, however, is practically the exact opposite—a "New World Dis-Order," that has brought untold suffering and insecurity to almost every corner of the globe.

The twentieth century was branded "the most terrible of centuries" by intellectual historian Isaiah Berlin,[49] but the death and violence that erupted to unspeakable levels as that century ended (Rwanda, Burundi, Bosnia-Herzogovina, Kosovo, East Timor, the AIDS crisis) have continued into this new century and seem to be increasing in scope and horror. The world has seen Israel and Palestine trapped in a deadly dance of violence. It has shuddered as Palestinians locked themselves into a deadly civil war, and as India and Pakistan—two nuclear powers—totter on the brink of war. Iraq has been wracked by vicious attacks of Shia and Sunni Muslims on each other in the wake of invasion by the United States. African nations such as Sierra Leone, Ivory Coast, and Liberia have seen wholesale violence for years, and the world has stood by helplessly as genocide continues in the Darfur province of Sudan. And what always has loomed ominously in the background is the memory of the terrorist attacks in East Africa, in the United States on September 11, 2001, in England on July 7, 2005, and in Madrid, Bali (Indonesia), and Turkey—and the possibility of further attacks anywhere.

As these new situations of violence have left their marks of hatred between peoples—between Israelis and Palestinians, Hamas and Fatah, Sunni and Shia, the West and the Muslim world, north and south Sudanese—the last several decades have unearthed the terrible crimes of governments in South Africa during the years of apartheid, or in Latin American countries such as Chile, Guatemala, and Argentina during years when democracy was suppressed. And countries like the United States, Canada, Australia, and New Zealand have become more and more conscious of the violence to their own original peoples that occurred with the founding of these nations. In the last several years— surfacing in the latter years of the last century but resurfacing even more clearly in the first years of the new one—the Catholic Church has been shaken to its core with the revelations about widespread sexual abuse of minors by its clergy, and shaken even more by the indifference to such abuse by church leaders. The epicenter of such revelations has been in the United States, but their shock waves have been felt in many other places in the world as well—Ireland, Canada, Austria, New Zealand, and Australia, to name just a few.

Such situations of violence and the revelation of violence form the context in which the church engages in mission today, and so perhaps more than in any age, mission and evangelization must include a commitment to working for reconciliation. Possibly the strongest advocate of the inclusion of reconciliation in the missionary task—indeed, one who sees it as perhaps the overall paradigm for mission work today—is Robert J. Schreiter, whose work has been seminal for a large body of literature on reconciliation—particularly doctoral dissertations—written over the last decade. For Schreiter, the possibility of reconciliation is "one of the most compelling forms the Good News of Jesus Christ takes on today."[50]

In the light of so much violence in the world and its scarring memories, this good news seems almost too good to be true, and yet—through God's grace—it can become credible through a Christian community that is committed to giving itself over to the possibility of reconciliation and of living it out in the authenticity of its life. Schreiter speaks of communities that can be "safe places" for victims of violence, of women and men who can be agents of reconciliation through patient listening, hospitality, and unselfish service, of places where a spirituality that is based on God's gift of reconciliation can flourish—places where this might seem impossible.[51]

Schreiter and others suggest that reconciliation as a work of evangelization today can be done on several different levels. First, and perhaps foremost, there is the *personal level* of reconciliation, where healing is prayed and worked for between victim and perpetrator, or for mothers and spouses of tortured or "disappeared" loved ones, or for victims of natural disasters or victims of genocide. Second, we can speak of *cultural* reconciliation, where Christians can be a reconciling presence among women and men of cultural groups whose cultural identity has been ignored, disparaged, or stolen from them altogether. Third, there is *political* reconciliation, such as that which has gone on in South Africa under the leadership of Archbishop Desmond Tutu, in Papua-New Guinea under the leadership of Bishop Doug Young, and in Argentina, Chile, and Guatemala. Finally, there is the effort of reconciliation within the church today—perhaps in regard to the sexual abuse crisis, or the treatment of women in the Roman Catholic Church, or the ordination of homosexual persons among members of the Anglican Communion.

Of course, the ministry of reconciliation has always been part of the church's mission. Paul writes in the second letter to the Corinthians that God has reconciled the world to Godself in Christ, and that this message has been entrusted to us as ambassadors for Christ (see 2 Cor 5:19–20). And yet in a world filled with unspeakable violence and still, ironically, one in which human dignity and human rights are protected and esteemed as never before in history, the ministry of reconciliation has emerged as a major task of mission, and a major topic of missiological reflection.

## THE LAITY IN THE MISSION OF THE CHURCH

In her monograph on Vatican II's decree on the laity and its declaration on education, Dolores Leckey has described the present state of the laity in today's Catholic Church as standing on a *threshold*—perhaps somewhat hesitant in the light of current scandals and the opposition of current church leadership, but nevertheless finding new ways of entering into the church's service.[52] This same metaphor of "threshold" applies in the same way to the question of the laity in mission today. Official documents (e.g., *RM*, 71–73) recognize the fact that "all the laity are missionaries by baptism" (the title of *RM*, 71), but one does not have to talk to many former lay missionaries to realize that, whether their missionary service was done at home or abroad, clericalism is still a major problem. Nevertheless, while it seems that—at least in the West—vocations to missionary congregations are dwindling, lay missionary groups of all kinds are thriving. It is this vitality that expresses the state of the question of laity in mission today.

One way in which laity are crossing the threshold of new forms of missionary cooperation is by their association with the various religious and missionary congregations. Leckey mentions lay associates of the Sisters of Mercy of the Americas "who are involved in Mercy missions and who experience a form of Mercy formation," and Jesuit lay collaborators, in particular women, who since 1995 have participated in Jesuit missions.[53] But there are many more. One of the largest is the Maryknoll Mission Association of the Faithful (MMAF), popularly called the Maryknoll Lay Missioners (MKLM). This organization has its origin in the 1970s and 1980s as an associate program of the Maryknoll communities of men and women, but since 1994 it has functioned as a separate entity, closely connected with the other two Maryknoll groups. Today it has over one hundred members—single women and men, married couples and children—who work in seventeen countries around the world. One can join the MKLM for a minimum of three and a half years, and this commitment can be renewed indefinitely. MKLM members describe themselves as "a lay Catholic community called through baptism to witness to the Gospel of Jesus Christ, crossing boundaries of culture, nationality, and faith to join our lives with impoverished and oppressed peoples of the earth. With them, we discern the presence of God's Spirit in all creation and in the world's many cultures and religions, and work toward human liberation and inter-religious dialogue in Africa, Asia and the Americas."[54]

Missionary congregations like the Spiritans, the Comboni Missionaries, the Columban Missionaries, the men's and women's branches of the Congregation of the Holy Cross, and the Claretians—to mention only a few!—also have groups of lay associates who work in missionary situations at home and around the world. In addition, the Volunteer Missionary Movement (VMM) is an independent and ecumenical lay missionary organization founded by the charismatic Edwina Gateley that since 1969 has sent out more than seventeen hundred lay women, men, and children to twenty-six countries around the globe.[55]

What all these lay missionary groups have in common is a fairly short-term commitment to actual missionary work. A person who joins VMM is considered a member for life, but his or her actual cross-cultural missionary service need only be for a limited time. In *Redemptoris Missio* 65, John Paul II emphasized the fact that those who commit themselves to mission work *"for life"* (the pope's italics) are the models of the church's missionary commitment, but—even among members of missionary congregations—this ideal is fulfilled less and less, and this is certainly true in regard to the laity. What is clear is that a new model of missionary service has emerged.

Perhaps even more current, however, and connected with lay missionary activity, is the trend both among Catholics and Protestants to do mission work in *very* short stints—a Holy Week trip to Appalachia, for example, or a three-week residence in Haiti or Mexico for dentists and doctors, or a summer vacation in Kenya for college students. This kind of short-term lay missionary activity has produced a considerable literature, particularly among Protestants, and it is also one of the areas of missiological reflection that is on the "cutting edge" of missiological thought today.[56]

### THREE ADDITIONAL ISSUES IN MISSION TODAY

As was mentioned at the beginning of this fourth part of our reflections on *Ad Gentes*, there are four questions that have emerged in the years following the close of the council that are integral questions about the nature and practice of mission in today's church: globalization, ecology,

migration, and women. We have treated the question of ecology in reflections on how issues of justice now include ecojustice or ecology.
The other three questions deserve at least some brief treatment as we
bring our discussion of the "state of the questions" to a close. Much
more could be said about them, of course, since they—along with several other themes we have discussed— represent some of the "cutting
edge" issues in mission. Our treatment, however, will be brief, only
because these are questions that have emerged since the publication of
*Ad Gentes*.


## Globalization

*Ad Gentes*, as we mentioned in Part 3, does not deal much with the situation of the world in which the church engages in mission. There are
certainly some hints in this direction—for example, when in paragraph
1 the document speaks of "the present state of affairs" in which "there
is arising a new situation for humanity" (my translation)—but there is
little else. *Gaudium et Spes* was the document that analyzed the world
situation, with all its "joys and the hopes,...griefs and the anxieties"
(*GS*, 1), while *Ad Gentes* dealt more with the theological foundations
and practical activities of the church's mission in that world. In the four
decades since, however, it has become increasingly apparent that any reflection on mission *must* deal with the context in which the church lives
and works, and in today's world, that context has been described more
and more precisely by the term "globalization."

Globalization is a complex phenomenon, with both positive and
negative aspects.[57] From one perspective, it is the result of the compres-
sion of space and time through the development in the last several
decades of advanced communications technologies (the Internet, cellu-
lar phones, satellite communications) and rapid and easily accessible
transportation. These real advances have connected the peoples of the
world as never before in history, and provided new levels of human, educational, economic, and political possibilities. But globalization has negative implications as well, because it threatens to exclude whole peoples
from economic and political participation and to extinguish traditional
languages and cultures. Robert Schreiter cites a United Nations report

that "notes that ... the disparity between rich and poor is growing worse in nearly all parts of the world, with roughly 20 percent enjoying the fruits of global capitalism, and the rest struggling to hold their ground and slipping away into deeper poverty."[58] And there is a tendency in globalization to create what Benjamin Barber has termed a "McWorld"—a standardization of local cultures by the introduction of McDonald's, KFC restaurants and the like, U.S. American rock music and clothing styles, with English as the common language.[59]

Despite the strong critique of globalization leveled by many Christians in general and many missiologists in particular,[60] globalization is a fact and is simply the context in which the church carries out its mission today. In his message for the annual World Day of Peace in 1998, Pope John Paul II recognized this fact, but noted soberly that "we are on the threshold of a new era which is the bearer of great hopes and disturbing questions." The pope called for the development of "a globalization *in solidarity*, a globalization *without marginalization*."[61] As it engages in mission, then, the church needs to be both "partner" with globalization's advantages for human and cosmic wholeness, and "prophet" against its excesses. It can use the wonders of contemporary means of communication, for example, to inform people quickly and accurately of events of importance or tragedy in all places of the world, and it can use today's possibilities of distance learning to educate clergy and laity throughout the world according to the highest standards of education. On the other hand, it is part of the mission of the church in the context of globalization to denounce any injustice that globalization brings about.[62]

Today, and in the years to come, globalization will be a major factor in any development of thinking in the area of mission theology and practice.

## Migration

*Ad Gentes* mentions the issue of migration only marginally (*AG*, 20, 38), but like globalization (and in some ways related to it) migration today forms a major context for the church's mission of evangelization and solidarity with the poorest of the earth's poor. "One of the most pervasive

features of the contemporary world," writes Professor Hugo Graeme of
the University of Adelaide, Australia, "...is greater human mobility."[63]
Graeme cites a United Nations report from 1998 that estimates that in
1990, 120 million people were living outside their country of birth, not
counting the millions more who were in other countries temporarily,
traveling, working, or studying. Today, one person in twelve in today's
world lives in a country other than the one in which she or he was
born, and a 1996 UN report stated that out of 184 countries surveyed,
"136 indicated that international migration was an important policy element"[64]— a statistic that is almost certainly still valid today as well. Add
to this the fact that the world contains, in some estimates, fifty million
refugees or internally displaced people and we see that the question of
migration—forced or unforced—is one of the burning issues in the
world today, and one that affects many countries and all parts of the
world in significant ways.

The situation of the world's migrants and refugees also represents,
said Pope John Paul II in 2003, "a vast field for the new evangelization
to which the whole Church is called."[65] This was perhaps not so evident
in 1965 when *Ad Gentes* was promulgated, but it was mentioned in John
Paul II's *Redemptoris Missio* as being among the new phenomena that
were transforming the world and the church's mission (*RM*, 37).
Especially in the world's more affluent countries, the church's pastoral
presence among migrants and refugees needs to be one of the major
commitments of the church's evangelizing mission today, but this is also
true of other countries like Kenya, the Sudan, and Mexico. Mission was
always understood classically as *going* to another place; now the people
of other places have come to our home countries!

Reflection on mission in the context of migration suggests that it
might be carried out in two ways. On the one hand, the church's mission is *to* migrants—that is, migrants should be the *objects* of the church's
pastoral care. On the other hand, however, the church's mission is *of* migrants—that is, the migrants in our midst are the *subjects* of mission.
They both call the local church to new ways of being church, and they
themselves need to be active *within* the church, serving the church
within and outside of their own communities, and serving the wider
world as well. Today there is a growing literature in this relatively new
area of missiological reflection and practice.[66]

## Women in Mission

Already in 1963, in his encyclical *Pacem in Terris*, John XXIII included the growing consciousness among women of their dignity and equality as one of the three characteristics of "the modern age" (*PT*, 39): "Far from being content with a purely passive role or allowing themselves to be regarded as a kind of instrument, they are demanding both in domestic and in public life the rights and duties which belong to them as human persons" (*PT*, 41). Since then there has been a steady growth in this area, and many—both women *and* men—are convinced that the women's movement throughout the world in the last four decades has indeed been a "transforming grace"[67] for both society in general and the church in particular.

What the women's movement (also called feminism) has emphasized is that, all over the world, women have been objects of oppression and marginalization and so are in desperate need of the liberation that the gospel proclaims and brings. It is common knowledge that women are among the world's least educated people, that they are victims of injustice and violence—especially spousal violence—and that they are among the world's poorest. Just to mention a few well-known but still shocking statistics: Women comprise only one-third of the world's paid labor force, but do two-thirds of the world's work; they earn one-tenth of the world's income, yet own only one one-hundredth of the world's property; two-thirds of the world's illiterate persons are women. One woman is beaten every fifteen seconds; one woman is raped every three to six minutes; 37 percent of women of every race, class, and educational background are physically abused during pregnancy.[68] As Marilyn Ann Martone, the Vatican delegate to the UN Commission on the Status of Women said in a report in March 2004: "My delegation is convinced that the road to ensure swift progress in achieving full respect for women and their identity involves more than simply the condemnation of discrimination and injustices, necessary though this may be. Such respect must first and foremost be achieved through an effective and intelligent campaign for the promotion of women, involving all sectors of human society."[69] This is why a kind of "preferential option for women" should be considered an essential part of the church's mission in today's world. The church should be in the forefront of such an "effective and intelligent campaign," by working for justice for women both within the church itself and in society at large.

One other aspect regarding women should be mentioned as we reflect on the state of the questions regarding mission today, and this is the emphasis on recovering the memory of the countless women who have worked as missionaries throughout history. Scholars such as Dana Robert, Cathy Ross, and Susan Smith—and many more—have in recent years produced important works that have helped historians of mission to recognize the essential role of women in spreading the gospel from the beginning of Christian history.[70] But as these and other scholars will agree, current scholarship has only scratched the surface of what is a rich and no doubt complex history, and so there is much hope for the future in this area.


### CONCLUSION


The state of the questions dealt with by *Ad Gentes* indicates that mission theology and mission practice have developed far beyond what the council envisioned. There are indications that mission has begun to move from the margins of church life and theological reflection toward the center. Issues such as the missionary nature of the church, inculturation, interreligious dialogue, the missionary nature of liturgy and prayer, and reconciliation figure prominently in contemporary theology, and reflection on these questions is calling for changes in the ways that the church is organized and the ways in which Christians live their lives. But the development of the questions with which *Ad Gentes* dealt does not mean that it has been surpassed or even outdated. Christians can still read the document with much profit, acknowledging that it came from a particular time period with particular theological and canonical restraints, yet marveling still at some of its fine turns of phrase (e.g., in *AG*, 2, 11, or 22) and challenged by its missionary vision. When all is said and done, *Ad Gentes* is a Vatican II document that is worth rediscovering.

# NOTES

1. Joseph Ratzinger, "La mission d'après les autres textes conciliaires," in *Vatican II: L'Activité Missionaire de l'Église*, Unam Sanctam 67, ed. Johannes Schütte (Paris: Éditions du Cerf, 1967), 121. Ratzinger's essay appeared originally in *Mission nach dem Konzil*, ed. Johannes Schütte (Mainz: Matthias-Grünewald-Verlag, 1967), 21–47. What is referred to here appears on p. 21. The need for a wider understanding of mission in the council's decrees is expressed as well by Thomas Corboy, "A Commentary on the Mission Decree," in *Missions and Religions*, ed. Austin Flannery (Dublin: Scepter, 1968), 9–10.

2. See John XXIII's opening speech at the Council in *Enchiridion Vaticanum*, 7th ed. (Bologna: Edizioni Dehoniane, 1968), 41.

3. "'Missionary outreach must give the direction to the Second Vatican Council,' wrote a bishop in his petition (*Eingabe*) at the Council." Johannes Schütte, "Vorwort," in Schütte, *Mission nach dem Konzil*, 7. "Perhaps it is the case that little by little, step by step, we will recognize in the Second Vatican Council a missionary Council of premiere importance...." Johannes Schütte, "Ce que la mission attendait du Concile," in Schütte, *Vatican II*, 120.

4. See "The Final Report: Synod of Bishops," *Origins* 15 (December 19, 1985): 444–450. A note in the introduction to Norman Tanner's volume in this series explains the fact that the various documents produced by Vatican II "are called, generically, 'decrees.' These 'decrees' were divided, according to a descending gradation of authority, into four 'constitutions' (*SC, LG, DV*, and *GS*), nine 'decrees,' and three 'declarations.' 'Decree,' therefore, has two meanings, a generic and a more specific one." Norman Tanner, *The Church and the World: Gaudium et Spes, Inter Mirifica* (New York/Mahwah, NJ: Paulist Press, 2005), xi. In the present volume, *Dignitatis Humanae* is a "declaration"; *Ad Gentes* is a "decree."

5. Ratzinger, "La mission," 122. Suso Brechter mentions in his commentary that in 1963 the council's Theological Commission had asked the Commission on Mission to draft a section on the church's mission for the

document on the church. A group of *periti* of the commission then drafted a text which is now found in *Lumen Gentium* 17. See Suso Brechter, "Decree on the Church's Missionary Activity," in *Commentary on the Documents of Vatican II*, vol. 4, ed. Herbert Vorgrimler (Freiburg: Herder/Montreal: Palm Publishers, 1969), 94.

6. See Stephen Schloesser, "Against Forgetting: Memory, History, Vatican II," *Theological Studies* 67, no. 2 (June 2006): 288.

7. Schütte, "Ce que la mission attendait du Concile," 108.

8. Ratzinger, "La mission," 145.

9. John W. O'Malley, "Vatican II: Did Anything Happen?" *Theological Studies* 67, no. 1 (March 2006): 3–33.

10. Ibid., 20.

11. Ibid., 22. De Smet's speech is found in *AS* I, IV, 142–144.

12. O'Malley, "Vatican II," 26.

13. See William R. Burrows, "Decree on the Church's Missionary Activity," in *Vatican II and Its Documents: An American Reappraisal*, ed. Timothy E. O'Connell (Wilmington, DE: Michael Glazier, 1986), 181.

14. Jan Grootaers, "The Drama Continues between the Acts: The 'Second Preparation' and Its Opponents," in *History of Vatican II, Volume 2: Formation of the Council's Identity, First Period and Intersession, October 1962–September 1963*, ed. Giuseppe Alberigo and Joseph A. Komonchak (Maryknoll, NY: Orbis Books/Leuven, Belgium: Peeters, 1997), 455. In his history of the decree, Saverio Paventi, the secretary of the Commission on Mission at the council, speaks of "le difficile chemin parcouru." See Saverio Paventi, "Étapes de l'élaboration du texte," in Schütte, *Vatican II*, 149.

15. Corboy, "A Commentary," 9; Brechter, "Decree on the Church's Missionary Activity," 87.

16. Peter Hünermann, "The Final Weeks of the Council," in *History of Vatican II, Volume 5: The Council and the Transition, The Fourth Period and the End of the Council, September 1965–December 1965*, ed. Giuseppe Alberigo and Joseph A. Komonchak (Maryknoll, NY: Orbis Books/Leuven, Belgium: Peeters, 2006), 445.

17. Ibid.

18. In what follows I am depending on several major sources, all of which present the same basic trajectory of development. These sources are: Giuseppe Alberigo and Joseph A. Komonchak, eds., *History of Vatican II*, 5 vols. (Maryknoll, NY: Orbis Books/Leuven, Belgium: Peeters, 1995, 1997, 2000, 2003, 2006); Brechter, "Decree on the Church's Missionary Activity"; Giovanni Caprile, ed., *Il Concilio Vaticano II*, volumes on the third and fourth sessions (Rome: Edizioni "La Civiltà Cattolica," 1965, 1969); and Paventi,

"Étapes de l'élaboration du texte." Only when there is a particular phrase that seems worth quoting will I refer to a particular source.

19. Paventi, "Étapes de l'élaboration du texte," 151. For the text of the propositions, see *Acta et Documenta Concilio Vaticano II apparando*, Series I (Antepreparatoria) (ADA), Volume III, 241–50.

20. Joseph A. Komonchak, "The Struggle for the Council during the Preparation of Vatican II (1960–1962), in *History of Vatican II, Volume 1: Announcing and Preparing Vatican Council II, Toward a New Era in Catholicism*, ed. Giuseppe Alberigo and Joseph A. Komonchak (Maryknoll, NY: Orbis Books/Leuven, Belgium: Peeters, 1995), 192n107. It should be noted that proposition 13 dealt with the question of the "lay" diaconate without the obligation of celibacy. The study group proposed that "an investigation be made regarding the establishment of the diaconate not connected with the presbyterate and without the obligation of celibacy" (ADA, III, 247).

21. Paulo Suess, "A Missão No Canteiro de Obras do Vaticano II: Contexto e Texto do Decreto Ad Gentes Revisitado 40 Anos depois de Sua Promulgação," *Revista Eclesiastica Brasileira* 66 (January 2006): 121n2.

22. Komonchak, "The Struggle for the Council," 192.

23. Ibid., 195; see note 120. The members of the commission are listed in Paventi, "Étapes de l'élaboration du texte," 176–77.

24. Brechter, "Decree on the Church's Missionary Activity," 88.

25. Ibid., 89.

26. Ibid., 90.

27. Komonchak, "The Struggle for the Council," 193.

28. Ibid., 193.

29. Ibid.

30. Henri Godin and Yvan Daniel, *France, pays de mission?* (Paris: Editions du Cerf, 1943).

31. Brechter, "Decree on the Church's Missionary Activity," 91.

32. See Burrows, "Decree on the Church's Missionary Activity," 182–83, and Brechter, "Decree on the Church's Missionary Activity," 93. During the two debates on the mission schema in the council's third and fourth sessions, however, the bishops from mission countries and several superiors general from missionary congregations evidenced a very strong presence and spoke quite forcefully.

33. Paventi, "Étapes de l'élaboration du texte," 157.

34. See note 23 above.

35. Brechter, "Decree on the Church's Missionary Activity," 93.

36. Ibid., 94.

37. Ibid. The text of the schema can be found in *AS*, III, VI, 659–676.

38. Brechter, "Decree on the Church's Missionary Activity," 95.

39. See *AS*, III, VI, 327–332. Caprile, *Il Concilio Vaticano II, Vol. 4, Terzo Periodo*, 377–80, lists fourteen propositions (listing the missionary obligation of the church separately from the obligation of bishops). This reflects an emendation of the text found in *AS*, III, VI, 347. Evangelista Villanova speaks of fourteen propositions as well, but summarizes only thirteen. See Villanova, "The Intersession (1963–1964)," in *History of Vatican II, Volume 3: The Mature Council, Second Period and Intersession, October 1963–September 1964*, ed. Giuseppe Alberigo and Joseph A. Komonchak (Maryknoll, NY: Orbis Books/Leuven, Belgium: Peeters, 1997), 392.

40. Villanova, "The Intersession (1963–1964)," 392.

41. For a digest of the congregation's history, see Horst Rzepkowski, *Diccionario de Misionología* (Estella, Spain: Editorial Verbo Divino, 1997), 131–32 ("Congregación para la Evangelización de los Pueblos").

42. The list of the five new members—four elected and one appointed by the pope—is found in Villanova, "The Intersession (1963–1964)," 390n132. Elected were Johannes Schütte, superior general of the Society of the Divine Word; Archbishop Eugene D'Sousa of Bophal, India; Bishop John Comber, superior general of Maryknoll; and Bishop Ignatius Dogget, apostolic vicar of Aitape, New Guinea. Appointed by the pope was Bishop Charles Cavallera of Nyeri, Kenya.

43. Norman Tanner, "The Church in the World (Ecclesia ad Extra)," in *History of Vatican II, Volume 4: Church as Communion, Third Period and Intersession, September 1964–September 1965*, ed. Giuseppe Alberigo and Joseph A. Komonchak (Maryknoll, NY: Orbis Books/Leuven, Belgium: Peeters, 2003), 369–70.

44. Ibid., 333.

45. Ibid., 335; Brechter, "Decree on the Church's Missionary Activity," 97. The text of the pope's address is found in *AS*, III, VI, 324–325.

46. See Tanner, "The Church in the World," 334–35.

47. Recorded in the journal of Yves Congar, *Mon Journal du Concile*, vol. 2 (Paris: Éditions du Cerf, 2002), November 19, 1964, p. 278.

48. For what follows I am relying especially on Tanner, "The Church in the World," 339–45, and Brechter, "Decree on the Church's Missionary Activity," 98–100. The texts of the speeches can be found in *AS*, III, VI, 357–447. All quotations in the text can be found in the pages indicated for these three sources.

49. The issue of a fourth session was a delicate one. Some wanted the council to end with the present third session, while others thought that a fourth session was necessary, especially for an adequate discussion of "Schema

XIII," which became the Pastoral Constitution on the Church in the Modern World. See Tanner, "The Church in the World," 369–72 for a discussion of this. A final decision for a fourth session was announced by Pope Paul VI on November 21, at the close of the council's third session.

50. Villanova, "The Intersession (1963–1964)," 391.

51. For these paragraphs on the intersession I have relied heavily on Brechter, "Decree on the Church's Missionary Activity," 100–104; Paventi, "Étapes de l'élaboration du texte," 164–67; and Riccardo Burigana and Giovanni Turbanti, "The Intersession: Preparing the Conclusion of the Council," in Alberigo and Komonchak, *History of Vatican II, Volume 4*, 573–84. As in my treatment in the previous paragraphs on the third session, all quotations will be from these three sources unless otherwise specified.

52. See note 286 in Burigana and Turbanti, "The Intersession," for an interesting quotation from Congar's journal for November 20, 1964. Bishop Riobé had come to see Congar with the news of his acceptance as a *peritus*. Congar wrote: "Agagianian did not refuse but said... 'Why change?... Why bring in others? Why Father Congar?' Because one of the complaints about the *De missionibus* is that it doesn't have a theological basis. And Fr. Congar has been on the theological commission, on the commission for the *De Ecclesia*, and is trusted by Cardinal Ottaviani and the Pope. In short, I have been accepted" (Congar, *Mon Journal du Concile*, vol. 2, p. 287).

53. Burigana and Turbanti write "Buijs"; in his journal, Congar writes "Buijk"; Brechter writes "Buys."

54. Burigana and Turbanti, "The Intersession," 581n300, quoting Congar's journal, vol. 2, March 24, 1965, p. 348.

55. Congar, *Mon Journal du Concile*, vol. 2, March 30, 1965, p. 354.

56. Ralph Wiltgen, *The Rhine Flows into the Tiber: The Unknown Council* (New York: Hawthorn, 1967), 258.

57. Hünermann, "The Final Weeks of the Council," 443–45.

58. See Hünermann, "The Final Weeks of the Council," 427. Hünermann here cites Wiltgen, *The Rhine Flows into the Tiber*, 254 (I have found the quote on 257).

59. Once again, I am depending heavily on several sources in the following paragraphs: Brechter, "Decree on the Church's Missionary Activity," 103–8; Hünermann, "The Final Weeks of the Council," 427–47; and Paventi, "Étapes de l'élaboration du texte," 168–75. The texts of the speeches of the Council members are found in *AS*, IV, III, 698–715; and *AS*, IV, IV, 134–172; 176–224; 287–332. Summaries of the speeches are found in Caprile, *Il Concilio Vaticano II, Vol. 5, Quarto Periodo*, 188–95; 197–202; 206–22. References are to these sources unless otherwise noted.

60. *AS* IV, III, 707.

61. The text of the revised schema, printed alongside the original schema, can be found in *AS*, IV, VI, 207–260.

62. The report of the commission, together with Fr. Schütte's report, can be found in *AS*, IV, VII, 11–96.

63. Hünermann, "The Final Weeks of the Council," 445.

### MAJOR POINTS

1. See Stephen Bevans, "The Church as Creation of the Spirit: Unpacking a Missionary Image," *Missiology: An International Review* 35, no. 1 (January 2007): 5–21.

2. See Suso Brechter, "Decree on the Church's Missionary Activity," in *Commentary on the Documents of Vatican II*, vol. 4, ed. Herbert Vorgrimler (Freiburg: Herder/Montreal: Palm Publishers, 1969), 113. Brechter's commentary (found on pp. 112–81 of Vorgrimler's *Commentary*, vol. 4) is one of the major sources for the material in the pages that follow. Other major sources I have used are Johannes Schütte, ed., *Vatican II: L'activité Missionnaire de L'Église*, Unam Sanctam 67 (Paris: Éditions du Cerf, 1967); Joseph Masson, *L'attività Missionaria della Chiesa* (Torino-Leumann: Elle Di Ci, 1966); Thomas Corboy, "A Commentary on the Missions Decree," in *Missions and Religions*, ed. Austin Flannery (Dublin: Scepter Books, 1968), 11–20; William R. Burrows, "Decree on the Church's Missionary Activity," in *Vatican II and Its Documents: An American Reappraisal*, ed. Timothy E. O'Connell (Wilmington, DE: Michael Glazier, Inc., 1986), 180–96.

3. Anthony J. Gittins, "Mission: What's It Got to Do with Me?" *The Living Light* 34, no. 3 (Spring 1998): 8.

4. For example, see Yves Congar, *I Believe in the Holy Spirit*, vol. 1 (New York: Crossroad Publishing Company, 1997), 15–25.

5. Yves Congar, "Principes doctrinaux," in Schütte, *Vatican II*, 186.

6. For a fuller development of the discussion of *Missio Dei*, see James A. Scherer, *Gospel, Church, and Kingdom: Comparative Studies in World Mission Theology* (Minneapolis, MN: Augsburg, 1987), 95–98, 119–21.

7. Peter Hünermann, "The Final Weeks of the Council," in *History of Vatican II, Volume 5, The Council and the Transition, The Fourth Period and the End of the Council, September 1965–December 1965*, ed. Giuseppe Alberigo and Joseph A. Komonchak (Maryknoll, NY: Orbis Books/Leuven: Peeters, 2006), 446. Hünermann's other criticism is that the document does not adequately present the critical and judgmental aspect of the gospel. What was not clearly

presented, he says, is that the preaching of the gospel always calls women and men to a radical decision.

8. For a more detailed history of the controversy alluded to here, see Karl Müller, *Mission Theology: An Introduction* (Nettetal, Germany: Steyler Verlag, 1987), 30–38. For a short overview of the history, see Brechter, "Decree on the Church's Missionary Activity," 118–19.

9. See Heribert Bettscheider, SVD, "Mission for the Twenty-First Century in Europe," in *Mission for the Twenty-First Century*, ed. Stephen Bevans and Roger Schroeder (Chicago: CCGM Publications, 2001), 110–28; see also the entire issue of *Spiritus* (Edición Hispanoamericana) 47, no. 4 (December 2006) entitled "Atreverse a la misión en una Europa en construcción. 3a Conferencia de las Asociaciones Europeas de Misionología."

10. D. T. Niles, *That They May Have Life* (New York: Harper and Brothers, 1951), 96. This famous phrase is quoted in Creighton Lacy, "D. T. Niles, 1908–1970: Evangelism, the Work of Disrupting People's Lives," in *Mission Legacies: Biographical Studies of Leaders of the Modern Missionary Movement*, ed. Gerald H. Anderson, et al. (Maryknoll, NY: Orbis Books, 1994), 362.

11. On *Nostra Aetate*, see Edward Idris Cardinal Cassidy's volume in this series: *Ecumenism and Interreligious Dialogue: Unitatis Redintegratio, Nostra Aetate* (New York/Mahwah, NJ: Paulist Press, 2005), 125–284.

12. Giuseppe Alberigo, "The Announcement of the Council: From the Security of the Fortress to the Lure of the Quest," in *History of Vatican II, Volume 1: Announcing and Preparing Vatican Council II, Toward a New Era in Catholicism*, ed. Giuseppe Alberigo and Joseph A. Komonchak (Maryknoll, NY: Orbis Books/Leuven, Belgium: Peeters, 1995), 1.

13. See Stephen Bevans and Roger Schroeder, eds., *Mission for the Twenty-First Century* (Chicago: CCGM Publications, 2001), 42, 385–86, and 409n35.

14. These were *Maximum Illud* (Benedict XV, 1919), *Rerum Ecclesiae* (Pius XI, 1926), *Evangelii Praecones* and *Fidei Donum* (Pius XII, 1951 and 1957), and *Princeps Pastorum* (John XXIII, 1959).

15. See Richard R. Gaillardetz's treatment of the diaconate in his commentary on *Lumen Gentium* in this series: *The Church in the Making: Lumen Gentium, Christus Dominus, Orientalium Ecclesiarum* (New York/Mahwah, NJ: Paulist Press, 2006), 17–18, 86–87, 139–42, and 184–86. An investigation into the possibility of restoration of the diaconate was also one of the recommendations of the initial study group at the Propaganda Fide in 1960. See ADA, III, 247.

16. On the council's full treatment of laity, see Gaillardetz, *The Church in the Making*, 22–24, 51–55, 98–100, 142–44, and 186–88. See also Dolores Leckey's volume in this series: *The Laity and Christian Education: Apostolicam Actuositatem, Gravissimum Educationis* (New York/Mahwah, NJ: Paulist Press, 2006).

17. See, for example, the Preface of Christmas III, Prayer Over the Gifts for Christmas Midnight Mass and Wednesday of the Second Week of Lent, and First Vespers of the Octave of Christmas (Mary, Mother of God), Antiphon 1.

18. See Gaillardetz, *The Church in the Making*, 74–82, 119–36, and 171–81.

19. The Synod of Bishops was instituted by Paul VI in the *motu proprio Apostolica Sollicitudo*, issued just before the start of the council's fourth session on September 15, 1965 (*AAS* 57 [1965], 775–780): "On our own initiative (*motu proprio*) and with our apostolic authority we erect and constitute in this beloved City a permanent Council of Bishops for the universal Church, directly and immediately subject to our power and which we call with the proper name *Synod of Bishops*." The pope goes on to say that the synod by nature has the task of giving information and advice, although when it is convoked by the pope it can have deliberative power, provided its decisions are ratified by him. The synod is also mentioned in *Christus Dominus* 5 and its canonical status is laid out in *CIC* 342–348. See Gaillardetz, *The Church in the Making*, 80, 130–32, and 179–80.

20. This congregation was originally under the Propaganda Fide, but has been an independent congregation since 1917, when it was called the Congregation for the Oriental Church (Congregatio pro Ecclesia Orientali). On August 15, 1967, Paul VI, with the apostolic constitution *Regimini Ecclesiae*, changed the name to Congregation for the Oriental Churches (Congregatio pro Ecclesiis Orientalibus). See <http://www.vatican.va/roman_curia/congregations/orientchurch/profilo/rc_con_corient_pro_20030320_profile.html>.

21. "Fasst man alles zusammen, so bleibt von dem Vorgriff, den das Missionsdikret hinsichtlich der Kurienreform als einziges Konzilsdokument gemacht hat, kaum etwas übrig....Im Alltag aber heißt das, dass praktisch alles beim Alten bleibt." Josef Glazik, *Kommentar*, in *Instruktionen der Kongregation für die Evangelisation der Völker* (Tübingen, 1970), 13–15. Quoted by Peter Hünermann in "Theologischer Kommentar zum Dekret über die Missionstätigkeit der Kirche: *Ad Gentes*," in *Herders Theologischer Kommentar zum Zweiten Vatikanischen Konzil*, ed. Peter Hünermann and Bernd Jochen Hilberath (Freiburg: Herder, 2005), 308.

22. Thomas C. Fox, *Pentecost in Asia: A New Way of Being Church* (Maryknoll, NY: Orbis Books, 2002); Jonathan Y. Tan, *"Missio inter Gentes*: Toward a New Paradigm in the Mission Theology of the Federation of Asian Bishops' Conferences (FABC)," *Mission Studies* 21, no. 1 (2004): 65–95.

23. Vicars apostolic and prefects apostolic are representatives of the pope and envoys of the Congregation for the Propagation of the Faith. The former are bishops, but they are not ordinaries. When a hierarchy is established, the bishops of the new territory—the bishops of the newly established dioceses—cease to be mere representatives or "vicars" of the pope and they exercise their charge over their dioceses in the name of Christ in communion with the pope, as head of the episcopal college. In this case, therefore, in the light of the council's theology of the episcopate the "Jus Comissionis," which is a contract made between a religious congregation and the Holy See, would cease to exist.

24. "Esiste ancora l'Istituto della 'commissio' nei territori di missione?" Editorial in *Euntes Docete* 45 (1992): 3–9.

25. See Horst Rzepkowski, "Jus Commisionis" and "Jus Mandati," in *Diccionario de Missionología* (Estella, Spain: Editorial Verbo Divino, 1997), 312–13; Paul Zepp, "Mission Law," in *Dictionary of Mission: Theology, History, Perspectives,* ed. Karl Müller, Theo Sundermeier, Stephen B. Bevans, and Richard H. Bliese (Maryknoll, NY: Orbis Books, 1997), 308–11; Patrick Taveirne, "The European Roots of the Modern Missionary Enterprise: The Nineteenth-Century Religious and Missionary Revivals : Liberal and Socialist Challenges," *Theology Annual* 13 <http://218.188.3.99/Archive/periodical/abstract/A013F2.htm>; Müller, *Mission Theology,* 105–9.

26. See Stephen Bevans, "Common Witness," in Müller, et al., *Dictionary of Mission,* 72–73.

27. Domenico Grasso, La Coopération Missionaire," in Schütte, *Vatican II,* 390.

## IMPLEMENTATION

1. Robert J. Schreiter, "Changes in Roman Catholic Attitudes toward Proselytism and Mission," in *New Directions in Mission and Evangelization 2: Theological Foundations,* ed. James A. Scherer and Stephen B. Bevans (Maryknoll, NY: Orbis Books, 1994), 113–25. The phrase "period of certainty" is discussed on 114–16. This article originally appeared in *Pushing the Faith: Proselytism and Civility in a Pluralistic World,* ed. Martin E. Marty and Frederick Greenspahn (New York: Crossroad Publishing Company, 1988), 93–108. What follows in this section owes much to Schreiter's article.

2. See Stephen B. Bevans and Roger P. Schroeder, *Constants in Context: A Theology of Mission for Today* (Maryknoll, NY: Orbis Books, 2004), 216.

3. See our brief discussion of this in the reflections on *Ad Gentes* 6 in Part 2 (pp. 35–36).

4. See Frederick R. Norris, *Christianity: A Short Global History* (Oxford: Oneworld, 2002), 240; David J. Bosch, *Transforming Mission: Paradigm Shifts in Theology of Mission* (Maryknoll, NY: Orbis Books, 1991), 479–80; Timothy Yates, *Christian Mission in the Twentieth Century* (Cambridge: Cambridge University Press, 1994), 24–33.

5. See Robert J. Schreiter, "The Impact of Vatican II," in *The Twentieth Century: A Theological Overview*, ed. Gregory Baum (Maryknoll, NY: Orbis Books, 1999), 160–61.

6. Schreiter, "Changes in Roman Catholic Attitudes," 116.

7. Ibid., 117.

8. This is evident in many of the articles cited in Suso Brechter's commentary on *Ad Gentes* in *Commentary on the Documents of Vatican II*, vol. 4, ed. Herbert Vorgrimler (Freiburg: Herder/Montreal: Palm Publishers, 1969), 87–181; in Louis J. Luzbetak's first edition of *The Church and Cultures: An Applied Anthropology for the Religious Worker* (Techny, IL: Divine Word Publications, 1963); and in the pioneering work of theologians like Heinz Robert Schlette in *Toward a Theology of Religions* (New York: Herder and Herder, 1966), which was originally published in German in 1963. Karl Rahner's groundbreaking work on "anonymous Christianity" goes back at least to the early 1960s. See his "Christianity and the Non-Christian Religions," in *Theological Investigations V* (Baltimore: Helicon Press, 1966), 115–34, which was originally a set of notes for a lecture given in 1961.

9. Schreiter, "Changes in Roman Catholic Attitudes," 120.

10. Bevans and Schroeder, *Constants in Context*, 251.

11. Johannes Schütte, "Relatio super Schema Decreti De Activitate Missionali Ecclesiae," *AS*, IV, III, 707.

12. It would seem that the Latin American bishops were also concerned with reflecting on the church's role in the light of Paul VI's encyclical *Populorum Progressio*, issued the previous year, in 1967. The encyclical is quoted liberally in the Medellín documents. The text of the encyclical can be found at <http://www.vatican.va/holy_father/paul_vi/encyclicals/index.htm>.

13. See Philip Berryman, *Liberation Theology* (Oak Park, IL: Meyer Stone Books, 1987), 22–24; see also Second General Conference of Latin American Bishops, *The Church in the Present-Day Transformation of Latin America in the Light of the Council*, 2nd ed. (Washington, DC: Division for Latin America— USCC, 1973). Gustavo Gutiérrez (one of the several theologians present at

Medellín), in his groundbreaking *Theology of Liberation*, levels a strong critique against the idea of development and proposes the idea of liberation as one more adequate to the Latin American situation. See *A Theology of Liberation: History, Politics and Salvation* (Maryknoll, NY: Orbis Books, 1973), 21–42.

14. Synod of Bishops, 1971, *Justice in the World*, in *Catholic Social Thought: The Documentary Heritage*, ed. David J. O'Brien and Thomas A. Shannon (Maryknoll, NY: Orbis Books, 1992), 289.

15. *Justice in the World*, 290, 295, 298, and 294.

16. On the controversies at the synod that led to this stalemate, see Stephen Bevans, "Witness to the Gospel in Modern Australia: Celebrating 30 Years of *Evangelii Nuntiandi*," *Australian E-Journal of Theology* 6 (February 2006), <http://dlibrary.acu.edu.au/research/theology/ejournal/aejt_6/bevans.htm>.

17. See Schreiter, "Changes in Roman Catholic Attitudes," 122.

18. Quotations from *Evangelii Nuntiandi* are from O'Brien and Shannon, *Catholic Social Thought*, 303–45, although the document's paragraph numbers are cited.

19. This statement is a bit controversial. I myself tend to equate "evangelization" with "mission," as does, I believe, the 1991 document issued jointly by the Pontifical Council for Inter-Religious Dialogue and the Congregation for the Evangelization of Peoples, *Dialogue and Proclamation*; see the document in *Redemption and Dialogue: Reading* Redemptoris Missio *and* Dialogue and Proclamation, ed. William R. Burrows (Maryknoll, NY: Orbis Books, 1993), 93–118. This document speaks of "evangelizing mission" (par. 8). See also Jacob Kavunkal, "Mission or Evangelization?" *Mission Studies* 21, no. 1 (2004): 55–64.

20. Federation of Asian Bishops' Conferences, "Evangelization in Modern Day Asia" (Briefer Statement of the Assembly), 9–21, in *For All the Peoples of Asia: Federation of Asian Bishops' Conferences Documents from 1970 to 1991*, ed. Gaudencio Rosales and C. G. Arévalo (Quezon City: Claretian Publications, 1997), 22–23.

21. On the development of *Evangelii Nuntiandi*, see John Prior, "Mission for the Twenty-First Century in Asia: Two Sketches, Three Flash-Backs, and an Enigma," in *Mission for the Twenty-First Century*, ed. Stephen B. Bevans and Roger Schroeder (Chicago: CCGM Publications, 2001), 81–84.

22. The quotations are from the full text of "Evangelization in Modern Day Asia," 12, 16, and 23 in Rosales and Arévalo, *For All the Peoples of Asia*, 14 and 16.

23. Paul VI, Lettera Apostolica Motu Proprio *Finis Concilio Oecumenico Vaticano II*, <http://www.vatican.va/holy_father/paul_vi/motu_proprio/documents/hf_p-vi_motu-proprio_19660103_finis-concilio_it.html>. *AAS* 58 (1966), 37–40.

24. Paul VI, Lettera Apostolica Motu Proprio *Munus Apostolicum*, <http://www.vatican.va /holy_father/paul_vi/motu_proprio/documents/hf_p-vi_ motu-proprio_19660610_munus-apostolicum_it.html>. *AAS* 58 (1966), 465–466.

25. Paul VI, Lettera Apostolica Motu Proprio *Ecclesiae Sanctae*, <http://www.vatican. va/holy_father/paul_vi/motu_proprio/documents/hf_p-vi_motu-proprio_19660806_ecclesiae-sanctae_en.html>. *AAS* 58 (1966), 757–787.

26. The designation "Introduction" or particular numbers in parentheses in the paragraphs that follow indicate numbers in the document.

27. Acta Congressus Internationalis de Theologia Concilii Vaticani II (Rome: Vatican Polyglot Press, 1968), 66, quoted in Pontificie Opere Missionarie, Direzione Nazionale Italiana, *Enchiridion della Chiesa Missionaria*, I (Bologna: Edizione Dehoniane, 1997), 694n7.

28. Sacred Congregation for Catholic Education, *The Basic Plan for Priestly Formation* (Washington, DC: National Conference of Catholic Bishops, 1970), paragraphs 77 and 96 (pp. 55 and 66).

29. See Sacred Congregation for the Evangelization of Peoples, *Puisque la "Ratio": La formation missiologique des futurs prêtres*, in *Enchiridion della Chiesa Missionaria*, I, 690–697. Reference is made in the document to the paragraph of *Ecclesiae Sanctae* referred to above.

30. United States Conference of Catholic Bishops, *Program of Priestly Formation*, 5th ed. (Washington, DC: United States Conference of Catholic Bishops, 2006), paragraph 202 (p. 71); United States Conference of Catholic Bishops, *Teaching the Spirit of* Ad Gentes: *Continuing Pentecost Today*, <http://www.usccb.org/wm/spiritofmission.shtml>.

31. For Catholic scholarship, see Francis Cardinal George, "The Promotion of Missiological Studies in Seminaries," *Mission Studies* 16, no. 2 (1999): 13-27; Stephen Bevans, "Wisdom from the Margins: Systematic Theology and the Missiological Imagination," in *The Catholic Theological Society of America: Proceedings of the Fifty-Sixth Annual Convention*, ed. Richard C. Sparks (2001), 21–42; Peter C. Phan, "Doing Theology in the Context of Mission: Lessons from Alexander de Rhodes for Comparative Theology," in *In Our Own Tongues: Perspectives from Asia on Mission and Inculturation* (Maryknoll, NY: Orbis Books, 2003), 153–73. For Protestant scholarship see Darrell L. Guder, "From Mission and Theology to Missional Theology," *The Princeton Seminary Bulletin* 24, no. 1, New Series (2003): 36–43; J. Andrew Kirk, *What Is Mission? Theological Explorations* (London: Darton, Longman and Todd, 1999), 7–22 and *The Mission of Theology and the Theology of Mission* (Valley Forge, PA: Trinity Press International, 1997); Robert J. Banks,

*Reenvisioning Theological Education: Exploring a Missional Alternative to Current Models* (Grand Rapids, MI: William B. Eerdmans Publishing Company, 1999).

32. See the committee's website at <http://www.usccb.org/wm/>. Some say that the importance of this committee will be lessened in the structures being developed in a current reorganization of the bishops' conference.

33. Sacred Congregation for the Evangelization of Peoples, *Relationes in Territoriis: De relationibus inter Ordinarios locorum et Instituta missionalia, Enchiridion della Chiesa Missionaria*, I, 630–645. *AAS* 61 (1969), 281–287.

34. See Part 1, p. 28.

35. Part 2, p. 48.

36. See *Regimini Ecclesiae Universae* at <http://www.vatican.va/holy_father/paul_vi/apost_constitutions/documents/hf_p-vi_apc_19670815_regimini-ecclesiae-universae_it.html>. The document consists of an introduction, seven major parts, and an appendix. The seven parts are entitled I. General Norms; II. Secretary of State and the Council for the Public Affairs of the Church; III. The Sacred Congregations; IV. The Secretariats; V. The Council of the Laity and the Pontifical Study Commission "Justitia et Pax"; VI. The Tribunals; and VII. The Offices.

37. Brechter, "Decree on the Church's Missionary Activity," 160.

38. Sacra Congregatio pro Gentium Evangelizatione seu de Propaganda Fide, Instructio *Cum in Constitutione* de membris adiunctis et de consultoribus Sacrae Congregationis pro gentium evangelizatione seu de propaganda fide, in *Enchiridion della Chiesa Missionaria* I, 608–617. Also found in *Bibliografia Missionaria* 31 (1967): 169–72.

39. Sacra Congregatio pro Gentium Evangelizatione seu de Propaganda Fide, Instructio *Quo Aptius* de ordinanda cooperatione missionali Episcoporum quoad Pontificalia Opera Missionalia necnon circa particularia diocesium pro Minsionibus; Instructio *Relationes in Territoriis* de quibusdam principiis atque normis circa relationes in territoriis Missionum inter Ordinarios locorum et Instituta Missionalia, in *Enchiridion della Chiesa Missionaria*, I, 618–629 and 630–645. Also in *AAS* 61 (1969), 276–281 and 281–287. We will discuss the second document in detail in the following section.

40. See <http://www.vatican.va/roman_curia/congregations/cevang/documents/rc_con_cevang_19971125_profile_it.html>. This profile, however, lists the number of archbishops and bishops as only eight, instead of the stated number of twelve. The organization profile of the Congregation on the Fides website (Fides is the news agency of the congregation) lists nine archbishops and three bishops (this according to *Ecclesiae Sanctae*) but only three national directors of the pontifical mission societies and three

superiors general. Since this website is slightly outdated (it refers to Cardinal Sepe as the prefect, but the prefect is now Cardinal Dias), the statistics at the Vatican website are probably more accurate as to the number of non-cardinal members. See <http://www.evangelizatio.org/portale/congregazione/istituzione/organizzazione.html>.

41. Brechter, "Decree on the Church's Missionary Activity," 164.

42. Viktor Dammertz, *Archiv für Katholiches Kirchenrecht*, 136 (1967), 59, quoted in Brechter, "Decree on the Church's Missionary Activity," 164n9.

43. Sacra Congregatio pro Gentium Evangelizatione seu de Propaganda Fide, Instructio *Quo Aptius* de ordinanda cooperatione missionali Episcoporum quad Pontificalia Opera Missionalia nec non circa incepta particularia diocesium pro Missionibus, 24 Februarii, 1969. *AAS* 61 (1969), 276–281.

44. See Peter Hünermann, "Theologischer Kommentar zum Dekret über die Missionstätigkeit der Kirche, *Ad Gentes*," in *Herders Theologischer Kommentar zum Zweiten Vatikanischen Konzil*, vol. 4, ed. Peter Hünermann and Bernd Jochen Hiberath (Freiburg: Herder, 2005), 308–9.

45. Sacra Congegatio pro Propaganda Fide, *Quum Huic*, *AAS* 22 (1930), 111–115.

46. Philip Sulumeti, "The Juridical System of the Mandatum," *African Ecclesiatical Review* 15, no. 4 (1973): 316–17.

47. *Relationes in Territoriis*, in *Enchiridion della Chiesa Missionaria*, I, 630-645. It should be recalled that this instruction was the result of the first Plenary Assembly of the Congregation for the Evangelization of Peoples or the Propagation of the Faith in June 1968.

48. See Sulumeti, "The Juridical System of the Mandatum," 322.

49. See Amand Reuter, "Religious and Mission according to the New Code of Canon Law," *Bibliographia Missionaria* 47 (1983): 367–78. It might be noted that Reuter was a member of the council's Preparatory Commission for the mission decree.

50. Sulumeti, "The Juridical System of the Mandatum," 328.

51. Amand Reuter, "The Missions in the New Code of Canon Law," *Bibliographia Missionaria* 46 (1982): 265.


THE STATE OF THE QUESTIONS


1. Peter Hünermann, "The Final Weeks of the Council," in *History of Vatican II, Volume 5: The Council and the Transition, The Fourth Period and the*

*End of the Council, September 1965–December 1965,* ed. Giuseppe Alberigo and Joseph A. Komonchak (Maryknoll, NY: Orbis Books/Leuven, Belgium: Peeters, 2006), 446.

2. The state of the question regarding the local church will not be dealt with here, since it is dealt with adequately in another monograph in this series. See Richard R. Gaillardetz, *The Church in the Making: Lumen Gentium, Christus Dominus, Orientalium Ecclesiarum* (New York/Mahwah, NJ: Paulist Press, 2006), 110–11, 159–62.

3. Roger D. Haight, "Mission: The Symbol for Understanding the Church Today," *Theological Studies* 37, no. 4 (December 1976): 620–51.

4. See, for example, Robert S. Rivers, *From Maintenance to Mission: Evangelizaton and the Revitalization of the Parish* (New York/Mahwah, NJ: Paulist Press, 2005); Donald G. LaSalle, Jr., "At the Threshold of the Assembly: Liturgy, the New Evangelization, and the New Millennium," *Liturgical Ministry* 8 (Fall 1999): 183–91; Philip Murnion, "Leadership for a Missionary Community," *Seminary Journal* 6, no. 2 (Fall 2000): 10–21.

5. Robert J. Schreiter, "The New Evangelization," in *Word Remembered, Word Proclaimed: Selected Papers from Symposia Celebrating the SVD Centennial in North America*, ed. Stephen B. Bevans and Roger Schroeder (Nettetal, Germany: Steyler Verlag, 1997), 53.

6. Avery Dulles, "The New Evangelization: Challenge for Religious Missionary Institutes," in Bevans and Schroeder, *Word Remembered, Word Proclaimed,* 19. Dulles quotes John Paul II's address on March 9, 1983, in Port-au-Prince, Haiti, where the term "new evangelization" was first mentioned. See John Paul II, "The Task of the Latin American Bishop," *Origins* 12 (March 24, 1983): 659–662, at 661.

7. Although the term "new evangelization" is not mentioned prominently, Ronald Rolheiser's edited book *Secularity and the Gospel: Being Missionaries to Our Children* (New York: Crossroad, 2006) is a fine example of contemporary thinking along this line. An influential book among Evangelical Protestants is Darrell L. Guder, ed., *Missional Church: A Vison for the Sending of the Church in North America* (Grand Rapids, MI: William B. Eerdmans Publishing Company, 1998).

8. Joint Working Group, "Christian Witness—Common Witness," in *New Direction in Mission and Evangelization 1: Basic Statements, 1974–1991,* ed. James A. Scherer and Stephen B. Bevans (Maryknoll, NY: Orbis Books, 1992), 18–26.

9. See the pope's interview during his flight to Brazil: <http://www.vatican.va/holy_father/benedict_xvi/speeches/2007/may/documents/hf_ben-xvi_spe_20070509_interview-brazil_en.html>. See also the article on the pope's

trip on the Catholic Online website (www.catholic.org): <http://www.catholic.org/international/international_story.php?id=23950>.

10. Edward Idris Cardinal Cassidy, *Ecumenism and Interreligious Dialogue: Unitatis Redintegratio, Nostra Aetate* (New York/Mahwah, NJ: Paulist Press, 2005), 110–11.

11. See, for example, the treatment of ecumenism in John Paul II's post-synodal exhortations: *Ecclesia in Asia* 27–30, <http://www.vatican.va/holy_father/john_paul_ii/apost_exhortations/documents/hf_jp-ii_exh_06111999_ecclesia-in-asia_en.html>; *Ecclesia in Africa*, 65, <http://www.vatican.va/holy_father/john_paul_ii/apost_exhortations/documents/hf_jp-ii_exh_14091995_ecclesia-in-africa_en.html>; *Ecclesia in America*, 49, <http://www.vatican.va/holy_father/john_paul_ii/apost_exhortations/documents/hf_jp-ii_exh_22011999_ecclesia-in-america_en.htm>; *Ecclesia in Europa*, 17, <http://www.vatican.va/holy_father/john_paul_ii/apost_exhortations/documents/hf_jp-ii_exh_20030628_ecclesia-in-europa_en.html>; *Ecclesia in Oceania*, 23, <http://www.vatican.va/holy_father/john_paul_ii/apost_exhortations/documents/hf_jp-ii_exh_20011122_ecclesia-in-oceania_en.html>.

12. Yves Congar, "Principes doctrinaux," in *Vatican II: L'activité Missionnaire de L'Église*, Unam Sanctam 67, ed. Johannes Schütte (Paris: Éditions du Cerf, 1967), 186.

13. What follows is based on the more detailed development found in Stephen B. Bevans and Roger P. Schroeder, *Constants in Context: A Theology of Mission for Today* (Maryknoll, NY: Orbis Books, 2004), 281–347.

14. Congregation for the Doctrine of the Faith, Instruction on Certain Aspects of the Theology of Liberation, *Liberationis Nuntius*, <http://www.vatican.va/roman_curia/congregations/cfaith/documents/rc_con_cfaith_doc_19840806_theology-liberation_en.html>; Instruction on Christian Freedom and Liberation, *Libertatis Conscientia*, <http://www.vatican.va/roman_curia/congregations/cfaith/documents/rc_con_cfaith_doc_19860322_freedom-liberation_en.html>. See especially *Libertatis Conscientia*, 61–70.

15. Jozef Tomko, "Proclaiming Christ the World's Only Savior," *L'Osservatore Romano* (April 15, 1991): 4.

16. See Bevans and Schroeder, *Constants in Context*, 348–52. See also Stephen B. Bevans and Roger Schroeder, "'We Were Gentle among You': Christian Mission as Dialogue," *Australian E-Journal of Theology*, Special Pentecost Issue, 2006 <http://dlibrary.acu.edu.au/ research/theology/ejournal/aejt_7/svd.htm>.

17. This phrase is a reference to a famous phrase by the great British missiologist Max Warren. See his introduction to John V. Taylor, *The Primal Vision: Christian Presence amid African Religion* (Philadelphia: Fortress Press, 1963), 10.

18. Bevans and Schroeder, "'We Were Gentle among You.'"

19. Gerhard Lohfink, *Jesus and Community: The Social Dimension of Christian Faith* (Philadelphia: Fortress Press, 1984). In previous publications, Roger Schroeder and I have written of only two dimensions of the prophetic stance of mission. The realization that there was a third dimension—listed as the first expression here—came as a result of a workshop that Roger and I conducted at the Divine Word School of Theology, Tagaytay City, Philippines, in July and August, 2006. I would like to thank the participants of the workshop for this important insight.

20. David J. Bosch, *Transforming Mission: Paradigm Shifts in Theology of Mission* (Maryknoll, NY: Orbis Books, 1991), 489.

21. "Agenda for Future Planning, Study, and Research in Mission," in *Trends in Mission: Toward the Third Millennium*, ed. William Jenkinson and Helene O'Sullivan (Maryknoll, NY: Orbis Books, 1991), 399–414.

22. Secretariat for Non-Christians, "The Attitude of the Church toward the Followers of Other Religions: Reflections and Orientations on Dialogue and Mission," *Bulletin. Secretariatus pro non christianis* 56:13 (1984/2). This is quoted in Pontifical Council for Inter-Religious Dialogue and Congregation for the Evangelization of Peoples, *Dialogue and Proclamation*, 2, <http://www.vatican.va/roman_curia/pontifical_councils/interelg/documents/rc_pc_interelg_doc_19051991_dialogue-and-proclamatio_en.html>.

23. Bosch, *Transforming Mission*, 368–510; J. Andrew Kirk, *What Is Mission? Theological Explorations* (Minneapolis, MN: Fortress Press, 2000); Donal Dorr, *Mission in Today's World* (Maryknoll, NY: Orbis Books, 2000); Anthony J. Gittins, *Reading the Clouds: Mission Spirituality for New Times* (Liguori, MO: Liguori Publications, 1999); Samuel Escobar, *Changing Tides: Latin America and World Mission Today* (Maryknoll, NY: Orbis Books, 2002); Robert J. Schreiter, "Globalization and Reconciliation: Challenges to Mission," in *Mission in the Third Millennium* (Maryknoll, NY: Orbis Books, 2001), 121–43.

24. Stephen Bevans and Eleanor Doidge, "Theological Reflection," in *Reflection and Dialogue: What MISSION Confronts Religious Life Today?* ed. Barbara Kraemer (Chicago: Center for the Study of Religious Life, 2000), 37–48.

25. Bevans and Schroeder, *Constants in Context*, 348–95.

26. Marcello Zago, OMI, "The New Millennium and the Emerging Religious Encounters," *Missiology: An International Review* 28, no. 1 (January 2000): 17.

27. Peter C. Phan, "Proclamation of the Reign of God as Mission of the Church," in *In Our Own Tongues: Perspectives from Asia on Mission and Inculturation* (Maryknoll, NY: Orbis Books, 2003), 41.

28. For an introductory discussion of these elements, see Bevans and Schroeder, *Constants in Context*, 361–68. See also Gregory Augustine Pierce, *The Mass Is Never Ended: Rediscovering Our Mission to Transform the World* (Notre Dame, IN: Ave Maria Press, 2007).

29. See James J. Stamoolis, "Orthodox Theology of Mission," in *Evangelical Dictionary of World Missions*, ed. A. Scott Moreau (Grand Rapids, MI: Baker Books, 2000), 715.

30. Robert J. Schreiter, "Mission for the Twenty-First Century: A Catholic Perspective," in *Mission for the Twenty-First Century*, ed. Stephen B. Bevans and Roger Schroeder (Chicago: CCGM Publications, 2001), 35.

31. 1971 Synod of Bishops, *Justice in the World*, Introduction, in *Catholic Social Thought: The Documentary Heritage*, ed. David J. O'Brien and Thomas A. Shannon (Maryknoll, NY: Orbis Books, 1992), 289.

32. See for instance, the document *Justice in the World*, cited above, 298; *EN*, 31; *RM*, 37; Kirk, *What Is Mission?* 143–63; Bosch, *Transforming Mission*, 118–19; Eliseo Mercado, "Responding to the Mission of Peacemaking," <http://www.mindanews.com/index.php?option=com_content&task=view&id =2671&Itemid=75>; Tan Kang-San, "Mission as Peacemaking," <http://theagora. blogspot.com/2007/04/ mission-as-peace-making.html>.

33. Paul VI, "Message for World Day of Peace," *Origins*, 1, no. 29 (January 6, 1972): 491.

34. The growing body of literature around the question of mission and the integrity of creation includes W. Dayton Roberts, *Patching God's Garment: Environment and Mission in the 21st Century* (Monrovia, CA: MARC, 1994); Heidi Hadsell, "Ecology and Mission," in *Dictionary of Mission: Theology, History, Perspectives*, ed. Karl Müller et al. (Maryknoll, NY: Orbis Books, 1997), 114–16; Fr. Stanislaus, "Ecology: An Awareness for Mission," <http:// www.sedos.org/english/stanislaus.htm>; Kirk, *What Is Mission?* 164–83; Calvin B. DeWitt and Ghillean T. Prance, eds., *Missionary Earthkeeping* (Macon, GA: Mercer University Press, 1992).

35. See, for example, Special Synod for Africa (1994), Proposition 55, in Africa Faith and Justice Network under the direction of Maura Browne, *The African Synod: Documents, Reflections, Perspectives* (Maryknoll, NY: Orbis Books, 1996), 106; Federation of Asian Bishops' Conferences, Final Statement of the Seventh Plenary Assembly, "A Renewed Church in Asia: A Mission of Love and Service," II.D, *FABC Papers* 93, 7; Fourth General Conference of Latin American Bishops, "Conclusions," 169–77, in *Santo Domingo and Beyond*, ed. Alfred T. Hennelly (Maryknoll, NY: Orbis Books, 1993), 119–22; John Allen, "Latin American Bishops Flag Poverty, Ecology and Indigenous Peoples," (June 9, 2007): <http://ncrcafe.org/node/1171>.

36. See <http://en.arocha.org/home/index.html>.

37. Alan Race, *Christians and Religious Pluralism: Patterns in the Christian Theology of Religions* (Maryknoll, NY: Orbis Books, 1983); Paul F. Knitter, *No Other Name? A Critical Survey of Christian Attitudes Toward the World Religions* (Maryknoll, NY: Orbis Books, 1985).

38. Challenging the adequacy of the categories are Andrew Kirk (see *What Is Mission?* 127–30) and Charles van Engen, "The Uniqueness of Christ in Mission Theology," in *Mission on the Way* (Grand Rapids, MI: Baker Books, 1996), 169–87. Knitter's four categories are spelled out in *Introducing Theologies of Religions* (Maryknoll, NY: Orbis Books, 2002); S. Mark Heim argues that to speak of "salvation" through other religions is ultimately to take an exclusivist perspective. Salvation, he says, is a particularly Christian perspective; other religions have other religious ends, and these must be respected. See his *The Depth of the Riches: A Trinitarian Theology of Religious Ends* (Grand Rapids, MI: William B. Eerdmans Publishing Company, 2001).

39. For this description, see the commentary on the document by Jacques Dupuis in *Redemption and Dialogue: Reading* Redemptoris Missio *and* Dialogue and Proclamation, ed. William R. Burrows (Maryknoll, NY: Orbis Books, 1993), 132.

40. The English text can be found at <http://www.vatican.va/roman_curia/congregations/cfaith/documents/rc_con_cfaith_doc_20000806_dominus-iesus_en.html>. The official Latin text can be found at <http://www.vatican.va/roman_curia/congregations/cfaith/documents/rc_con_cfaith_doc_20000806_dominus-iesus_lt.html>.

41. In 2007 these statements regarding Protestant communities were repeated in the Congregation for the Doctrine of the Faith's document *Some Responses Regarding Certain Aspects of the Doctrine of the Church*, Third Question and Fifth Question. See <http://www.vatican.va/roman_curia/congregations/cfaith/documents/ rc_con_cfaith_ doc_20070629_responsa-quaestiones_en.html>. This controversial wording, however, appears as a quotation from Vatican II's *Unitatis Redintegratio* 3, as it does in *Dominus Iesus* 17.

42. For a spectrum of views, see Stephen J. Pope and Charles Hefling, eds., *Sic et Non: Encountering* Dominus Iesus (Maryknoll, NY: Orbis Books, 2002).

43. See Francis X. Clooney, "The Emerging Field of Comparative Theology: A Bibliographical Review (1989–1995)," *Theological Studies* 56, no. 3 (March 1995): 521–50; Francis X. Clooney, "La Prassi della teologia comparata: Con riferimento ad alcune recenti pubblicazioni," in *Verso l'India Oltre l'India: Scritti e ricerche sulle tradizione intelletuali sudasiatiche*, ed. Federico Squarcini (Milan: Mimesis, 2001); *Theological Studies* 64, no. 2 (June 2003),

thematic issue: "The Catholic Church and Other Living Faiths in Comparative Perspective"; James L. Fredericks, *Faith among Faiths: Christian Theology and Non-Christian Religions* (New York/Mahwah, NJ: Paulist Press, 1999); James L. Fredericks, *Buddhists and Christians: Through Comparative Theology to Solidarity* (Maryknoll, NY: Orbis Books, 2004). For a general introduction to comparative theology, see <http://www2.bc.edu/~clooney/Comparative/ct.html>.

44. I refer in particular to the late Belgian theologian Jacques Dupuis and the U.S. theologian Roger Haight. See <http://www.vatican.va/roman_curia/congregations/cfaith/documents/ rc_con_cfaith_doc_20010124_dupuis_en.html> (Dupuis) and <http://www.vatican.va/roman_curia/congregations/cfaith/documents/rc_con_cfaith_doc_20041213_notification-fr-haight_en.html> (Haight).

45. See Robert J. Schreiter, *Constructing Local Theologies* (Maryknoll, NY: Orbis Books, 1985), 6–12; Stephen B. Bevans, *Models of Contextual Theology* (Maryknoll, NY: Orbis Books, 2002), 37–53.

46. See Bevans, *Models of Contextual Theology*, 61. I heard this phrase in conversation with veteran missionary and anthropologist Jon Kirby, SVD, on a visit to Ghana in 1996. For what follows, see my book *Models of Contextual Theology*.

47. Schreiter, *Constructing Local Theologies*, 4.

48. See <http://www.vatican.va/holy_father/benedict_xvi/speeches/2006/September/documents/hf_ben-xvi_spe_20060912_university-regensburg_en.html>.

49. Quoted in Schreiter, "Mission for the Twenty-First Century," 34.

50. Schreiter, "Mission for the Twenty-First Century," 35.

51. See Robert J. Schreiter, "Globalization and Reconciliation: Challenges to Mission," 141–42.

52. Dolores R. Leckey, *The Laity and Christian Education: Apostolicam Actuositatem, Gravissimum Educationis* (New York/Mahwah, NJ: Paulist Press, 2006), 86–91.

53. Ibid., 90–91.

54. See the MKLM web page at <http://www.mklaymissioners.org/laymissioner/index.php>.

55. See <http://www.vmmusa.org/id10.htm>.

56. See, for example, the October 2006 issue of *Missiology: An International Review* (34, no. 4) which is devoted to short-term missions. Each article provides a rather extensive bibliography. There are no Catholic contributions, which is unfortunate; but Catholic reflection on this issue is quite sparse. The Catholic organization "From Mission to Mission" has published

two booklets on short-term mission entitled *What about Short-Term Mission?* and *Remaining Faithful: How Do I Keep My Experience Alive?* They may be ordered from <http://www.missiontomission.org/page6.html>.

57. The best introduction to the phenomenon of globalization is Malcolm Waters, *Globalization* (New York: Routledge, 1995). See also Robert J. Schreiter, *The New Catholicity: Theology between the Global and the Local* (Maryknoll, NY: Orbis Books, 1997). See *Theological Studies* 69, no. 3 (March 2008), which is a thematic issue on globalization. Richard R. Gaillardetz treats the question of globalization briefly in his monograph in this series, *The Church in the Making*, 158–59.

58. Schreiter, *The New Catholicity*, 7.

59. Benjamin R. Barber, *Jihad vs. McWorld* (New York: Times Books, 1995). See also Tissa Balasuriya, "Globalization," in *Dictionary of Third World Theologies*, ed. Virginia Fabella and R. S. Sugirtharajah (Maryknoll, NY: Orbis Books, 2000), 91–94.

60. See Balasuriya, "Globalization"; *Spiritus* (Latin American edition), 38, no. 1 (March 1997): thematic issue: "La Globalización: Nuevos Desafíos para la Misión."

61. John Paul II, "From the Justice of Each Comes Peace for All," Message for the Celebration for the World Day of Peace, 1 January 1998, 3. See <http://www.vatican.va/holy_father/ john_paul_ii/messages/peace/documents/ hf_jp-ii_mes_08121997_xxxi-world-day-for-peace_en.html>.

62. See Stephen Bevans, "Partner and Prophet: The Church and Globalization," *Verbum SVD* 41, no. 2 (2000): 177–98.

63. Hugo Graeme, "Key Issues in International Migration Today: Trends," in *Migration at the Threshold of the Third Millennium: IV World Congress on the Pastoral Care of Migrants and Refugees* (Vatican City: Pontifical Council for the Pastoral Care of Migrants and Itinerant People, 1998), 31.

64. Robert J. Schreiter, "The Changed Context of Mission Forty Years after the Council," *Verbum SVD* 46, no. 1 (2005): 80.

65. John Paul II, "Address of Pope John Paul II," *People on the Move* 35, no. 93 (December, 2003): 9. This volume contains the Proceedings of the fifth World Congress for the Pastoral Care of Migrants and Refugees.

66. Two of the most important books to appear are Gioacchino Campese and Pietro Ciallella, eds., *Migration, Religious Experience, and Globalization* (New York: Center for Migration Studies, 2003) and Daniel G. Groody and Gioacchino Campese, eds., *A Promised Land, A Perilous Journey* (Notre Dame, IN: University of Notre Dame Press, 2008).

67. This is the title of the fine book by Ann Carr, *Transforming Grace: Christian Tradition and Women's Experience* (New York: Harper and Row, 1988).

68. The source for these statistics is my colleague Barbara Reid; some of the data is from the United Nations Commission on the Status of Women.

69. Holy See's Address on Status of Women. ZENIT News Agency, <http://www.zenit.org/> March 8, 2004.

70. Dana L. Robert, *American Women in Mission: A Social History of Their Thought and Practice* (Macon, GA: Mercer University Press, 1996); Cathy Ross, *Women with a Mission* (Auckland: Penguin Books, 2007); Susan E. Smith, *Women in Mission: From the New Testament to Today* (Maryknoll, NY: Orbis Books, 2007).

# PART V
# FURTHER READING

## GENERAL

Alberigo, Giuseppe, and Joseph Komonchak, eds. *History of Vatican II, Volume 1: Announcing and Preparing Vatican Council II, Toward a New Era in Catholicism.* Maryknoll, NY: Orbis Books/Leuven, Belgium: Peeters, 1995. *History of Vatican II, Volume 2: Formation of the Council's Identity, First Period and Intersession, October 1962–September 1963.* Maryknoll, NY: Orbis Books/Leuven, Belgium: Peeters, 1997. *History of Vatican II, Volume 3: The Mature Council, Second Period and Intersession, October 1963–September 1964.* Maryknoll, NY: Orbis Books/Leuven, Belgium: Peeters, 2000. *History of Vatican II, Volume 4: Church as Communion, Third Period and Intersession, September 1964–September 1965.* Maryknoll, NY: Orbis Books/Leuven, Belgium: Peeters, 2003. *History of Vatican II, Volume 5: The Council and the Transition, The Fourth Period and the End of the Council, September 1965–December 1965.* Maryknoll, NY: Orbis Books/Leuven, Belgium: Peeters, 2006.

Alberigo, G., J-P Jossua, and J. Komonchak, eds. *The Reception of Vatican II.* Washington: Catholic University of America Press, 1987.

Congar, Yves. *Mon Journal du Concile.* 2 vols. Paris: Les Éditions du Cerf, 2002.

———. "The Theological Significance of the Council." *Report from Rome: The First Session of the Vatican Council,* 9-18. London: Geoffrey Chapman, 1963.

Hebblethwaite, Peter. *John XXIII. Pope of the Council.* London: Chapman, 1984.

———. *Paul VI: The First Modern Pope.* New York/Mahwah, NJ: Paulist Press, 1992.

Hünermann, Peter, ed. *Das Zweite Vatikanische Konzil und die Zeichen der Zeit Heute.* Freiburg: Herder, 2006.

Hünermann, Peter, and Bernd Jochen Hilberath. *Herders Theologischer Kommentar zum Zweiten Vatikanischen Konzil.* 4 vols. Freiburg: Herder, 2005.

Legrand, Hervé, Julio Manzanares, and Antonio García y García, eds. *Reception and Communion among Churches.* Washington, DC: Catholic University of America Press, 1997.

Miller, J. H., ed. *Vatican II: An Interfaith Appraisal.* Notre Dame, IN: Association Press, 1966.

Rush, Ormond. *Still Interpreting Vatican II: Some Hermeneutical Principles.* New York/Mahwah, NJ: Paulist Press, 2004.

Vorgrimler, Herbert, ed. *Commentary on the Documents of Vatican II.* 5 vols. New York: Herder and Herder, 1968.

Weigel, George. *Witness to Hope.* New York: HarperCollins Publishers, 1999.

Wiltgen, Ralph M. *The Rhine Flows into the Tiber: The Unknown Council.* New York: Hawthorn Books, Inc., 1967.

Yzermans, Vincent, ed. *American Participation in the Second Vatican Council.* New York: Sheed and Ward, 1967.

## EVANGELIZATION

### Evangelization and Vatican II

*Acta et Documenta Concilio Oecumenico Vaticano II Apparando.* Series I (Antepreparatoria), Volume III: Proposita et Monita SS. Congregationum Curiae Romanae, 239–250. Vatican City: Vatican Polyglot Press, 1960.

*Acta Synodalia Sacrosancti Concilii Oecumenici Vaticani II.* Volume III, VI. Vatican City: Vatican Polyglot Press, 1975.

*Acta Synodalia Sacrosancti Concilii Oecumenici Vaticani II.* Volume IV, III and IV. Vatican City: Vatican Polyglot Press, 1977.

*Acta Synodalia Sacrosancti Concilii Oecumenici Vaticani II.* Volume IV, VI and VII. Vatican City: Vatican Polyglot Press, 1978.

Burrows, William R. "Decree on the Church's Missionary Activity." In *Vatican II and Its Documents: An American Reappraisal,* edited by Timothy E. O'Connell, 180–96. Wilmington, DE: Michael Glazier, 1986.

Caprile, Giovanni. *Il Concilio Vaticano II. Vol. 4: Terzo Periodo (1964–1965); Vol. 5: Quarto Periodo (1965).* Rome: Edizioni La Civiltà Cattolica, 1965, 1969.

Corboy, Thomas. "A Commentary on the Missions Decree." In *Missions and Religions,* edited by Austin Flannery, 9–20. Dublin: Scepter Publishers, 1968.

Masson, Joseph. *L'attività missionaria della chiesa.* Torino-Leumann: Elle Di Ci, 1967.

Schütte, Johannes, ed. *Mission nach dem Konzil.* Mainz: Matthias-Grünewald-Verlag, 1967. French translation: *L'activité Missionnaire de l'Église.* Paris: Les Éditions du Cerf, 1967.

## On Missiology and Mission Theology

Anderson, Gerald H., ed. *The Theology of Christian Mission*. Nashville, TN: Abingdon Press, 1961.

Bevans, Stephen B., and Roger P. Schroeder. *Constants in Context: A Theology of Mission for Today*. Maryknoll, NY: Orbis Books, 2004.

Bosch, David J. *Transforming Mission: Paradigm Shifts in Theology of Mission*. Maryknoll, NY: Orbis Books, 1991.

Bueno, Eloy. *La Iglesia en la Encruciajada de la Misión*. Pamplona, Spain: Editorial Verbo Divino, 1999.

Dorr, Donal. *Mission in Today's World*. Maryknoll, NY: Orbis Books, 2000.

Gittins, Anthony J. *Ministry at the Margins: Strategy and Spirituality for Mission*. Maryknoll, NY: Orbis Books, 2002.

———. *Reading the Clouds: Mission Spirituality for New Times*. Liguori, MO: Liguori Publications, 1999.

———. "Mission: What's It Got to Do with Me?" *The Living Light* 34, no. 3 (Spring 1998): 6–13.

———. *Bread for the Journey: The Mission of Transformation and the Transformation of Mission*. Maryknoll, NY: Orbis Books, 1993.

Karotemprel, Sebastian, et al., eds. *Following Christ in Mission: A Foundational Course in Missiology*. Boston: Pauline Books and Media, 1996.

Kirk, J. Andrew. *What Is Mission: Theological Exploration*. London: Darton, Longman and Todd, 1999.

Legrand, Lucien. *Unity and Plurality: Mission in the Bible*. Maryknoll, NY: Orbis Books, 1990.

Moreau, A. Scott, Harold Netland, and Charles van Engen, eds. *Evangelical Dictionary of World Missions*. Grand Rapids, MI: Baker Books, 2000.

Müller, Karl. *Mission Theology: An Introduction*. Nettetal, Germany: Steyler Verlag, 1987.

Müller, Karl, Theo Sundermeier, Stephen B. Bevans, and Richard H. Bliese, eds. *Dictionary of Mission: Theology, History, Perspectives*. Maryknoll, NY: Orbis Books, 1997.

Oborji, Francis Anakwe. *Concepts of Mission: The Evolution of Contemporary Missiology*. Maryknoll, NY: Orbis Books, 2006.

Okoye, James Chukwuma. *Israel and the Nations: A Mission Theology of the Old Testament*. Maryknoll, NY: Orbis Books, 2006.

Pontificie Opere Missionarie Direzione Nazionale Italiana. *Enchiridion della Chiesa Missionaria*. 2 vols. Bologna: Edizioni Dehoniane, 1997.

Scherer, James A., and Stephen B. Bevans, eds. *New Directions in Mission and Evangelization. Vol. 1, Basic Documents*; *Vol. 2, Theological Foundations*. Maryknoll, NY: Orbis Books, 1992, 1994.

Schroeder, Roger P. *What Is the Mission of the Church? A Guide for Catholics*. Maryknoll, NY: Orbis Books, 2008.

Senior, Donald, and Stuhlmueller, Carroll. *The Biblical Foundations for Mission*. Maryknoll, NY: Orbis Books, 1983.

Wright, Christopher J. H. *The Mission of God: Unlocking the Bible's Grand Narrative*. Downer's Grove, IL: InterVarsity Press, 2006.

### Witness and Proclamation

Burrows, William R. *Redemption and Dialogue: Reading* Redemptoris Missio *and* Dialogue and Proclamation. Maryknoll, NY: Orbis Books, 1993.

Finch, Ray. "Missionaries Today." *Origins* 30, no. 21 (November 2, 2000): 327–332.

John Paul II. *The Mission of the Redeemer* (*Redemptoris Missio*). <http://www.vatican. va/edocs/ ENG0219/_INDEX.HTM>.

Pontifical Council for Interreligious Dialogue and Congregation for the Evangelization of Peoples. *Dialogue and Proclamation*. <http://www.vatican. va/roman_curia/pontifical_councils/interelg/documents/rc_pc_interelg_ doc_19051991_dialogue-and-proclamatio_en.html>.

Zago, Marcello. "The New Millennium and the Emerging Religious Encounters." *Missiology: An International Review* 28, no. 1 (January, 2000): 5–18.

### Liturgy, Prayer, and Contemplation

LaSalle, Donald G., Jr. "At the Threshold of the Assembly: Liturgy, the New Evangelization, and the New Millennium." *Liturgical Ministry* 8 (Fall 1999): 183–91.

Pierce, Gregory Augustine. *The Mass Is Never Ended: Rediscovering Our Mission to Transform the World*. Notre Dame, IN: Ave Maria Press, 2007.

Schattauer, Thomas H. *Inside Out: Worship in an Age of Mission*. Minneapolis, MN: Fortress Press, 1999.

Schreiter, Robert J. *The Ministry of Reconciliation: Spirituality and Strategies*. Maryknoll, NY: Orbis Books, 1998.

### Justice, Peace, and the Integrity of Creation

Cejka, Mary Ann, and Thomas Bamat, eds. *Artisans of Peace: Graceroots Peacemaking among Christian Communities*. Maryknoll, NY: Orbis Books, 2003.

Daneel, Marthinus L. *African Earthkeepers: Wholistic Interfaith Mission*. Maryknoll, NY: Orbis Books, 2001.

Gensichen, Hans-Werner. "Peace and Mission." In *Dictionary of Mission:*

*Theology, History, Perspectives*, edited by Karl Müller et al., 348–50. Maryknoll, NY: Orbis Books, 1997.

Hadsel, Heidi. "Ecology and Mission." In *Dictionary of Mission: Theology, History, Perspectives*, edited by Karl Müller et al., 114–17. Maryknoll, NY: Orbis Books, 1997.

O'Brien, David J., and Thomas A. Shannon, eds. *Catholic Social Thought: The Documentary Heritage*. Maryknoll, NY: Orbis Books, 1992.


**Interreligious Dialogue**

Dupuis, Jacques. *Toward a Christian Theology of Religious Pluralism*. Maryknoll, NY: Orbis Books, 1997.

Kendall, Daniel, and Gerald O'Collins, eds. *In Many and Diverse Ways: In Honor of Jacques Dupuis*. Maryknoll, NY: Orbis Books, 2003.

Knitter, Paul F. *Introducing Theologies of Religions*. Maryknoll, NY: Orbis Books, 2002.

Pope, Stephen J., and Charles Hefling, eds. *Sic et Non: Encountering* Dominus Iesus. Maryknoll, NY: Orbis Books, 2002.

Sherwin, Byron L., and Harold Kasimow, eds. *John Paul II and Interreligious Dialogue*. Maryknoll, NY: Orbis Books, 1999.


**Inculturation**

Bevans, Stephen B. *Models of Contextual Theology*. Rev. and expan. ed. Maryknoll, NY: Orbis Books, 2002.

Irarrázaval, Diego. *Inculturation: New Dawn of the Church in Latin America*. Maryknoll, NY: Orbis Books, 2000.

Magesa, Laurenti. *Anatomy of Inculturation: Transforming the Church in Africa*. Maryknoll, NY: Orbis Books, 2004.

Phan, Peter C. *In Our Own Tongues: Perspectives from Asia on Mission and Inculturation*. Maryknoll, NY: Orbis Books, 2003.

Schreiter, Robert J. *Constructing Local Theologies*. Maryknoll, NY: Orbis Books, 1985.


**Reconciliation**

Schreiter, Robert J. "Mission as a Model of Reconciliation." *Neue Zeitschrift für Missionswissenschaft* 51 (1996): 243–50.

———. *Reconciliation: Mission and Ministry in a Changing Social Order.* Maryknoll, NY: Orbis Books, 1992.

Volf, Miroslav. *Exclusion and Embrace: A Theological Exploration of Identity, Otherness and Reconciliation*. Nashville, TN: Abingdon Press, 1996.

### Laity

Federation of Asian Bishops' Conferences. "The Vocation and Mission of the Laity in the Church and in the World of Asia." In *For All the Peoples of Asia: Federation of Asian Bishops' Conferences Documents from 1970 to 1991*, edited by Gaudencio Rosales and C. G. Arévalo, 177–98. Maryknoll, NY: Orbis Books, 1992.

Hahnenberg, Edward P. *Ministries: A Relational Approach*. New York: Crossroad, 2003.

Lakeland, Paul. *The Liberation of the Laity: In Search of an Accountable Church*. New York: Continuum, 2003.

### Globalization

Beyer, Peter. *Religion and Globalization*. London; Thousand Oaks, CA; New Delhi: Sage Publications, 1994.

Schreiter, Robert J. "Globalization and Reconciliation: Challenges to Mission." In *Mission in the Third Millennium*, edited by Robert J. Schreiter, 121–43. Maryknoll, NY: Orbis Books, 2001.

———. *The New Catholicity: Theology between the Global and the Local*. Maryknoll, NY: Orbis Books, 1997.

Waters, Malcolm. *Globalization*. New York: Routledge, 1995.

### Migration

Campese, Gioacchino, and Peter Ciallella, eds. *Migration, Religious Experience and Globalization*. New York: Center for Migration Studies, 2003.

Daniel G. Groody and Gioacchino Campese, eds. *A Promised Land, A Perilous Journey*. Notre Dame, IN: University of Notre Dame Press, 2008.

### Women and Mission

*Missiology: An International Review* 33, no. 3 (July 2005). Thematic Issue: Women and Missions.

Robert, Dana L., ed. *Gospel Bearers, Gender Barriers: Missionary Women in the Twentieth Century*. Maryknoll, NY: Orbis Books, 2002.

Smith, Susan. *Women in Mission: From the New Testament to Today*. Maryknoll, NY: Orbis Books, 2003.

# Dignitatis Humanae

Jeffrey Gros, FSC

# PART I

# THE DOCUMENT

The Declaration on Religious Freedom marks a watershed in Catholic history. The English-speaking world often neglects this document's significance because of the Anglo-Saxon traditions of tolerance, constitutional protections of human rights—including religious freedom—and the separation of church and state in countries like the United States.[1] However, the document's significance in Christian history and for the life of the Catholic Church was clear at the time of the council. In the words of a young theological expert to Cologne's Cardinal Frings, Joseph Ratzinger:

> The debate on religious liberty will in later years be considered one of the most important events of the Council already rich enough in important events. To use the catch-phrase once again, there was in St. Peter's the sense that here was the end of the Middle Ages, the end event of the Constantinian age.[2]

The theme, religious freedom, has meant a variety of things in Christian history. However, questions of church and state, pluralism, tolerance, freedom of conscience or religious freedom were not part of the Christian vocabulary or the way of thinking of human societies for the first millennium and a half. Civil society existed within a universal church, and princes were responsible in one way or another for the spiritual care of their subjects.

### HISTORICAL PERSPECTIVE

Both religion and civil society were seen as integrally related realities from ancient times. Both the Hebrew scriptures and the Greco-Roman world into which Christianity was born knew no separation between religion and civil society. The Roman world executed Jesus and martyred his apostles because the gospel message was subversive to the religious ideology of the Empire.

Christians have killed more of their fellow believers through the murder of heretics, wars of religion, and persecution of one another than the imperial Romans ever did. More Christians have given their lives for their faith in the last century than in the first three.[3]

Since the fourth-century changes in the Roman Empire, the principle developed that unity in religion was necessary in civil society for the peace, public order, and common good of all of the people. This principle continued in Orthodox, Protestant, Anglican, and Catholic parts of Europe, Africa, and the Middle East until early modern times. The ideas of tolerance, individual conscience, and even a "state" that was not religious only gradually entered the Christian imagination.[4]

During the sixteenth-century Reformation, only the Anabaptists raised the issue of religious freedom and the independence of the church from civil society. They questioned the identification of the Christian faith with and Christian legitimation of the wider civil society. For them, one had to respond to grace by a free conviction in faith. Only adult baptism initiated one into the community. Membership in a "Christian society" was not sufficient for church membership.

In both Byzantine East and Latin West, church and society were part of one sacred whole in which kings and emperors played a sacred role and bishops and abbots had civil responsibilities. The church often relied on the power of the secular arm of society to enforce uniformity of faith and practice. In some cases there was harmony between the civil and religious dimensions of Christian society. Often, however, there were tensions between leaders in the political and ecclesiastical realms, and frequently issues relating to power overshadowed the positive role of the church in society. Both ecclesiastical and civil leaders were subject to financial and political ambitions that inhibited the mission of the church and the freedom of Christians in the exercise of their faith. However, during most of this period no one questioned the integration of a social whole, Christendom.

Only with the Enlightenment and the eighteenth-, nineteenth-, and twentieth-century revolutions in Europe and the New World did Catholicism begin to face the challenge of differentiating the role of the church as believing community and the state as giving order to the society. The eighteenth-century revolutions in the United States (1776) and France (1793) raised the issues of religious freedom, the separation of religion from the state, and human liberty, but in very different contexts and with very different social and political results.

On the one hand, French Enlightenment thinkers represented a variety of understandings of the human person, liberty, equality, and human solidarity (fraternity). Many of these thinkers did not have a place for religion, and some that did developed an anti-Christian form of rational faith that excluded revelation and the hierarchical authority of church teaching. France established this rationalist faith for a brief period in the late eighteenth century. Reason replaced Christ as the focal point of faith and worship for a time in some of the churches and cathedrals of France.

On the other hand, the U.S. Bill of Rights did not establish a federal state church. Neither, however, did it prohibit local state-established churches. For example, Congregationalism was established in Massachusetts until 1833, more than forty years after the writing of the American constitution and the ratification of its first amendment, and the final vestiges of religious discrimination were not removed from the New Hampshire constitution until 1877. Separation of church and state eventually became a fact, if not a constitutional imperative. In the U.S. context, religious freedom did not entail state control of religion, secularization of schools and other institutions, or the ideal of human autonomy from God and the church. By a century after the passage of the Bill of Rights, the variety of believing communities and even unbelievers was protected by law. However, "[t]he distinction between the rationale and dynamic of the American Revolution and that of the French Revolution was never a significant aspect of the Holy See's response to democracy."[5]

*Dignitatis Humanae* deals, on the one hand, with an issue faced by the church in every generation of its history and, on the other, with one that demands new solutions as history develops. In both East and West from the fourth century to the sixteenth century there were few who challenged the political theology of sacral kingship. The Reformation challenged the unity of church and empire, but the identification of the religion of the people with a state and with the religion of the ruler was not challenged, except by the Anabaptists.

*Dignitatis Humanae* represents one stage in the long pilgrimage of Christian reflection on faith, freedom, and society. "A fundamental and essential element of every culture which has been shaped by Christianity is the recognition of the dignity of the human person.... This is the most important contribution which Christianity has made and can in the future continue to make to the culture of Europe and the culture of humanity as a whole."[6]

## A NEW CONTEXT

To understand *Dignitatis Humanae*, it is important to look at this longer history of Christianity and its commitment to tolerate only the Christian religion (understood differently by Protestants, Catholics, and the Orthodox, of course) for the preservation of the common good; the more recent situation of the early modern world with Catholicism's different experiences in the European and American revolutions; and the immediate experience of preconciliar, twentieth-century global Catholicism.

The traditional Catholic position, and that of many of the Orthodox and Protestant churches, was that the ideal situation was for the state to support the one, true faith, to control error, and to suppress heretical groups. That a church or a religion is "established"[7] means that the particular religious tradition is the privileged faith of the state. The civil authorities give moral, financial, and often military support to the established religion; and, by law, leaders are members of and often officials in the established religion or church. Such an established religion may or may not allow for the religious freedom of other believers.

In the modern world there are three models of the relationship of church and society: (1) a church is established by law in the state; (2) the secular state may affirm or be neutral toward religion, where the religion is disestablished; and (3) the secularist state seeks to eliminate or at least control religion. Separation of church and state has quite different meanings for a secularist—sometimes called "laicist,"[8]—state and for a secular, neutral state.

The laicist (*laïcité*) position asserts that religious liberty entails the suppression and control of all religion and the marginalization of religious institutions in society. The premise of this position is the absolute autonomy of the individual conscience and the juridical supremacy of the state. The human person is free of any dependence on or responsibility to God. In some such societies, religious institutions are subject to tax, religious personnel are subject to the draft, private religious institutions are not allowed, and often religious dress or insignia are not tolerated in public. In some of these societies, churches are forbidden to own property. Where religion is allowed, it is held to be a private option that should carry no weight in public discourse, and churches are permitted no witness in public debate. In the secularist state—for example Marxist, Nazi, or laicist French Revolution–style governments—a rationalist, anti-religious bias often functions as if it were an established religion.

The second and third models were unimaginable for most of Christian history, and are still quite alien for many people today, as is evident in Islamicized societies and the tensions in India and other parts of the world.

In the American colonies, religion was established, except in Pennsylvania and Rhode Island. Maryland, under Catholic leadership, started with religious toleration (1639), but when the Protestant population could dominate, the Act of Toleration was repealed (1654). The colonial American Catholic minority was quite supportive of the American Revolution and subsequent developments of religious freedom and separation of church and state.

Catholic Charles Carroll of Maryland signed the Declaration of Independence; and his cousin John Carroll, who was to become the country's first bishop, traveled to Quebec with Benjamin Franklin to try to bring the French Catholics on board with the revolution. As bishop, Carroll favored English as the language of worship. He also favored a democratic church polity and introduced a form of lay leadership into the Catholic parishes of the new country. Later waves of immigration from France after its revolution, and from Ireland, would cause church leaders to be more wary, especially as nineteenth-century anti-immigrant and anti-Catholic sentiments emerged.

As a result of the revolution in France and subsequent revolutions in many of the Latin American colonies of Spain and Portugal, a very different relationship between religion and civil society developed. The leaders of these revolutions professed a commitment to freedom in the abstract, but fearing that the Catholic Church would be an enemy of the liberty and the individualism they espoused, they saw the church as something that had to be eliminated or at least controlled. So persecution was the order of the day early in the French Revolution and in certain new Latin American states such as Mexico. These secularist states were severely anti-clerical. They confiscated religious institutions and property and dispersed religious orders.

## Pius IX

In this context of suppression and persecution of the Catholic Church, religious leaders in the Vatican became very wary of claims of democracy, toleration, and "religious liberty." Pius IX, who during his long pontificate (1846–1878) suffered many of the radical changes in European society, including the loss of the Papal States in 1870, judged that the church should withstand all of these innovations in thought and law. In 1864, along with the encyclical *Quanta Cura*, he published a Syllabus of Errors, which listed a set of erroneous propositions to be condemned. Among these propositions were:

15. Every man is free to embrace and profess that religion which, guided by the light of reason, he shall consider true.

16. Man may, in the observance of any religion whatever, find the way of eternal salvation, and arrive at eternal salvation...

24. The Church has not the power of using force, nor has she any temporal power, direct or indirect...

30. The immunity of the Church and of ecclesiastical persons derived its origin from civil law...

55. The Church ought to be separated from the State, and the State from the Church...

77. In the present day it is no longer expedient that the Catholic religion should be held as the only religion of the State, to the exclusion of all other forms of worship.

78. Hence it has been wisely decided by law, in some Catholic countries, that persons coming to reside therein shall enjoy the public exercise of their own peculiar worship...[9]

In the United States there was a rabid anti-immigrant, anti-Catholic climate. There were even anti-Catholic parties, like the Know-Nothings, who tried to make the case that Catholicism was incompatible with a democratic society. Some Catholic communities and their institutions experienced anti-Catholic violence. From the midst of all this there emerged new voices to provide a positive apologetic for Catholicism and the American democratic system with its relationship of church and state.

Among the most prominent United States Catholic apologists were converts Orestes Brownson (1803–1876) and Isaac Hecker (1819–1888), the founder of the Paulist Fathers. Both developed a theological position that made the case for Catholicism, not Protestantism, as a better basis for democracy and the common good. The anti-democratic statements of Catholic leaders in Europe embarrassed such Catholic apologists. They attempted to interpret them more positively.

When the first Vatican Council (1869–1870) was convened, some feared that a majority of the council fathers, mostly European, would support the positions of Pius IX. British prime minister William Gladstone and the liberal Catholic leader Lord Acton, among others, placed their hopes in American leadership, as Gladstone noted to Acton in 1870: "Of all the prelates at Rome, none have a finer opportunity, to none is a more crucial test now applied, than to those of the United States."[10] The forty-nine bishops from the United States were not as opposed to the definition as was the leadership from Germany and France. However, there were Americans in the minority who opposed a statement on papal infallibility as inopportune for their pastoral settings at home. In the nineteenth-century American context, Protestants would have interpreted this doctrine as a reaffirmation of Catholic claims to dominance, not only in Catholic consciences but also in society. "They [U.S. bishops] opposed the definition [of infallibility] on the very pragmatic grounds that it would worsen relations between Catholics and the dominant Protestant majority of their homeland."[11]

The First Vatican Council did not take up the issue of church and society. European Catholics debated the issue in terms that had little bearing on the American experience. However, the American bishops were quite prepared to speak their own views (as they would later do at Vatican II) on this significant issue. Cincinnati's Archbishop John Purcell expressed his views at home, after returning from the council:

In it [his proposed statement before the Council that he did
not have the opportunity to deliver] I took occasion to show
that ours is, I believe, the best form of human government.
...I said that our civil constitution grants perfect liberty to
every denomination of Christians...and that I verily believe
this was infinitely better for the Catholic religion, than were it
the special object of the State's patronage and protection; that
all we want is a free field and no favor.... Truth is might and will
prevail.... If they approve our religion, they will embrace it;
if not they will stay away from it. I believe this is the best
theory.[12]

With the loss of the Papal States in 1870, and with the emergence
of pluralistic societies in the United States, England, Canada, and parts
of Europe, French Bishop Dupanloup developed a new distinction.
The ideal situation or "thesis" is the classical position: a Catholic
Church, the only true church, is established in a Catholic state, and
other churches cannot be in the same position, since error has no
rights. But where, in de facto pluralistic societies, the Catholic Church
is a minority, and the citizens and state do not recognize this ideal thesis, toleration of other religions, though erroneous, is possible and
Catholicism is to be accorded its freedom among other religious bodies. This situation, the "hypothesis," does not hold when Catholicism
becomes a majority and has the political power to introduce the "thesis." By the time of Vatican II, this nineteenth-century development of
"thesis/hypothesis" had become the "traditional" position of almost all
canon lawyers.

In the United States, the Catholic Church was thriving in a pluralistic context of religious freedom and separation of church and state.
This experience was the ideal, not a "hypothesis." The distinction be-
came a burden, an embarrassment, and a cause of debate among
Catholic theologians, canon lawyers, and political scientists who were
writing on subjects having to do with church and society. It was a dis-
tinction that made the church appear opportunist and manipulative.
Many Catholics were particularly perplexed when they saw their fellow
Catholics being persecuted in "most Catholic" Spain and Latin
America, or suffering disabilities in France, "the eldest daughter of the
Church."

Later in the century, Archbishop John Ireland (1838–1913) of St. Paul, Minnesota, circulated in Europe information on some of the more positive evaluations of the American experience, of democracy and the freedom of religion. Pope Leo XIII (whose papacy spanned the years 1878 to 1903) criticized certain aspects of American church-state relations in *Longinqua Oceani Spatia* (1895) and *Testem Benevolentiae* (1898). Yet the same pope also initiated the church's approach to modern social teaching and began opening the door to relations with the new republican forms of government.

## IMMEDIATE CONTEXT

By the time Pope John XXIII announced a general council of the Catholic Church, on January 25, 1959, the world context had changed. The concerns of Europe were still dominant in the Catholic Church, to be sure, but even those concerns were shifting.

Europe had just emerged from the Second World War, where totalitarian Nazism had been defeated and the horrors of the Jewish Holocaust were only beginning to be fully grasped. During the war and in the years leading up to it, Pius XII (who was pope from 1939 to 1958) and his predecessors had positively affirmed democratic governments and rights to religious freedom—meaning freedom for the church primarily, but also humane treatment of other religions and groups. Church leaders did not seem to see the inconsistency between, on the one hand, the advocacy of human dignity and constitutional government and, on the other, the thesis/hypothesis position and the church's cautions about democracy inherited from the traumas of modern anticlerical revolutions and the loss of the Papal States in 1870.

Nevertheless, the church still saw "religious liberty" (meaning suppression of public religious expression) as a threat. It was precisely this language that was used in the French laws by which a secularist government dissolved religious orders and Catholic institutions in 1905. Refugees from laicist France were dispersed throughout the Catholic world. Marxism was enveloping Eastern Europe after the war. It was also advocating freedom *of* religion, which meant freedom *from* religion and often outright persecution. In Mexico and in Spain there had been bloody civil wars, with anticlerical revolutionary governments killing many Catholics, especially priests and nuns.

## World War II

Ironically, the triumph of the Allies in the Second World War and the Cold War on the eve of the council gave American Catholics a confidence about their democratic institutions and the freedoms they experienced—including religious freedom—over against the tragedies of Nazism, Marxism, and the struggles of their fellow believers in Mexico and Spain. Likewise, the war veterans' benefits bill began to help integrate returning Catholics into the mainstream of American education, culture, and economic life. Anti-Catholicism began to subside. During the 1960 presidential campaign of John F. Kennedy (the first Catholic to win the White House), the specter of the thesis/hypothesis teaching of Catholic leadership became an increasing embarrassment, as it was explicitly used against Catholics' claim to be good U.S. citizens capable of holding national public office with integrity.

However, Europe and North America were not the only venues in which a new situation was calling for Catholic reflection on the relationship of the church with society and culture. Many nations of Africa, Asia, and the Middle East were freeing themselves from colonialism.[13] Between 1960 and 1967 (the years during which the Second Vatican Council was held as well as those immediately preceding and following it), more than thirty new nations emerged from colonial rule. In many of these nations not only were Catholics a minority but the religion of the majority was one of the great world religions, some of which, like Hinduism and Islam, did not have a heritage of the separation of religion and civil society.

There were certain situations, as in some African nations, where no one religion held social dominance. In these situations Catholicism existed in a pluralistic context where collaboration in nation building was absolutely essential for the common good. In the United States, the post-war debates on Catholicism and society were often occasioned by the need to collaborate with fellow believers in post-war reconstruction and in resistance to encroachments of secularism in society.

In 1948 the United Nations put forward its Universal Declaration on Human Rights, with a strong affirmation of freedom of religion:

> Article 18. Everyone has the right to freedom of thought, conscience and religion; this right includes freedom to change his

religion or belief, and freedom, either alone or in community with others and in public or private, to manifest his religion or belief in teaching, practice, worship and observance.[14]

At the same time, people living in countries where the Catholic Church was dominant, in places such as Portugal, Spain, Italy, or Latin American countries, articulated a strong feeling of oppression and manipulation:

> [In a variety of political situations] the Roman Catholic Church has acted in accordance with its traditionally asserted right to serve as the final arbiter of issues which affect the moral and spiritual well-being of peoples who, either actually or nominally, are overwhelmingly Catholic. Church insistence upon the exercise of this right has frequently led to difficulties in Latin America, where individualistic Catholic laymen are apt to consider themselves competent to make moral judgments free from clerical influence. Even if the lay faithful are willing to accept the authority of the Church in the spiritual realm, friction can result from the fact that churchmen claim the power to define what constitutes moral and spiritual issues. Matters which some churchmen regard as having moral and spiritual implications are often considered by lay political leaders as purely political and secular in nature and therefore removed from the Church's competence.[15]

One of the most urgent drives for a strong affirmation of the freedom of the church, and of religious freedom, came from the "church of silence," the Catholic churches from the various nations of Eastern Europe which had fallen under the pall of Communist domination. In these contexts, the official thesis/hypothesis position was irrelevant, since even toleration was not an option.

## The Eve of the Council

The modern ecumenical movement blossomed in the Christian world during the post-war years, with the founding of the World Council of

Churches (WCC), which held its first Assembly in Amsterdam, August 1948. Religious freedom was among the organization's earliest concerns. The Amsterdam Assembly issued a strong Declaration on Religious Liberty, which provided an important resource for the work of the Second Vatican Council. Many Christian leaders were involved in both the United Nations and the WCC drafting on human rights and religious freedom.[16] The WCC also sponsored studies on religious freedom and the Catholic Church.[17]

Some Catholics who were concerned with ecumenical questions and followed the WCC agenda through the Catholic Conference on Ecumenical Questions,[18] approved by the Holy See, were figures who became influential in the Vatican Council: Johannes Willebrands (1909–2006), Gustav Weigel, SJ (1906–1964), Yves Congar, OP (1904–1995), and Jérôme Hamer, OP (1916–1996). In September 1960 the Conference discussed religious freedom, in the context of reviewing the draft text of the WCC in preparation for its third Assembly (November 1961).

The specialized Catholic Action movements, with their concern for the role of the laity and new models for the church's influence and understanding of religion and culture, social teaching, church-state relations, and theological education of the laity, laid a receptive ground for the council's initiatives, including religious freedom.

French philosopher Jacques Maritain (1882–1973), although not present at the council, had a very important influence through his relationship with Pope Paul VI, who consulted him directly in 1964. As a Thomistic philosopher who favored democracy and religious freedom, Maritain was an important bridge between the classical Catholic tradition in anthropology and natural law and the pressing concerns of human rights, constitutional government, and church-state relations in the mid-twentieth century. Also, along with a group of European Catholic intellectuals, some of whom who had immigrated to the United States, he was critical of the Catholic hierarchy's stance in relation to Nazism, French collaborators, and the fascism of Italy, Portugal, and Spain.[19] Maritain's influence in Latin America, especially through the rise of Christian Democratic parties, also aided in fostering receptivity to developments favoring democratic, constitutional governments that would support religious freedom.[20] Furthermore, in 1961 Pope John XXIII's challenge to the Latin American bishops to pastoral renewal, especially in catechetics and human rights, set the stage for a new openness among some of the hierarchy there.[21]

If the churches—Catholic, Orthodox, and Protestant—were to have any rapprochement, the issue of religious freedom in the Catholic Church would need precise clarification. If the Catholic Church itself was to make its appropriate contribution to democracies such as the United States and the newly emerging nations in the postcolonial world, or to the reconstruction of post–World War II Europe, it would need to address its stance toward other churches and toward other religions, as well as its position on the social and civil right to religious freedom.

In the years preceding the council, the Roman silencing of some of the more creative thinkers on the subject, Yves Congar and John Courtney Murray (1904–1967) among them, made it impossible to have open discussion on the questions of religion and society, religious freedom, and church and state. The silencing of Murray on church-state issues fueled the anti-Catholic propaganda of Paul Blanshard and his organization, Protestants and Other Americans United for the Separation of Church and State (since renamed Americans United for the Separation of Church and State). Blanshard became particularly vocal during the 1960 John F. Kennedy presidential campaign. Citing the thesis/hypothesis position, the unwillingness of Catholic authorities to allow free discussion of church-state issues, and closed Catholic societies like Spain, Blanshard said it was impossible for Catholics to be good Americans, to hold public office responsibly, or to contribute to a democratic society.[22] The first American to call for a statement on religious freedom at the council was Cincinnati's Karl Alter, who quoted Blanshard by name.[23] Like his predecessor at Vatican I, Archbishop John Purcell, Alter made a strong case for the American arrangement of church and society.

## THE COUNCIL[24]

The official opening of the Second Vatican Council took place in Rome on October 11, 1962, with more than twenty-four hundred fathers and their experts in attendance. Commissions largely composed of members of the Roman curia and their academic consultants from the Roman universities had done the preparatory work, hoping to present their initial drafts for council debate.

The draft on the church (*De Ecclesia*) prepared by the Theological Preparatory Commission had included a final chapter entitled "The Relations between Church and State, and Religious Tolerance." It repeated the standard position—privileging the Catholic Church where the thesis could be realized but allowing toleration in the hypothetical case of a Catholic minority, and affirming the state's responsibility to the truth for the sake of the common good:

> The ideal State is the "Catholic State," and in such a State "the civic power should protect its citizens from seducing errors and thus preserve the unity of faith—the highest good..." The civic power "can temper public manifestations of other (i.e., non-Roman Catholic) cults and defend its citizens against the diffusion of false doctrines which, in the Church's judgment, place external salvation in danger."[25]

This chapter was never presented to the council for debate. Before the first session, the commission dropped the entire chapter from the schema on the church.

On Pentecost Sunday 1960, Pope John XXIII established a Secretariat for Promoting Christian Unity (SPCU) (known since 1989 as the Pontifical Council for Promoting Christian Unity), with Augustine Bea, SJ (1881–1968) as president and Johannes Willebrands as secretary. Its mandate was rather open: welcoming and informing the ecumenical observers, receiving their feedback, and assisting other commissions with the ecumenical dimension of their work.

At its first plenary meeting of members and consultors in November 1960, the SPCU set up a subcommission chaired by Bishop Émile de Smedt of Bruges, Belgium. He was to remain the SPCU's spokesperson on religious freedom throughout the duration of the council and would be a key contributor in drafting and presenting the text. In December 1960 the subcommission—which included Father Jérôme Hamer, who was to have a central role in the history of the text, and Bishop Charrière of Fribourg—met to begin work on a draft document addressing religious freedom. Two years earlier, in 1958, the Vatican secretary of state, Cardinal Tardini, had asked the bishops of the world to freely suggest council themes. In the responses to this solicitation, only thirty-six bishops—most of them Americans—suggested topics having to do with political, civil, and religious freedom. The SPCU's decision to develop a draft on religious freedom was unrelated to the bishops' survey. Preparation of the draft was seen as simply a step in establishing a foundation for ecumenical collaboration. The SPCU plenary completed a first draft on religious freedom in August 1961.

The SPCU also began to draft a document on a Catholic approach to ecumenism and the ecumenical movement. At this time the SPCU had no right to present its own work to the council's Central Preparatory Committee, and indeed Cardinal Alfredo Ottaviani (1890–1979), president of the Theological Preparatory Commission and secretary of the Sacred Congregation of the Holy Office (known until 1908 as the Inquisition and since 1965 as the Congregation for the Doctrine of the Faith) was opposed to its being given that right. On February 1, 1962, the pope made it clear to Cardinal Bea that the SPCU could present texts directly to the 110 members of the Central Preparatory Commission.

### First Session (October 11 to December 8, 1962)

When the bishops from around the world converged on Rome in October 1962, not even Pope John XXIII was able to predict how long the council would last. He and some others projected only one or two sessions lasting perhaps a few weeks or a few months. No one foresaw four long sessions, with extended intercessions, over a four-year period.

Also, it was unclear who would lead the council fathers, and in what direction. Would they approve, modify, or set aside the initial preparatory texts, or would they try to draft their own? If the preparatory texts were to remain the focus of the agenda, would discussion of an issue like religious freedom and a new opening to the ecumenical community of Christians become possible?

During the first period of the council, leadership from the bishops outside Rome clearly emerged. Bishops largely from central Europe introduced ideas that would expand and redirect the original agenda. Shortly after the first session began, Pope John XXIII raised the SPCU to the same rank as other commissions, with full authority to submit draft texts. All the preparatory commissions had been dissolved, the bishops had elected new members and the pope had appointed others, but the original members of the SPCU continued.

The rejection of certain texts presented to the fathers and the severe criticism of others made it necessary for the pope to intervene and create a mixed commission of the SPCU and the Theological Commission. As the council proceeded, membership in the SPCU would expand and its role would continue to grow in importance.

Even as he opened the council, Pope John XXIII knew that his death was approaching. Between the first and second sessions of the council, before he died on June 3, 1963, he wrote his last encyclical. *Pacem in Terris*, which was issued on April 11, 1963, appealed not only to Catholics and Christians but to all persons of good will.

It is said that right after the fall 1962 Cuban missile crisis, the confrontation between the United States and the Soviet Union during which the world came terrifyingly close to the brink of nuclear war, Pope John XXIII asked the help of Pietro Pavan, an expert in international law, in crafting a letter the content and style of which would be such that Washington and the Kremlin might read it with equal attentiveness. Among the encyclical's affirmations is a plea for freedom of religion:

> Also among one's rights is that of being able to worship God in accordance with the right dictates of a person's own conscience, and to profess his or her religion both in private and in public. …Hence, too, Pope Leo XIII declared that "true freedom, freedom worthy of the sons of God, is that freedom which most truly safeguards the dignity of the human person. It is stronger than any violence or injustice. Such is the freedom which has always been desired by the Church, and which she holds most dear. It is the sort of freedom which the Apostles resolutely claimed for themselves. The apologists defended it in their writings; thousands of martyrs consecrated it with their blood."[26]

In this papal text we see a clear transition in the Catholic approach to rights and religious freedom from an emphasis on error to a focus on the human person and conscience.

## Second Session (September 29 to December 4, 1963)

The newly elected pope, Paul VI, began the second session with a strong call for religious freedom in his inaugural address to the council.[27] He also expanded the various commissions. Originally there had been no Americans on the SPCU. The pope, however, approved the appointment of Cardinal Sheehan of Baltimore and the council fathers elected Bishops Helmsing of Kansas City and Primeau of Manchester to the SPCU.

The SPCU had attached chapters on Judaism and religious freedom to its text on Christian unity. Because of the large number of texts emerging from the first session, it was deemed advisable to join the three themes in one text so that freedom and Catholic-Jewish relations would not be removed from the agenda. Both of these issues were important to the majority the world's bishops. So important was the issue of freedom, for example, that Cardinal Spellman of New York and more than two hundred fathers petitioned the pope for the preparation of a special text on religious freedom.[28]

Bishop de Smedt indicated that the reason for addressing the topic of religious freedom in the text on Christian unity was that many fellow Christians distrusted the Catholic Church because of the duplicity apparent in its thesis/hypothesis approach, which denied others their rights whenever possible. Unless religious freedom were affirmed, no honest and equal collaboration would be possible.

General discussion of the text on Christian unity began late in the session, but debate on specifics and voting were deferred to the third session. In his reports to the council fathers, de Smedt attempted to deal with the objections of the majority throughout the sessions of the council by making it clear how the text avoided: (1) religious indifferentism, (2) laicism, (3) doctrinal relativism, and (4) complacency about truth.[29]

During the second session, the council fathers indicated that the SPCU chapter on religious freedom would require further discussion, and they proposed specific changes; it was not at all clear that there would be a positive outcome to all this, nor that there would be a freestanding text on the subject.

A powerful minority held out until the end for the classical position that error has no rights and that the human person is bound to seek the truth, which exists only in the Christian faith, and that therefore the state has an obligation to support the Catholic Church. This minority had a clear and consistent position, one that had been formally articulated for over a century and claimed its foundation in a tradition dating back to the Constantinian shift in the fourth century.

A number of Italian, Spanish, and Portuguese bishops as well as some bishops from Latin America were adamant on this position. On the other hand, those who wanted a statement on religious freedom came from various backgrounds and had wide-ranging reasons for their position: the theological reflection in central Europe; the suffering church of Marxist Eastern Europe; the political heritage of the United States, the United Kingdom, and Canada; the embarrassment of Catholic minorities with the official position; and the emerging post-colonial churches with no clear direction and no natural allegiance to the nineteenth-century position. These bishops did not have a common mind, a common set of experiences, or a history of theological reflection on the issue. Although they were in the majority, would there be enough consensus among them to put forward a coherent position? On what theological basis would such a position be grounded?

The American theologian who had done the most work in the field, John Courtney Murray, had not been present at the first session of the council. However, his Maryland colleague, Gustav Weigel, SJ, was a consultor to the SPCU subcommission on religious freedom, and he had undoubtedly kept his confrere informed of the debates and documents of the council.

Another set of considerations was emerging as well. If the Catholic Church were to enter into the modern ecumenical movement, an affirmation on religious freedom would be absolutely essential. (Pope Paul himself, as noted above, was a strong proponent of religious freedom; his first encyclical, *Ecclesiam Suam*, written after the council's second session and issued on August 6, 1964, focused on the importance of dialogue in the church, among the churches, and with the world: "The Christian life, as encouraged and preserved by the Church, must resist every possible source of deception, contamination, or restriction of its freedom."[30]) Also, if the Catholic Church were to present a witness to the world on human dignity, justice, and peace, it would have to be able to do so with an affirmation of the civil right of the human person and of human communities to freedom in matters of religion. Early discussion of *Gaudium et Spes* (the Constitution on the Church in the Modern World) had already included formulations on the dignity of the human person.

The majority of bishops wanted a strong and forthright statement. But how should they ground the content? What credible arguments could counteract the formidable minority and make a strong case to the world and to the Christian community?

During the second session of the council there were multiple responses to the initial ecumenical text of the SPCU. A number of bishops and influential theological advisors suggested that the chapter on religious freedom in the document on ecumenism might better be placed in the document on the Church in the Modern World. The majority, however, favored a separate declaration. Many were advocates of freedom for the Catholic Church, without yet advocating the religious freedom of all persons based on a consistent theology of conscience and human dignity.

Between the second and third sessions of the council, John Courtney Murray and the previously mentioned Italian international law expert Pietro Pavan began working with the SPCU on the text. The SPCU plenary then corrected and approved its second draft, now an appendix to the Decree on Ecumenism. The council bishops received the text before the September 1964 opening of the third session, along with an SPCU report outlining the definitions and methods employed.[31] There was no voting on this second text, though numerous recommendations for revision were gathered, including many positions that contradicted one another.

### Third Session (September 14 to November 21, 1964)

The council debated the draft sent out in April 1964, now a separate text. Discussion followed the careful presentation delivered by Bishop de Smedt, which emphasized the lengthy report from the SPCU circulated with the text. He noted the shift from religious tolerance to religious freedom grounded in the nature of the human person.

Cardinal Ritter of St. Louis suggested that the text simply affirm religious freedom without debating and including the reasons for it. Some members of the minority seized on this proposal, but they did not prevail. Cardinal Silva Henríquez of Santiago, Chile, representing forty-eight Latin American bishops, strongly supported the draft, citing the importance of religious freedom in the process of evangelization in

Latin America. While the bishops and theologians of central Europe continued to make substantive contributions to the discussion and drafting, Ratzinger recognized that, "[i]n a critical hour, council leadership passed from Europe to the young churches of America and the mission countries. It was now as never before unmistakably clear that the Church had become an international Church, drawing on the treasures of all nations and showing the meaning of plurality within the unity of the Church."[32]

In October Archbishop Felici, the secretary general of the council, transmitted a message from Pope Paul VI: a new mixed commission would redraft the religious freedom text. In response to protests from fourteen cardinals, however, the Holy Father returned to conciliar procedures and the text remained under the direction of the SPCU.

In November 1964 the Theological Commission co-approved a third draft of the now freestanding text on religious freedom. This text emphasized the importance of modern persons becoming aware of their human dignity and the development of freedom in all spheres of life. It also introduced the notion of the limited character of the state and the significance of constitutional government. It focused the discussion on religion and society, not on the state-church relationship. This "watershed event" shifted the church's "emphasis from a church-state dialogue to an appreciation of a new partner: civil society."[33]

The text affirmed the personal right of religious freedom, stating that governments are not to coerce a person to act against his or her conscience, or to prevent a person from acting according to conscience. It spelled out the duties of the state to safeguard this right and referred to the limits of government. Religious freedom is a social and civic right not only of individuals but also of families and communities. Natural law and divine revelation ground this freedom.

Certain voices, among them those of some French bishops and other fathers, wanted a more prophetic, theological text.[34] However, others wanted a text that would speak to governments, the international community, and all persons of good will, as well as to Catholics. The latter line of argument prevailed. The emphases were on the ethical doctrine of religious freedom as a human right, the political position on limited government, and the theological principles of the church's freedom in relation to civil society. Murray feared over-theologizing the argument, because that approach would have problems similar to those of the minority's inflexible position, which sought to create a universal theological rationale.

The secretary general announced that there would be a vote on this schema in two days, November 19, 1964. Some judged the revised draft to be substantially a new text in length and content. The presidents, moderators, and leaders of the council, with the concurrence of Pope Paul VI, agreed to a delay in the voting until the fourth session, encouraging recommendations to be sent in for improving the text during the intersession. The decision particularly disturbed American bishops such as Cardinal Meyer of Chicago. However, it was not only the resistive minority that judged the text insufficiently mature for debate, as Joseph Ratzinger noted at the time:

> Anyone wholeheartedly in favor of its purpose would scarcely have wanted [this schema] passed in the form in which it was re-submitted. This is not merely because of the many compromises which considerably diluted the original statement, but also because of the bad and unhistorical point of departure, based not on the Gospel and what the Church as Church can say with full authority, but on doubtful natural law constructions.... As a matter of fact, the American model came perhaps too clearly through these supposedly timeless natural-law doctrines.[35]

This week in November 1964 is referred to as "black week" in histories of the council because of the angry frustration among a majority of the bishops.[36] The Holy Father had intervened to make certain changes in the Decree on Ecumenism, to add introductory notes to the Dogmatic Constitution on the Church, and to allow for delayed voting on the Declaration on Religious Freedom. The applause that accompanied Bishop de Smedt's oral presentation of the text, however, was a testimony to the world of the mind of the council. In retrospect, those who were responsible for assisting the bishops in drafting the document admit that the final result is a better text with a larger proportion of the council fathers understanding it and voting positively for its final draft, even if the motive and manner of the decision to delay may have been flawed. "What was unhappily delayed was happily perfected."[37]

In the next draft, sections were added on salvation history and on the necessity of educating people to deal with religious freedom. The text was also tightened. On April 18 the Coordinating Committee approved the text and it was sent out to the bishops. At the same time, the pope accepted an invitation from the United Nations to address its full assembly in October.

## Fourth Session (September 14 to December 8, 1965)

Pope Paul VI opened the fourth and last session of the council with a visit to the catacombs, thereby giving witness to solidarity with the church of silence in Eastern Europe and symbolically demonstrating his own personal commitment to religious freedom. Because he would be addressing the United Nations in October while the council was still in session, he requested an initial vote on the church's position with regard to religious freedom. Through his personal theologian, Archbishop Colombo of Milan, assisted by John Courtney Murray and Pietro Pavan, the pope had contributed to the drafting of the document, and had followed the discussions closely. The new text clearly restricted the theme to civil rights in society and to governmental implications. This restriction avoided any direct implications for freedom within the church.

The session began on September 15 with four days of debate on this draft. The majority wanted a preliminary vote to see what direction the revisions would take. The pope himself had to intervene to assist the majority in their desire to proceed in this fashion. While highlighting the importance of the document, he also wanted to ensure that the revised text emphasized the obligation to seek the truth as well as the importance of avoiding a basis grounded solely in freedom of conscience, being clear on the traditional role of the magisterium, and taking care to make sure that the lay state's obligation to the church was strengthened. Venice's Cardinal Urbani spoke out in the name of a number of Italian bishops in support of the declaration. The outcome of this preliminary sounding of the fathers was 1,997 in agreement, with some 224 voting *no*. The voting by paragraph produced a majority of 90 percent or more in favor of each section, with, however, a large number of suggestions for final revisions. The vote was, in effect, "the pope's passport of credibility at the United Nations." In his address to that organization he praised its initiative on human rights, especially religious freedom:

You proclaim here the fundamental rights and duties of the human person, their dignity, their freedom, above all religious freedom. We think you are the interpreters of this, the highest of human wisdom. We also affirm this sacred character. It is above all, about human life, the life of the person which is sacred, no one can dare to go against it.[38]

Cardinal Beran of Prague, recently released from a Communist prison, made one of the most dramatic interventions in the debate. He talked of the tragic history of his people, in what was then Czechoslovakia, as a result of the church's execution of Jan Hus and the forced reconversion of the Bohemian people to Catholicism. This declaration would be an essential contribution to his country in healing the painful memories of church-sponsored violence and coercion of consciences.

During this fourth session of the council, debates on religious freedom were no longer about whether there should be a declaration, though the minority did not cease its resistance till the final vote, and some not even then. The debate among the majority, all of whom wanted the declaration, was on what would serve as the basis for such an affirmation. In contrast to earlier sessions, the Latin Americans for the most part no longer followed the line of some Italian, Portuguese, and Spanish bishops in the minority.

The drafters of the current text opted for a very narrow juridical argument based on the dignity of the human person and the limited competency of the state, acknowledging the obligation of the individual to the truth and the claims of the Catholic Church to that truth. French and German bishops preferred an argument based more firmly on divine revelation. Some bishops wanted to include an affirmation of the right to religious freedom of partners in mixed marriages.

The SPCU enlisted scholars for a stronger biblical base. The French and other bishops accepted the wisdom of avoiding discussion of church and state and the theology of Christian freedom as a response to divine grace. A longer piece interpreting the history of the modern magisterium in support of the declaration's affirmations was finally dropped.[39] At the request of the Polish bishops, clarifications were added to ensure that "public order" could not be used as a pretext for government interference in the freedom of the church; the declaration clearly stated that public order was grounded in the objective moral order.[40]

In presenting the draft, Bishop de Smedt emphasized that the declaration does not compromise the responsibility of the Christian to the truth. Rather, the subject of the declaration is freedom in human, political society. The declaration does not deal with freedom of Catholics in the church, but rather with social relations in the public sphere. Therefore, the declaration does not question or undermine the truth of revelation, the claims of the Catholic Church, or the obligation of conscience to seek the truth and adhere to it. In this draft the section on salvation history was deleted and the biblical material reshaped.

Implicit throughout the debate, though not explicitly treated in the document, was the question of development of doctrine. Can the Catholic Church change its formulations, its positions on society, and recognize that earlier positions and policies are no longer adequate? Many of the voices of the minority, when they had lost the debate on the substance of the matter, still held that this position would be a departure from the fixed tradition of the church. Bishop de Smedt spoke explicitly to this objection when he pointed out that the position taken in the proposed text reflected continuity as well as progress.[41] The question of the development of the church's teaching was one of the many issues left to postconciliar theological discussion.[42]

Bishop de Smedt in his presentations and the drafters in their work with the interventions of particular bishops tried to set a context to show that such development is consistent with the natural law tradition and divine revelation, though departing from some of the formulations and policies of the nineteenth century. This sense of development was to lend credibility to the church for the ecumenical observers and for many Catholics, though it would also lead to the integrist schism that followed the council.

On October 27 the fathers began to vote on the new text by section. A vote also allowed for provisional approvals with suggested improvements. In both cases there were clear majorities for the document and for its articles. Now the bishops were ready to produce a final text.

The final draft incorporated some emendations of the fathers but rejected suggested substantial revisions. The text stressed the limitation of government. An affirmation of the teaching of "recent" popes on the subject replaced the review of recent magisterial pronouncements. A statement on the responsibility of government to support the rights of religion was added in order to assuage the fathers concerned about an implicit affirmation of the secularist state.

On November 19 the fathers voted 1,954 in favor and 249 opposed. A final vote of 2,308 in favor and 70 opposed was taken December 7, 1965, and the pope promulgated the Declaration on Religious Freedom on the eve of the close of the second Vatican Council. The same day Pope Paul expressed himself to an international audience:

> ...in a declaration which will undoubtedly remain one of the greatest documents of the Council, the Church echoes the aspirations to civil and social freedom in religious matters, so universally felt today; i.e., that no one should be forced to believe; that no longer should anyone be prevented from believing or professing his or her faith, since it is a fundamental right of the human person. (December 7, 1965)[43]

# PART II

# Major Points

*Dignitatis Humanae* is intentionally brief, consisting of fifteen articles. It attempts a very precise task for the church: reinterpreting a burdensome past and opening up a more effective and consistent approach to the future. In the light of the Catholic Church's affirmation of religious freedom, *Unitatis Redintegratio* articulates future relations with other Christians, *Nostra Aetate* with other believers, and *Gaudium et Spes* with the modern world. The last of these incorporates a more complete Catholic understanding of the dignity of the human person (*GS*, 11–45).[1]

The American reader of the declaration often misses the fact that it does not treat (1) pluralism, (2) Vatican diplomatic treaties with states, called concordats, or (3) the separation of church and state, a theme so dear to the American experience.[2] All of these areas of Catholic life evolved under the influence of this new policy on religious freedom. The text does not discuss relations among Catholics themselves and how ecclesiastical structures and processes do or do not honor the dignity of the human person. Thus the subtitle of the declaration best summarizes its content: "On the Right of the Person and of Communities to Social and Civil Freedom in Matters Religious." This text has a restricted and focused purpose in Catholic teaching. The outline of the document is as follows:

Introduction
    1. Contemporary dignity/obligations of conscience

Chapter 1—The General Principle of Religious Freedom
    2. Definition of religious freedom
    3. Role of divine and human law

## INTRODUCTION

**Article 1.** The introductory paragraphs read the signs of the times: "A sense of the dignity of the human person impresses itself more and more deeply on the consciousness of the peoples of our times. In their actions more and more people are demanding that they should use their own responsible freedom and judgment, not driven by coercion but by a sense of duty."[3] And they "demand constitutional limits on the powers of government, in order that there may be no encroachment on the rightful freedom of the person and of associations." The church attends to both the personal right and to the civil and legal conditions in societies and states.[4]

However, the nature of the human person and the signs of the times are only part of the argument. The declaration is also attentive to the sources of divine revelation: it "searches into the sacred tradition and doctrine of the church—the treasury out of which the church continually brings forth new things that are in harmony with the things that are old."

This affirmation of freedom in the civil sphere diminishes neither the truth claims of Catholicism—"one true religion subsists in the Catholic and Apostolic Church"—nor the obligations of conscience—"...persons are bound to seek the truth, especially in what concerns

God and God's Church, and to embrace the truth they come to know, and to hold fast to it. . . . It is upon the human conscience that these obligations fall and exert their binding force."

But the council affirms that "the truth cannot impose itself except by virtue of its own truth," and that religious freedom has to do with "immunity from coercion in civil society." The explanation of this theological position is provided in the next section of the document and is shorter than that proposed in earlier drafts.

The council then sees this new insight and affirmation as being in continuity with the faith of the church through the ages, as leaving "untouched traditional Catholic doctrine on the moral duty of persons and societies toward the true religion and toward the one Church of Christ." The document's introduction finally places this affirmation of "the rights of the human person and the constitutional ordering of society" within the context of the teachings of the "recent popes," without giving a detailed account of this development.[5] At the time of the council, Joseph Ratzinger expressed regrets about the formulations in this section of the document: "This text [*DH*, 1] attempts to emphasize a continuity in the statements of the official Church on this issue. . . . It would have been better to omit these compromising formulas or to reformulate them in line with the later text. Thus the introduction changes nothing in the text's content; therefore, we need not regard it as anything more than a minor flaw."[6]

Article 1 holds together with a careful balance the concerns for the obligation of conscience to be guided by truth, which is proclaimed by the Catholic Church, and the social obligation of society not to coerce the individual in matters of religion.

### CHAPTER 1—THE GENERAL PRINCIPLE OF RELIGIOUS FREEDOM

**Article 2.** The first chapter of the declaration outlines the foundation in reason, and the requirements of civil, governmental protections for religious freedom.

Article 2 presents the key thesis of the entire declaration:

This Vatican Council declares that the human person has a right to religious freedom. This freedom means that all persons are to be immune from coercion on the part of individuals or of social groups and of any human power, in such wise that no one is to be forced to act in a manner contrary to his own beliefs, whether privately or publicly, whether alone or in association with others, within due limits.

The council further declares that the right to religious freedom has its foundation in the very dignity of the human person as this dignity is known through the revealed word of God and by reason itself. This right of the human person to religious freedom is to be recognized in the constitutional law whereby society is governed and thus it is to become a civil right.

It is in accordance with their dignity as persons—that is, beings endowed with reason and free will and therefore privileged to bear personal responsibility—that all persons should be at once impelled by nature and also bound by a moral obligation to seek the truth, especially religious truth. They are also bound to adhere to the truth, once it is known, and to order their whole lives in accord with the demands of truth. However, people cannot discharge these obligations in a manner in keeping with their own nature unless they enjoy immunity from external coercion as well as psychological freedom. Therefore the right to religious freedom has its foundation not in the subjective disposition of the person, but in his very nature. In consequence, the right to this immunity continues to exist even in those who do not live up to their obligation of seeking the truth and adhering to it and the exercise of this right is not to be impeded, provided that just public order be observed.[7]

These paragraphs parallel very closely the United Nations Universal Declaration on Human Rights (December 10, 1948) and the WCC Declaration on Religious Liberty approved at its first Assembly in August 1948. *Dignitatis Humanae* 2 outlines a clear definition of the type of freedom under consideration, and its "foundation in the very dignity of the human person." While the council recognizes that the experience of pluralism and the rise of consciousness of individual liberties is an occasion for recognizing this right, it grounds the argument in the concept of human dignity. This acknowledged right in civil society is embodied in "constitutional law."

The text avoids the objection of the classical position, that error has no rights and that the common good demands support of only the truth of the Catholic faith. The dignity of the person requires the civil right without denying the moral obligation of the person to seek the truth. The community must honor the fact that the "right to this immunity continues to exist even in those who do not live up to their obligation of seeking the truth"—a clear departure from the preconciliar position. In the subtitle the council uses the language "freedom in matters religious" rather than "religious freedom" precisely to guarantee the rights of atheists as well as believers.

There are limits to the freedom of individuals and communities, even in the area of religion, as noted by the phrase "provided that just public order be observed." "Public order" defines a minimal legal framework for ensuring a peaceful society. Use of the term "public order" does not provide an implicit affirmation of secularist states or encourage undue restriction of religion.[8] Likewise, the public order is not as comprehensive as seeking the common good, which is the function of the whole society and the variety of communities within it, and cannot be reduced to legislation.

**Article 3.** This section outlines, in detail, the argument from "divine law—eternal, objective and universal—whereby God orders, directs and governs the entire universe." The characteristic of the human person that makes religious freedom an imperative is that "every person has the duty, and therefore the right, to seek the truth in matters religious in order that he or she may with prudence form for themselves right and true judgments of conscience."

The argument is based on the dignity of the human person and not on an analysis of conscience. Yet it is conscience which is an inherent element of this dignity that society must respect. While truth is an objective reality of which the church is the custodian, "truth, however, is to be sought after in a manner proper to the dignity of the human person." Thus the text carefully balances the demands of freedom, human dignity, conscience, and truth.

This right is not only an individual one. Many countries that recognize the liberty of individual conscience proscribe or control the rights or public activities of either all religions or of those religions not established in the particular state. It is for this reason that the declaration is clear on the "social nature" of this right to religious freedom as well.

Catholicism no longer sees uniformity of religion as a necessary or even an ideal basis for the common good of society. According to the council, the state is neither to "command or inhibit" the free exercise of religion, whether by communities or individuals. It will remain for postconciliar debate to interpret pluralism in God's design for the human family.

**Article 4.** Religious freedom extends to those who "act in community," so that they may be free to "govern themselves according to their own norms, honor the Supreme Being in public worship, assist their members in the practice of the religious life, strengthen them by instruction, and promote institutions in which they may join together for the purpose of ordering their own lives in accordance with their religious principles."

These statements, of course, were in contradiction to some of the laws in traditionally Catholic countries and would require considerable adjustment in societies in which the church had been established for centuries. The statements also, however, challenged Marxist and Islamic societies where various religions, including the Catholic religion, suffered under severe restrictions.

Further, religious groups are "not to be hindered...in the selection, training, appointment, and transferral of their own ministers, in communicating with religious authorities and communities abroad, in erecting buildings for religious purposes, and in the acquisition and use of suitable funds or properties." This means that government should not interfere in such matters.

For centuries in some Catholic countries (e.g., Spain and Portugal) the sovereigns and civil authorities had played formal roles in the selection of candidates for the episcopacy and in deciding which decrees of the Holy See could be promulgated within their borders; an example of the latter would be Russia and the suppression of the Jesuits in the eighteenth century. Likewise, in many Catholic countries (e.g.,

Colombia and some other Latin American countries) governments controlled the status of other religious bodies. This admonition is thus addressed to such countries as well as to Marxist and other secularist states that control and limit religion.

The declaration then challenges the kind of state censorship that inhibits religious communities in the "public teaching and witness to their faith, whether by the spoken or by the written word." It admonishes governments to "refrain from any manner of action which might seem to carry a hint of coercion . . . especially when dealing with poor or uneducated people."

The council calls on both governments and religious groups to avoid the unworthy witness called proselytizing. This is as much of an admonition to Catholics who have profited by state support of their education and evangelism as to secularist states or assertive religious groups that rely on coercive tactics in their evangelism. As we shall see in Part 3, proselytism and common witness would be fruitful areas of debate and development following the council.

The article concludes by noting that states should provide protections in the public sphere so as not to exclude religious voices. States are to allow religious bodies to contribute to the debates in society in order to "show the special value of their doctrine in what concerns the organization of society." This means that religious groups should be able to "hold meetings and to establish educational, cultural, charitable and social organizations."

**Article 5.** The family deserves the protection of the state and the wider civil society in its exercise of religious freedom. It should have the "right freely to live its own domestic religious life under the guidance of parents. Parents, moreover, have the right to determine, in accordance with their own religious beliefs, the kind of religious education that their children are to receive."

This affirmation is of particular importance in countries like the United States, where all support a common system of schools and the parents have the freedom to choose a public or religious school for their children. The government does not provide for financial support of the parents in this free choice of religious schools. Catholics and others continue to advocate for provisions under which parents would not be subject to unjust burdens as a result of having exercised their right to opt for the religious school of their choice. It is worth noting that the council did not, however, accept a proposal for explicit support of government aid to Catholic schools.

In a number of societies the state provides education and sometimes enforces attendance in such a way that parents do not have the "free choice of schools," a right affirmed by the council. Children are "forced to attend lessons or instructions that are not in agreement with their religious beliefs."

The council was particularly concerned about the secularist governments of Western Europe and the Marxist world. There were also parts of the world, nations such as Italy or countries in Latin America where, at that time, study of the Catholic religion was required of non-Catholic students in state-sponsored schools. There had been attempts in the United States to impose a "single system" that would have been obligatory and would have excluded Catholic schools, but the U.S. Supreme Court had struck this down as an infringement on the religious freedom of parents to educate their own children.

**Article 6.** The document outlines the responsibilities of states and the preference for constitutional government—a preference that is itself a development in Catholic thinking. Religious freedom is viewed as a matter of "common welfare" and therefore the responsibility of all members of society, not just governments.

Churches and other nongovernmental institutions in society are to "care for the right to religious freedom [which] devolves upon the whole citizenry, upon social groups, upon government, and upon the Church and other religious communities, in virtue of the duty of all toward the common welfare."

Governments have a special responsibility for religious freedom. "Government is also to help create conditions favorable" to the free exercise of religion and to create an environment where religion can flourish. The declaration uses the terms "civil authorities," and "governments" rather than the word "states" because such terms are more comprehensive and avoid the church-state question.

The establishment of churches, including the Catholic Church in certain countries continues. Yet, the establishment of the church and its particular privileges in a society are not to override the religious freedom now affirmed by the church universal.

If, in view of peculiar circumstances obtaining among peoples, special civil recognition is given to one religious community in the constitutional order of society, it is at the same time imperative that the right of all citizens and religious communities to religious freedom should be recognized and made effective in practice.

The affirmation made here is a statement of historical fact; it makes no value judgments, positive or negative. This compromise did not fully please either those who favored establishment or those who favored separation of church and state. Bishops from Islamic nations were concerned that the recognition of a confessional state might cause pastoral problems in their situations.[9] As the established churches in the United States eventually became disestablished in the early nineteenth century, so many of the nations where the Catholic Church was established with certain privileges in law have not only enacted religious freedom under the influence of the council but have also created separation of church and state.

However, freedom under law is not the only value that states serve in supporting religious freedom. They should also strive to diminish "discrimination among citizens" on the basis of religion. Enacting constitutional religious freedom is one thing. Contributing to a culture that supports religion and diminishes intergroup tensions is quite another. Many societies have a long way to go in providing legal and cultural supports that would enhance the constitutional protection of religious freedom.

The council is very explicit that it is "wrong," a violation of the will of God and the integrity of the human person, to inhibit the "profession or repudiation of any religion." A government is not to use force or fear to limit the religious freedom of its people. The family of nations has the responsibility for holding accountable governments that violate these rights.

**Article 7.** As with any personal right, the right to freedom in religious matters may be "subject to certain regulatory norms." In exercising their religious "rights, individual persons and social groups are bound by the moral law to have respect both for the rights of others and for their own duties toward others and for the common welfare of all."

The declaration then adds: "Society has the right to defend itself against possible abuses committed on the pretext of freedom of religion." In a free society, any right can be subject to abuse, or developed out of the context of the concomitant responsibility that attends to those rights. The state is to oversee and protect the "rights of all citizens and provide for the peaceful settlement of conflicts of rights," but not in an arbitrary or unfair manner.

It is this limitation of coercion by the state, and the very strict concern to preserve the public peace, that is "meant by public order...freedom of the person is to be respected as far as possible and is not to be curtailed except when and insofar as necessary." As noted above, the concept of public order is narrower than that of the common good, used in earlier drafts. Public order is the legal minimum that is necessary for a society, while the common good is the wider goal of the collaboration of government and other key elements of society, such as families, churches, and voluntary organizations. One cannot legislate the common good. It is served only by the free cooperation of members of a society working together in mutual support.

In an age of suicide bombers and even state-sponsored religious violence, it becomes particularly evident that limits must be set even on religious expressions when they violate the rights of others or the peace of society. However, the criterion by which the government limits religious rights must be clear and compelling. The government must avoid arbitrary decisions.

At the council, the churches of Eastern Europe were particularly concerned that the declaration not offer pretexts to totalitarian governments to exert arbitrary restrictions on religion in the name of the public order.

**Article 8.** The council fathers were aware of the modern individualistic affirmation of freedom and antisocial dimensions of behavior to which such individualism can give rise. There was every effort to avoid confusing the church's position with this Enlightenment Western stream of individualism, the view of "freedom as the pretext for refusing to submit to authority and for making light of the duty of obedience."

The bishops also recognized that, as certain cultures that had at one time claimed to be "Catholic" now became open to religious freedom,

Catholics would have to take increasing responsibility for their own faith, institutions, and education. Freedom requires responsibility, both personal and corporate.

Therefore, the council affirmed, society will have to work at "educating others, to do their utmost to form persons who on the one hand will respect the moral order and be obedient to lawful authority, and on the other hand will be lovers of true freedom."

This will press people not to become more subjective, relativistic, and autonomous, but rather to "come to decisions on their own judgment and in the light of truth [and] govern their activities with a sense of responsibility." Rather than fostering less responsibility, this new sense of freedom espoused by the Catholic Church will call persons to "act with greater responsibility in fulfilling their duties in community life."

### CHAPTER 2—RELIGIOUS FREEDOM IN THE LIGHT OF REVELATION

**Article 9.** Chapter 2 begins by stating that the right to religious freedom has "its foundation in the dignity of the person." But it also affirms that this freedom has "roots in divine revelation." It does not initially provide a set of biblical texts because it recognizes that scripture "does not indeed affirm [religious freedom] in so many words." Rather, scripture "gives evidence of the respect which Christ showed toward the freedom," and "gives us lessons in the spirit which disciples of such a Master ought to adopt and continually follow."

The witness of Christ and the apostles in scripture is "consonant with the freedom of the act of Christian faith."

**Article 10.** The theological understanding of the act of faith in the Catholic tradition supports this biblical witness. It is one of the major tenets of "Catholic doctrine that the person's response to God in faith must be free." The writings of the "Fathers of the Church" demonstrate the consistent tradition that freedom is necessary for authentic faith.

So, in addition to the argument from natural law and from the witness of the ministry of Christ and the apostles, it is the "nature of faith that in matters religious every manner of coercion on the part of persons should be excluded." This understanding of the faith is such that Christians must contribute to the "creation of an environment in which persons can without hindrance be invited to the Christian faith, embrace it of their own free will, and profess it effectively in their whole manner of life."

**Article 11.** The witness of Jesus, calling for a free response to the gospel, and a doctrine of faith that presupposes religious freedom do not release the Christian from the responsibility of conscience and the obligation to truth. "God calls people to serve Him in spirit and in truth, hence they are bound in conscience but they stand under no compulsion...truth appears at its height in Christ Jesus." In this way the council dissociates its teaching on religious freedom from any form of indifferentism, which levels the truth claims of all religions, making Catholicism merely one option among many.

However, in bringing persons to affirmation of this truth, Christ and his disciples "used patience" and not coercion. Christ "denounced the unbelief of some who listened to him, but he left vengeance to God." When challenged to use coercion and violence in service of his mission, he "refused to be a political messiah, ruling by force." He was critical of the religious and political injustices of his day, but he "acknowledged the power of government."

The church maintains that tradition: "Taught by the word and example of Christ, the apostles followed the same way." They "showed respect for those of weaker stuff even though they were in error," but they "did not hesitate to speak out against governing powers."

The council goes on to acknowledge the members of the church who have given their lives for their commitment to the gospel and its freedom as "martyrs and other faithful [who] have walked through all ages and over all the earth."

**Article 12.** This paragraph affirms the traditional character of this teaching on religious freedom in which the "Church is following the way of Christ and the apostles." However, it makes a remarkable statement of fact, recognizing the failures of the past.

Up until the time of this and other Vatican II documents, the church had never before offered in its magisterial statements so explicit an admission of having departed from the spirit of the gospel. Almost immediately, however, the declaration also affirms that the doctrine has stood firm, even when the practice has failed:

> In the life of the People of God, as it has made its pilgrim way through the vicissitudes of human history, there has at times appeared a way of acting that was hardly in accord with the spirit of the Gospel, or even opposed to it. Nevertheless, the doctrine of the Church that no one is to be coerced into faith has always stood firm.

The declaration goes on to note how the church, in spite of the failures, has been brought back to authentic doctrine: "in the course of time persons have come more widely to recognize their dignity as persons."

Distancing the Catholic Church from centuries of dominance— through inquisitions, wars of religion, ecclesiastical monopoly in service of the truth, claiming to serve the common good by having the state ensure the uniformity of the true faith and suppression of error—may be considered one of the most dramatic turns in the teaching of the council.

**Article 13.** The text then goes on to affirm the freedom that should be accorded to the church itself in human society: "The Church should enjoy that full measure of freedom which her care for the salvation of humanity requires."

This affirmation challenges specifically the secularist governments and those religious states which do not provide freedom for the Catholic Church. The declaration asserts that to "act against the Church is to act against the will of God." Nevertheless, the Catholic Church seeks no privileged place, but only "claims freedom for herself in her character as a society of persons who have the right to live in society in accordance with the precepts of the Christian faith." This is a departure from the traditional claim of the Catholic Church for a favored place in societies where it could be a dominant force.

Like the rights of the individuals, the freedom of the church should be "incorporated in law but also given sincere and practical application." In most Marxist states of the time and in some Muslim countries, there was a constitutional place for religious freedom, but in practice, actual experience was marked by a secular uniformity and religious disability or a second-class status for Christians and other religions.

Religious freedom is a civil right in both the legal and the practical order. "Christian faithful, in common with all other persons, possess the civil right not to be hindered in leading their lives in accordance with their consciences." Thus a "harmony exists between the freedom of the Church and the religious freedom which is to be recognized as the right of all." This freedom for the church, as well as freedom of individual conscience, is to be sanctioned by "constitutional law."

**Article 14.** In traditional Catholic societies, the culture, the state, and the leadership of the church have been responsible for providing a religious atmosphere. As the church departs from this religious monopoly— whether in the concrete form of an established Catholicism, the pervasive Catholicism of a majority in society, or the mindset of a minority hoping for the ideal thesis in which Catholicism will dominate the rest of society—the church will have to provide education in pluralism, religious freedom, and a Catholic faith founded on personal conviction.

In the "formation of their consciences, the Christian faithful ought carefully to attend to the sacred and certain doctrine of the Church." Some Latin American fathers in particular affirmed the direction toward religious freedom, recognizing that a veritable revolution would be necessary in the catechetical practice of the Catholic Church in order to prepare the people for living in a society where this new understanding of religious freedom would prevail.

Religious freedom, however, does not relieve the Christian of the responsibility of providing an appropriate witness in a pluralistic world. "It is [the Church's] duty to give utterance to and authoritatively to teach that truth, which is Christ himself, and also to declare and confirm it by her authority." Religion is not to be relegated to the privacy of individual conviction. Religious freedom is a right to activity as well as a right to personal conviction.

This teaching has to do with more than just the inner life of the church and its convictions about the content of divine revelation. It also entails the Catholic Christian's responsibility to advocate for the social and ethical positions that are among its contributions to the common good, the "task of spreading the light of life with all confidence."

This means that Christians should have the freedom to carry out their own evangelizing mission "even to the shedding of their blood."

However, the gospel mission proceeds without proselytism or disrespect for the freedom of others. The church is "faithfully to proclaim [the truth received from Christ], and vigorously to defend it, never—be it understood—having recourse to means that are incompatible with the spirit of the Gospel."

The council has departed dramatically from the earlier position: that error has no rights and therefore coercion is acceptable. The Catholic is now to exercise the evangelizing mission with "prudence and patience in dealing with those who are in error or in ignorance with regard to the faith." Catholic evangelization is now to be carried out in the context of human dignity, calling "persons who are invited freely to accept and profess the faith."

**Article 15.** The final paragraph of the declaration summarizes the whole document, recalling the contemporary situation of "persons of the present day [who] want to be able freely to profess their religion in private and in public," and the fact that religious freedom has "already been declared to be a civil right in most constitutions." In a general way, citing "international documents," the council acknowledges the 1948 United Nations' Universal Declaration on Human Rights.

The council affirms governments and the international community for having codified the right to religious freedom. It also challenges those that have not, as well as those that have demonstrated only a nominal commitment to the rights of their citizens, noting that certain "governments are engaged in the effort to deter citizens from the profession of religion and to make life very difficult and dangerous for religious communities."

The declaration recognizes the pluralism in modern societies, while making no value judgment, positive or negative, on it. The council fathers note that peace among peoples calls for an affirmation of religious freedom. Although the current situation draws the attention of modern persons to the need for this affirmation, the argument of the council is based not on historical circumstances but on the dignity of the human person.

Advocacy for the rights of all persons to religious freedom is now a central element of Catholic identity. The council exhorts "Catholics, and it directs a plea to all people, most carefully to consider how greatly necessary religious freedom is, especially in the present condition of the human family." This exhortation to all persons not only articulates the value, but also calls for an institutionalization of this right so that "religious freedom be everywhere provided with an effective constitutional guarantee."

The declaration ends with a prayer: "May the God and Father of all grant that the human family, through careful observance of the principle of religious freedom in society, may be brought by the grace of Christ and the power of the Holy Spirit to the sublime and unending and 'glorious freedom of the sons of God' (Rom. 8:21)."

# PART III

# IMPLEMENTATION

In discussing the implementation of the Declaration on Religious Freedom we will note four dimensions of the church's life following Vatican II: (1) reception of religious freedom, (2) incorporation of the principles in the declaration into the treaties (concordats) of the Holy See with civil governments and the responses of some states, (3) interpretation by the popes, and (4) ecumenical reception.

As James Burtchaell notes in introducing the declaration: "A Church Council is less an initiative than a sanction. Its enactments must be read as vindications of insights and arguments that had been elaborated earlier by scholars and pastors, and were sustained against vigorous opposition even from many of the bishops who in Council had been brought to accept them."[1]

## RECEPTION

After each great council of the church a long process of reception has occurred. Reception can be defined as the process whereby new formulations of the Christian faith are incorporated into the faith, life, and witness of the church.

### Reception in History

Statements made by church councils, such as the Council of Nicea (325) with its definition of the divinity of Christ, took decades—sometimes centuries—to become the clear and universal teaching of the church. Even the books in the New Testament took several centuries to be received and clearly enumerated.

Reception is a normal process, entailing debate, reformulation, and interpretation. For example, the Council of Trent (1545–1563) produced reform and doctrinal decrees. The reform decrees were not implemented or received in France until the fall of the monarchy in the French Revolution and the concordat with Napoleon in 1801, and some bishops were still working to have the Tridentine Mass utilized in certain parts of France in the late nineteenth century.

We will learn how the Second Vatican Council is interpreted as the centuries progress. Will it be seen as the end of the Tridentine era, as Trent was seen as the end of the Middle Ages? Or will the council be interpreted as the capstone of an era, completing the biblical and liturgical work of Trent, finalizing the ecclesiological work begun in Vatican I (1870), and initiating the openness of recent popes to ecumenism and the modern world?

## Interpretation

The debates on the interpretation of Vatican II are background for implementation, reception, and interpretation of the Declaration on Religious Freedom. There are four interpretative perspectives to consider in situating the story in its historiographical landscape.

First, during the council, there were a number of organized networks of council fathers from all continents and most countries of the world. One of these, the conservative International Group of Fathers (*Coetus Internationalis Patrum*), was dedicated to reaffirming recent papal teaching and restraining any modification of the pre–Vatican II position on religious freedom. One of their number, Archbishop Marcel Lefebvre, left the Catholic Church after the council and founded a new church. Most of this group—some in very high places with influence on the appointment of bishops—did not leave but remained to resist the conciliar initiatives.

A second perspective comes from those who see the council itself as having been unable to make the decisions that were in the best interest of the church's renewal, and therefore as an event the "spirit" of which can be discerned only in postconciliar creativity. From this point of view, the council texts are inherently defective and call for more radical reforms of which the institution itself may be incapable. The declaration is seen as defective because it did not unambiguously reject established churches, did not abolish the papal diplomatic corps and the concordat system, did not address freedom within the church, and made no judgment on a pluralistic social situation.

Within the progressive council majority and the historians they have spawned, many tendencies have emerged over the past forty-plus years. One school of interpretation emphasizes the continuity of the sixteen texts of the council with the councils of Trent and Vatican I in particular and with the popes who immediately preceded John XXIII, especially Pius XII.

The other school emphasizes the *aggiornamento* theme of Pope John's opening address, highlighting the discontinuity and the new elements that were developed in the course of the council's debates and drafting. For this school, religious freedom is particularly significant, since the debates point so clearly to a theology of the development of doctrine. Both of these last two perspectives are necessary and have important contributions to make to the history of Christianity.[2]

The process of implementing the declaration has taken place on many levels, and its effects can be seen in many areas, including (1) canonical and constitutional changes in the universal church and in local Catholic churches (national episcopal conferences, Eastern Catholic synods, and dioceses/eparchies), (2) educational changes to incorporate the commitment to formation for freedom, and (3) new perspectives on the human person and the church that inform Catholic teaching and theological reflection.

Study of reception and nonreception in each of these areas and in a variety of contexts is necessary for a full understanding of implementation of the declaration. In this part we will review (1) nonreception of the declaration, (2) its reception in selected contexts, (3) emphases of the papacies since the council, and (4) ecumenical reception. These themes open the discussion, but hardly do justice to the massive study that is needed to fully comprehend this seismic change in Catholicism and the societies in which it lives.

## NONRECEPTION

There were seventy bishops who voted against the Declaration on Religious Freedom. A substantial number of others had serious reservations about its fidelity to the tradition of the church, about its applicability in their local situation, and about its explicit theology of the church and its relationship to human dignity and the truth claims of Catholicism.

## Rejection of Vatican II

In the conciliar debates, many of the fathers had only two models of society in mind: (1) the secularist state, which did not support religion and (2) the confessional state, where the Catholic Church or some other religion was established. However, those drafting the document had a third model in mind, (3) the constitutional state, where religious rights of both persons and institutions are protected and positive collaboration with religions is possible. Much of the nonreception came from a lack of understanding of the presuppositions of the declaration.[3]

The story of the integrist schisms and the founding of a new denomination by Archbishop Marcel Lefebvre are well known and will not be recounted here. As in the case of the formation of the Old Catholic Church by those who resisted the teaching of Vatican I, or the Oriental Orthodox Churches by those who did not receive the Council of Chalcedon in 451, the emergence of such new churches is a common phenomenon in the conciliar history of the church.

Lefebvre's new denomination has bishops in various parts of the world, including the United States. It is based on an integrist ecclesiology that rejects religious freedom, constitutional government, and ecumenism. In its view the church is not able to change. Dialogue with fellow Christians grants credence to their errors, and the state should be supportive of the truth of the Catholic faith.[4] Lefebvre's followers in the United States tend to be those opposed to the liturgical reforms of Vatican II, preferring the liturgical innovations of the Council of Trent. However, separation from Catholicism over such issues is not the only aspect of resistance to the declaration or elements within it.

In fact, the debates over the nature of the church—over the meaning of the use in this and other conciliar texts of the phrase "subsists in" for describing the relationship between the one, true church and the Catholic Church—are examples of the lack of uniformity in the reception of as well as of resistance to the formulations and intent of the council. Ecclesiological self-understanding has critical implications for the interpretation of religious freedom among Christians and especially for Catholic ecumenical relations. Even now, more than forty years after the council, debates over the nature of the church are ongoing at the highest levels of Catholic leadership.

## Resistance to the Council's Teaching on Religious Freedom

There were undoubtedly many among those who voted for the Declaration on Religious Freedom with conviction who did not have the political or canonical skills to make the declaration effective; the educational vision or pedagogical influence to lead in its commitment to formation for freedom; the ecumenical zeal to ensure that witness to freedom became part of their dialogue with fellow Christians; or the social commitment to make advocacy for the religious rights of all part of their pastoral program. Some bishops told their people that the declaration would not change their particular situation. Others did not see the importance of educating for a new understanding of personal rights and responsibilities in the pluralism that would inevitably emerge in predominantly Catholic societies with the coming of religious freedom. Still others were cautious about admitting a new understanding of the relationship of the Catholic Church to the one true church, or entering into ecumenical dialogue with fellow Christians.

This does not mean that many who voted in the majority actively resisted the Catholic commitment to religious freedom with its educational, legal, ecumenical, social, and theological implications. It means, rather, that reception and implementation is a process, one that—as the declaration itself attests—is the task of the whole people of God and indeed of all persons of good will.

However, as we shall see, the declaration involved such a dramatic shift that it could be implemented only gradually, depending on the intellectual, legal, and financial resources of the local churches for effective change. In reviewing the more than forty years of implementation, we can only marvel that so much has been done.

We have already mentioned the integrist denominations; we are not surprised by their persistence or by pockets of nonreception of religious freedom that may continue for decades or even centuries. Furthermore, we are not surprised to find that the declaration's various elements were received unevenly and interpreted differently in different Catholic contexts. The following section will focus on a few examples to illustrate the complexity and diversity of this reception.

## CONTEXTUAL RECEPTION

The declaration challenges the constitutional arrangements of governments to provide for religious freedom. It also challenges the canonical arrangements of the Catholic Church where it has not provided for or encouraged the promotion of religious freedom, especially in its treaty arrangements through concordats with various states. Since the time of the council, Catholic practice has shifted dramatically, calling forth enormous changes in societies where the Catholic Church was established for centuries.

There are other societies, of course, in which governments are hostile to the Catholic Church, or where other religions are established and Catholics are not guaranteed religious freedom. There are also societies in which governments are positive toward religion and do guarantee religious freedom. Each of these situations demands a different diplomatic and pastoral approach from the church. Furthermore, the reception of religious freedom by the various nations of the world— both those in which religion and/or the Catholic Church has significant influence and those in which it is a minority—varies considerably.

Each society negotiates its relationship between religion and society according to its own culture, history, and demography. There are various examples that can be used. Societies emerging from Marxist domination in Eastern Europe after 1989, where predominantly Catholic countries like Poland and Slovakia, or Orthodox societies like Russia and Romania, had no experience of pluralism or religious freedom before Marxist secularization, present particular challenges.[5] Countries that remain Communist, such as China, require regular attention from religious groups and states committed to religious freedom.[6] The 1993 Vatican-Israel Fundamental Agreement illustrates Catholic advocacy of the rights and freedoms of all religious groups in the Holy Land: Muslim, Jewish, and Christian. The 1994 Memorandum on "The Significance of Jerusalem for Christians," following up the Fundamental Agreement attests to the Catholic Church's commitment to the religious rights of all parties, not singling itself out for special treatment.[7] Also, the debates concerning religion, Islamic immigration, and other religious minorities in Europe present a rich array of discussions on the question. The reemergence of proselytizing religious societies, not only in the Muslim world but also in some Buddhist nations and India, presents unique challenges that also merit exploration.

A thorough study of the reception of the Declaration on Religious Freedom would entail a detailed review of the last forty years of church-state relations in all of the countries around the world in which the Catholic Church is present. In this section, however, we will provide overviews of only three examples of particular societies: Spain, the United States, and Latin America. This will be followed by a brief treatment of the formal treaty relationships with which the Catholic Church has been involved. The major work of the church universal in implementing the declaration has been carried out through such diplomatic relationships and concordats with different governments, so it is important to take these into account, even if we cannot explore them in depth. Finally, we will end this section with comments on the reception of the Declaration of Religious Freedom in modern states, pointing out the ways in which the social teaching of the church on religious freedom has been a resource for people of good will in their advocacy for the religious freedom of all.[8]

## Examples

### Spain[9]

On the eve of the Second Vatican Council, Spain was an example of the ideal thesis, where harmony between a Catholic establishment and a Catholic ruler could effectively root out institutions promoting error and merely tolerate the presence of dissenting non-Catholics who in good conscience remained believers in other religions or were nonbelievers.

When the 1953 concordat was signed by Generalissimo Francisco Franco and the Holy See, Cardinal Ottaviani used the occasion to give a talk elaborating on the Catholic thesis/hypothesis position. John Courtney Murray responded to this address in a presentation at Catholic University of America and eventually found himself silenced.

At the council the Spanish bishops were among the most vocal opponents of the theology and social policy of the Declaration on Religious Freedom. Even with the strong support of traditional church-state arrangements, however, voices were raised in support of the majority and even criticized the Franco regime early in the council.[10] Still, when the bishops returned to Spain after the council, some of them assured their people, especially their people in public service, that the declaration had no bearing on their situation and would not entail any change in the arrangements between church and state. The published introduction to the declaration at the time said in relating it to the 1953 concordat with the Holy See that there was "perfect harmony between the principles of the two documents."[11]

This was clearly not the understanding of Pope Paul VI and the prefect of the Congregation of Bishops, Cardinal John Wright. Some very pointed letters were exchanged between Franco and the Holy See. In some ways, the bishops were caught between a changing Catholic Church and a resistant, traditional dictator. There were many in the Spanish Catholic Church who were quite ready for change. This was true both for the reception of conciliar teaching and for the modern quest for democracy and human rights in their own society, a quest so eloquently reinforced in the declaration. The Jesuits in particular were anxious to study the work of their American confrere John Courtney Murray and to find ways of making the council have an impact in Fascist Spain. Several conferences were held and a variety of publications were circulated.

Ironically, Spanish law promulgated in 1958 had required that national legislation should be inspired by the doctrine of the Catholic Church. This caused something of a problem when Catholic doctrine stated that religious freedom was to be written into constitutional provisions where possible, and the Spanish dictator was not sympathetic to this Catholic doctrine. As early as 1967 provisions for civil religious freedom began to be written into Spanish law, though these provisions were still quite restrictive. By 1973 a large gathering of the bishops with their clergy explored the issue and began to affirm Catholic teaching on religious freedom for Spain. There was no mechanism yet for incorporating religious freedom into Spanish law and life.

With the passing of Franco, serious constitutional revision and open dialogue in Spanish society could begin. In 1976 an accord was signed between the Vatican secretary of state and the undersecretary for foreign affairs of the Spanish government, beginning the process toward developing a constitutional state in Spain and a new concordat with the Catholic Church. This basic accord signaled a profound transformation for Spanish society, after more than five hundred years of the union of Catholicism with Spanish regimes and culture. This process led to the constitution of 1978 and the signing of four accords with the Catholic Church in 1979. Accords were also signed with Muslim, Jewish, and Protestant communities.

The fact that Spanish society has begun this transition with hope for peaceful church-state relations after a period of civil war in the 1930s, almost forty years of dictatorship, and half a millennium of religious monopoly is a testimony to the power of the vision of the declaration and the determination of the Spanish people. Some Spanish commentators have made note of the maturation of the Spanish society in the last half century. The elected party in power in the early years of the constitutional government was the same socialist party that had persecuted the church during the civil war era. The socialists have mellowed to become less anti-clerical and the Catholic Church has become less militant in its claim to hegemony in Spanish society.

Collaboration has become possible. The seeds of religious freedom have now been sown in Spanish soil and embodied in Spanish constitutional law. Instruments of dialogue are firmly in place. Only the course of future history will determine how this young plant flourishes.

### United States[12]

Reception of Vatican II and its Declaration on Religious Freedom in the United States was quite another matter. Catholics in the United States are a minority in the church universal, representing about 6 percent of Catholics worldwide. They are used to living as a minority in a situation where they are the largest religious body and the largest Christian church but are outnumbered by other Christians in the general population. For many historians, "American" reception "of religious freedom took place before and during the Council, which affirmed what had been the American tradition."[13]

"It was as if the great battle had been won, and it was enough to bask in the warmth of the victory. It may also be that the success of 'the

American schema,' and the applause with which it was greeted in the United States, led people to assume that the notion of religious freedom in *Dignitatis Humanae*, and the notion of the state's competence and duties that follows from it, coincided with those of the American political system. Events have proven this not to be the case, and with this realization have come new reflections on the conciliar declaration."[14] In the postconciliar years, Catholics were caught up implementing the liturgical and catechetical reforms of the council, building ecumenical and interreligious contacts, establishing programs of lay ministry and diaconate training, and initiating structures of collegiality and lay leadership in the local church.[15]

Those who attended to the social teachings of the church were for the most part engaged in building peace during the Vietnam era, promoting civil rights for Hispanic and African Americans, and developing local peace and justice commissions and education programs. Religious freedom was taken for granted.

The declaration laid a strong basis for the bishops' advocacy for the rights of parents in seeking resources from the states for freedom of choice for Catholic schooling as well as for Catholic collaboration in advocating for religious freedom, redressing the Supreme Court's extension of the government's "compelling interest" in restricting religious freedom in the 1990s. Supported by the declaration, Catholics made an important contribution to the Religious Freedom Restoration Act. The Catholic position that only "public order" should allow for the restriction of religious freedom was a basic contribution to this debate, which continues as Congress attempts to craft a new law that will stand up to Supreme Court scrutiny.[16] Periodically the engagement of the state in church support through tax relief, zoning privileges, and a host of other benefits is questioned by the secular press or separationist groups. There is in fact an amazing amount of U.S. legislation that does provide for protection, collaboration, and favor for religious institutions that serve the common good.[17]

Thus the tasks of ensuring an appropriate role for religion in society, advocating the religious rights of all, and resisting tendencies toward secularist monopolies in education, public media, and legislation remain as important in American Catholic life as they are in any other part of the Catholic world.

### Latin America[18]

Reception of religious freedom, its constitutional implementation, and the declaration's impetus for education for freedom has developed in a diversity of ways in the twenty-two countries and the bishops' conferences of Latin America and the Caribbean.

At the council, there were some Latin American bishops in support of the Spanish position; some were from countries with a history of concordats favoring the establishment and support of the Catholic Church in a confessional state. There were other Latin American bishops who supported religious freedom, who made contributions to the drafting of the text and recognized the need for educating Catholics to live their responsibility in a new context.[19]

In all of the Latin American countries and many in the Caribbean, Catholicism was demographically dominant, even where not established. From colonial times, the Spanish monarchs had appointed bishops and controlled the church. When the nineteenth-century revolutions came, the church leadership was unprepared to identify with the peoples of the new states of Latin America. Many Spanish-born colonial bishops returned to Spain or were exiled. Even though the initiators of the Mexican revolution were popular priests who were advocates of the indigenous and African elements of the population, they were finally executed as heretics by civil authorities. The Latin American revolutions were not populist uprisings of the poor, but middle/upper class separations led by Europeans born in the New World. Governments of secularist, French Revolution, anticlerical style alternated with conservative clericalist regimes.

Popular religious devotions, often untouched by the Catholic reforms of the sixteenth-century Council of Trent, were primary bearers of the gospel for the majority of people. This made catechesis in the new values of the council extremely difficult, in spite of a vibrant catechetical renewal in many countries. In some nations, the church was persecuted and severely controlled by the state. It was only in 1992 that the Catholic Church was legalized again in Mexico, though the persecution had stopped in the 1930s, the Mexican president had greeted the pope on his 1979 visit, and even during the most virulent times of persecution the Basilica of Our Lady of Guadalupe was never closed down!

In some countries implementation of the council was intentional and well planned. Brazilian bishops, for example, began work on a five-

year "General Pastoral Plan" while still in Rome during the final session of the council.[20] Most of the states of Latin America constitution-
ally affirm religious freedom and separation of church and state.
However, the Catholic Church has a long road ahead in terms of developing a culture that welcomes religious pluralism, nurturing a community of Catholics catechized in such a way as to be able to share their
faith with others and to defend it when attacked by proselytizing evangelicals, and taking up Catholic ecumenical initiatives.

Religious minorities often suffer in places where the population is
dominantly Catholic, whatever the ecumenical policy of church leaders.
Technical, constitutional religious freedom or the position of the council and the bishops does not immediately translate into a culture of advocacy for freedom of the other, ecumenical openness, or a welcome to
pluralism.

Liberation theologies have been one venture in implementing the
Second Vatican Council's call to an option for the poor and the creation
of a culture of freedom. The father of liberation theology, Gustavo
Gutiérrez, for example, commenting on the declaration soon after the
council, noted its implications:

> It certainly seems that a theology of the freedom of [persons] in
> religious matters ought to benefit from a deepening of the
> theme of awareness of the New Testament, and from recent
> thought on the historical conditions of [persons'] march towards
> truth, the duality of subject and object, and the role of human
> mediation in the salvific dialogue between God and [the human
> person].[21]

It still remains to be seen, however, if the Catholic Church will be
open to allowing the freedom of other Christians, for example, to practice divorce where it is outlawed, or to adjust to schools where the
Catholic religion is not taught, or to societies that give equal treatment
to military chaplains from a variety of religions or cemeteries not under
church control. Each country works out new legislation, and it is an
open question whether, based on conciliar principles, the Catholic majority will advocate the freedom of all persons.

The reception of Vatican II and the acceptance of a culture of freedom among the Catholic people is not yet a forgone conclusion.

Immigrants arriving in the United States from Latin America are often not prepared culturally or catechetically to live and dialogue in the pluralistic culture that typifies American church life. As the fifth largest Spanish-speaking country in the world, the United States is faced with the particular challenge of integrating the Hispanic community into its mainstream; of teaching the heritage of the council to its entire people; and of building bridges, ecumenical and intercultural, among all the people of this country.

The 1997 Roman Synod for America began a substantive dialogue among the episcopal conferences of Canada, Latin America, and the United States. Church-state relations, ecumenical priorities, and educating for freedom are among the most challenging issues for this hemispheric Catholic dialogue.

## Civil Society

### New Concordats[22]

Since AD 1122, the pope routinely sent legates to represent him before the kings and emperors of Christendom and even earlier to councils and to the patriarchs of the Eastern churches. Many of the civil-ecclesiastical arrangements included formal accords. With the breakdown of Catholic hegemony during the sixteenth-century Reformation, legates or ambassadors (called papal nuncios, or apostolic delegates when they do not have ambassadorial rank) from the Holy See became a regular feature of the church's relationships with civil powers and national hierarchies. Treaties called concordats accompanied these diplomatic arrangements.

### The System

From time to time specific mutually agreed upon concordats have been drawn up between civil governments and the Holy See. For the most part, these concordats have the force of treaties in international law.[23] They usually clarify the rights and privileges of the Catholic Church in a particular nation and reflect the provisions of the laws of a particular government and the canon law of the Catholic Church.

The council fathers had a wide range of views on the diplomatic corps and the concordat system, views that can be grouped into three categories. (1) Some of the council fathers were all for concordats, especially those giving the church a privileged role in a particular society. (2) Others objected to concordats and nuncios in principle as unduly restricting the function of bishops and bishops' conferences and interfering in the freedom of the local church—and even of the Holy See—in the process of nominating bishops and overseeing Catholic schools. (Certain Latin American and Asian bishops reported interference of nuncios in local political and ecclesiastical affairs.) (3) There were still others who preferred no a priori policy, recognizing the variety of histories and needs of local churches and the necessity of dealing with different contexts in a case-by-case way. The council did not address the issue of nuncios and concordats in the declaration, but the third point of view was the majority position.[24]

For example, in Eastern Europe both before and after the fall of Marxism, the diplomatic system made it possible both to unify divided Catholic jurisdictions in complex countries like Romania and to speak for the local Catholic community when the political situation made it impossible for the local bishops to do so freely. It is a widely held conviction that, because of its diplomatic system and its universal community of believers, the Holy See is often a much more reliable source of information than the high tech, well funded intelligence systems of many of the world's major powers.

### Changes

As noted above, the declaration touches neither on the concordat system nor on the diplomatic corps. Nevertheless, during years of Pope Paul VI's papacy up to August of 1978, more than 31 agreements regulating church and state were revised and signed, all in the light of the declaration, with many explicitly citing its text.[25] As of the year 2000, 115 of these agreements had been rewritten taking into account the teachings of the council.[26] According to the Holy See's secretary for external affairs, in these concordats "the Church seeks above all to have recognized or illustrated the freedom of religion inscribed on the human conscience and to advocate for the public expression of the faith."[27] With regard to changes in the diplomatic corps, during the pontificate of Pope John Paul II alone, the number of nuncios had risen from 85 to 173 as of the year 2000.[28]

The technical diplomatic and legal work entailed by all these changes does not disclose the depth or breadth of the spiritual renewal, pedagogical programming, or clerical formation involved. It does document the seriousness of the Catholic Church's determination to institutionalize its theology of the human person and role in society. This technical task lays the groundwork for the church to have freedom in collaborating on an equal footing with the state and with other entities in the society in a commitment to the common good.

Revision of the agreements plants the seeds for the flowering of dialogue with other persons of good will, of renewed ecumenical relations, and of shaping a new mode of evangelization. These new concordats, like the declaration, provide a necessary prelude to a new beginning which cannot be realized by legal technicalities, but which is impossible without them.

### The Reception of Religious Freedom in Modern States

Before providing theological arguments for the Catholic faithful, the council based the Catholic argument for religious freedom on juridical and natural law foundations and on appeals to governments and all people of good will. This means that exploring the impact of the declaration on civil society and secular governments is an integral element in the study of the reception of religious freedom. While this is not the place for a state-by-state evaluation of the incorporation of religious freedom into the constitutional structure of society and of its values into the culture and mores of the peoples of each nation, it is important to examine in a general way the progress and challenges of this new social teaching of the church. Cardinal Kasper, president of the Pontifical Council for Promoting Christian Unity, notes the reciprocal relationship between religion and society: "The state must, so to speak, have an interest in religion, because it is itself dependent on human and social values which it cannot itself guarantee. In return, the Christian churches have always recognized and respected the state as an independent authority. It is not a question of a state church or of a church state, but of a free church in a free state."[29]

Ironically, in places where the Catholic Church had been established or enjoyed exclusivist hegemony—for example, in countries such as Brazil, Chile, the Philippines, Poland, and the nations of Central America—incorporation of this human right seems to have happened more easily.[30]

However, in the ever-changing global political and cultural scene there are some who say that there are more restrictions placed on religious freedom among the nations of the world today than at the time of the promulgation of the declaration. This is attributable to a variety of reasons: postcolonial destabilization where the constraints of dominant Western powers have been removed; the dissolution of oppressive Marxism, allowing traditional religious rivalries or nostalgia for religious hegemonies to flourish; or the emergence of national security states where governments feel the need to repress their own people. Such restrictions show up as limitations in the allocation of visas and permits to build churches; discrimination in appointments to public office and in hiring for public school teaching; narrowing of access to public media; special funding for particular religions; and lack of freedom to preach and publish, as well as intergroup violence and outright persecution.

On the other hand, the common witness of the churches together, of Christians in collaboration with people of other religions and people of good will, the pressure brought to bear by the United Nations, and the desire of certain nations to enter the European Union have contributed to the positive development and monitoring of religious freedom around the world. The World Council of Churches and, since the council, the Catholic Church have supported the United Nations Universal Declaration on Human Rights, with its call for religious freedom. Christians and people of other religions have collaborated with and supported the United Nations High Commission for Human Rights and its Special Rapporteur on freedom of religion.[31] However, in 1966 the phrase "freedom to change one's religion" could not be used in a draft UN text because of objections from Saudi Arabia and Pakistan, and in 1981 the formula stipulating freedom "to adopt a religion" was also suppressed.[32] Only the United States and the Vatican (as a city-state and as the church) have made this UN text part of their policy.[33] So "there is still no consensus on the international level about what is really meant by religious freedom."[34]

The World Council of Churches regularly reports violations of religious freedom in its Ecumenical News International.[35] The Evangelical Protestant community monitors persecution of Christians around the world.[36] Some churches, such as the Seventh-day Adventists, have a special denominational commitment to religious freedom, a commitment that includes producing regular publications and sponsoring a Washington lobbying office.[37] Catholics work closely with other Christians in this important social witness of the church. It has been an important element of many ecumenical dialogues. Collaborating with Evangelicals, the church has found the declaration helpful in arguing the case for situating the right to religious freedom neither in mere tolerance nor in advocacy for Christians alone, but in the dignity of the human person. Unlike some groups, Catholics bring to their advocacy a commitment to equal rights for all believers and even nonbelievers, not just for the rights of the Christians or their churches. This has enabled them to make a very important contribution to the recently legislated International Religious Freedom Act of 1998[38] establishing the United States Commission on International Religious Freedom, a commission on which two Catholic bishops along with representatives of a wide variety of religions sit.[39]

The challenges in countries like China, Sudan, or Pakistan are continuing concerns for the churches' witness for religious freedom. The groups mentioned in the previous paragraph and other organizations provide both religious and secular advocacy for a world in which people are able to profess and celebrate their faith without government coercion, inhibition, or control.[40]

## PAPAL RECEPTION

Understanding of reception of the Declaration on Religious Freedom entails a review of the catechetical material over the last forty years to determine how education for freedom was carried out in various parts of the Catholic world. It also entails an analysis of the pastoral letters of bishops' conferences and individual bishops to understand how the formal teaching of the church embodied the teaching of the council. A survey of the papal World Day of Peace messages, and the statements of the nuncios to the United Nations are also important in documenting the reception of religious freedom and its advocacy. Such surveys go beyond the scope of this volume. However, we will treat one dimension of the teaching church: the positions taken by the three major postconciliar popes.

All the popes who experienced the council, including John XXIII, had also experienced the horrors of oppression and the suppression of religious freedom. Roncalli was papal ambassador in Turkey during the Nazi era and facilitated the rescue of Jewish children. He served in Paris during the era of reconstruction after the Second World War. Montini came to leadership during the dire days of Fascist leadership in Italy. Wojtyla grew up in the world of Nazi-occupied Poland and served as a priest and a bishop in a Communist country until being elected pope. Ratzinger was a youth during the Nazi regime and saw Eastern Europe, including a large part of Germany, fall under the sway of Marxism. All of them came to be champions of democracy, constitutional government, and religious freedom in their own ministry. None of them grew up in an American-style democracy, with its constitutional separation of church and state.

## Paul VI[41]

Pope Paul was elected pope by the emerging conciliar majority. He was a champion of religious freedom from the beginning of his pontificate. His inaugural encyclical promoted dialogue, including dialogue with modern society.[42]

During his pilgrimage to the Holy Land between the second and third sessions of the council he committed the church most forcefully to a position that had yet to be articulated by the council fathers: "Our only concern is to proclaim our faith. We ask nothing more than to embrace this religion, the new bond instituted between human beings and God through Jesus Christ, our Lord" (Bethlehem, January 6, 1964).[43]

We noted earlier the urgency of the vote in the last session of the council in October 1965, when Pope Paul VI and many of the council fathers wanted a clear sounding on religious freedom before the pope's speech at the United Nations. His word of peace is the note most often recalled from that historic moment, but the council vote and the pope's personal affirmation of Catholic commitment to religious freedom was also central to the event. Before the council ended he had already set in motion many of the plans for its implementation. Revisions of concordats and policies of the Holy See began in rapid succession with the return of the bishops to their countries.

The theology of human dignity continued to be a central theme in the pope's pontifical teaching. His emphasis focused more strongly on divine revelation than on the juridical and natural law elements of the declaration: "'True freedom in a human being is the greatest sign of the divine image.'.... Remove this deliberately free and morally binding relationship with God for human beings and one would take away the most cogent reason for human freedom" (words spoken during an audience, August 18, 1971).[44]

Even as the council was drawing to a close, Pope Paul VI began to feel the pressures for more freedom within the church, and for interpreting the declaration in light of enlightenment individualism. Both the conservative minority within the council and voices in the wider society and church were disposed to misinterpret the implications of religious freedom, so he felt the need to keep the position of the council clear:

> The Council has spoken of freedom, referring to it many times. Freedom is a wonderful word.... None of you will want to confuse freedom with ideological and religious indifference, nor with individualism set up as a system. (1969)

> The religious freedom considered by the Council—which is based on freedom of conscience—is valid for the personal decision in a response of faith, but is not absolutely valid when it comes to determining the content and extent of divine revelation. (1979)[45]

In his inaugural discourse opening the 1968 Eucharistic Congress in Bogotá, Pope Paul VI emphasized the dangers of secularization and of the misunderstanding of freedom.[46]

## Pope John Paul II[47]

In the long and productive quarter-century of John Paul II's papal ministry, he distinguished the Catholic Church for its witness to human rights and personal freedom. His encyclicals highlight the dignity of the human person. His social teaching is founded on this integral Christian humanism.

Natural law, interpreted personalistically—especially in the areas of human sexuality, bioethics, and international relations—are integral to the worldview he put forward for society on behalf of the church. His views on solidarity and the organic ordering of society contrast with the individualistic liberal understanding of the person. The experience and intellectual foundation that shaped his concept of the limits of the state came from a world that differed greatly from the world of liberal Western Enlightenment. Indeed, the Polish bishops at the council were very strong in support of the declaration on the one hand, but insistent that it be formulated in such a way that Marxists could not use it to impose a "public order" that would inhibit the freedom of the church. During the council's third session, Cardinal Wojtyla suggested two declarations: one as a theological statement directed at Christians, Catholics, and their ecumenical partners; and the other as a witness to the world of secular governments and persons of good will.[48]

In his contributions to the debates within the international community —especially in the United Nations, to which the Catholic Church is firmly committed—the pope attempted to change the focus from individual rights to spiritual and material values. For this pope, religious freedom was the basis for other freedoms:

> The civil and social right to religious freedom, inasmuch as it touches the most intimate sphere of the spirit, is a point of reference of the other fundamental rights and in some way becomes a measure of them...religious freedom in so far as it touches the most intimate sphere of the spirit, sustains and is as it were the raison d'etre of other freedoms. (World Day of Peace Message, 1988)[49]

The declaration emphasizes both the dignity of the human person and the person's religious rights as a result, even when that person is in error. It also highlights the importance of truth and the rights of the church to articulate its position in society, especially on behalf of the most vulnerable. In balancing these three dimensions, Pope John Paul II emphasized truth and the importance of the church publicly presenting its own understanding of society's responsibility, even when the rights of individuals would need to be curtailed.[50] This assertive, often confrontational style was particularly important in confronting hostile Communist regimes. However, "[i]n the less stark, more subtle task of shaping a moral consensus, under conditions of religious and cultural pluralism, he may come across as too sure, too impatient, and immune to compromise on forging a civil consensus for a diverse populace. The very characteristics that enhance his role in stark confrontation may be less usable after the battle for democracy has been won."[51]

In his encyclical *Evangelium Vitae*, the pope states the contrast between Christian freedom in solidarity and the subjective individualist ideology of freedom embodied in many contemporary cultures:

> At another level, the roots of the contradiction between the solemn affirmation of human rights and their tragic denial in practice lies in a notion of freedom which exalts the isolated individual in an absolute way, and gives no place to solidarity, to openness to others and service of them. While it is true that the taking of life not yet born or in its final stages is sometimes marked by a mistaken sense of altruism and human compassion, it cannot be denied that such a culture of death, taken as a whole, betrays a completely individualistic concept of freedom, which ends up by becoming the freedom of "the strong" against the weak who have no choice but to submit.[52]

During Pope John Paul's long papacy, several debates touching on religious freedom emerged in the Catholic Church. One of these had to do with Latin American liberation theologies. These theologies can be interpreted as attempts to apply the principles of the declaration in societies where the church has traditionally claimed hegemony because of its Iberian ecclesiastical history and its large number of adherents.

Liberation theologies articulate the church's solidarity with the poor, its witness to religious and social freedom stemming from below, rooted in the whole people of God, moving beyond the traditional clerically focused leadership. Some of these theological streams were more confrontational than others, some more reliant on radical economic and social analysis or individualist anthropologies. In the 1980s the Congregation of the Doctrine of the Faith issued two texts critical of liberation theology. Eventually, however, Pope John Paul in a statement to the Brazilian bishops affirmed the contribution of liberation theology.[53]

During this pontificate the Holy See also intervened in particular political discussions in the United States. In 1992 the Congregation of the Doctrine of the Faith issued directives to U.S. bishops advising them on how to deal with a variety of state legislative initiatives relating to civil rights for persons with a homosexual inclination. Some interpreted this as a Vatican move back from its affirmation of the dignity of the human person, in that the directives seemed to indicate that employment and housing discrimination was appropriate in this particular case.[54]

The affirmations of Pope John Paul II and the complexities involved in dealing with the variety of situations in which religious freedom is an issue give some indication of how this commitment of the Catholic Church will continue to be discussed, interpreted, and applied in the decades and centuries to come.

## Pope Benedict XVI

Some presume that this relatively new pontificate will be a mirror of the work that emerged from the Congregation of the Doctrine of the Faith in the last pontificate. However, looking at the theological corpus of Joseph Ratzinger's work, his engagement in the council, and the social and ecumenical context from which he emerged, it is clear that such a presumption cannot be a foregone conclusion. One will need to be very attentive to see how Catholic leadership evolves during the pontificate of Benedict XVI.[55]

As president of the Congregation of the Doctrine of the Faith and in the weeks leading up to the 2005 papal election, then Cardinal Ratzinger was a consistent champion of a Christocentric approach to truth in the face of contemporary relativism, a tendency he perceived as intruding into the Catholic Church. In this, one can expect continuity with the previous pontificate.

In his inaugural encyclical on charity, after recounting the teaching of his predecessors and reaffirming it, Benedict XVI outlines his understanding of the roles of state and church, making clear his firm commitment to the principles of the declaration:

> Love—*caritas*—will always prove necessary, even in the most just society. There is no ordering of the State so just that it can eliminate the need for a service of love.... The State which would provide everything, absorbing everything into itself, would ultimately become a mere bureaucracy incapable of guaranteeing the very thing which the suffering person—every person—needs: namely, loving personal concern. We do not

need a State which regulates and controls everything, but a State which, in accordance with the principle of subsidiarity, generously acknowledges and supports initiatives arising from the different social forces and combines spontaneity with closeness to those in need. The Church is one of those living forces: she is alive with the love enkindled by the Spirit of Christ.[56]

In his public statements the pope also continues his sharp critique of the individualist idea of freedom and the marginalization of religion in society, even in a country with as deep a Catholic history as Italy, which, he says:

> ... participates in the culture that predominates in the West... by which only what is experiential and calculable would be rationally valid, while on the level of praxis, individual freedom is held as a fundamental value to which all others must be subject. Therefore, God remains excluded from culture and from public life, and faith in him becomes more difficult, also because we live in a world that almost always appears to be of our making, in which... ethics is brought within the confines of relativism and utilitarianism with the exclusion of every moral principle that is valid and in itself binding.[57]

### ECUMENICAL RECEPTION[58]

The influence of the ecumenical observers at the council was substantive. The staff and a number of the experts and bishops involved with the Secretariat for Promoting Christian Unity (SPCU) had followed the World Council of Churches (WCC) work on religious freedom very carefully. Therefore, it is not a surprise that the declaration was well received by many of the observers and in the WCC.[59]

## Types of Reception

United Church of Christ theologian Douglas Horton noted at the time of the first ballot that this was "a vote with endless consequences," and

United Methodist theologian Albert Outler exclaimed that it was "the most important victory" of the council.[60]

In fact, there have been three distinct types of Christian responses to the declaration. We will examine each of these to illustrate the effect of reception of the council's teaching on the unity of Christians. The declaration's contribution to interreligious relations, especially with the Jewish and Muslim communities, is also important but will not be examined here.[61]

First of all, there were those who held to the old nativist agenda in the United States and some other parts of the world. This group was largely represented by Protestants who had a commitment to democratic institutions and constitutional government, with a "wall of separation" bias in interpreting the Bill of Rights. For persons and groups with this perspective, the Catholic Church cannot adapt to American-style democracy because of its authoritarian, hierarchical, and closed leadership style; its commitment to separatist institutions such as Catholic schools; and its support of totalitarian governments, as seen in Spain. On the eve of the council, in the context of John F. Kennedy's campaign for the presidency, these voices were very strong. Seminarians often read the anti-Catholic literature that was produced by this group, precisely to prepare an apologetic to counter it in their ministry with their people and in the wider arena of American society. Catholics needed to understand the arguments, not to caricature them. Ironically, this apologetic interest contributed to a Catholic receptivity to the changes articulated in the declaration.

Paul Blanshard was a principal spokesperson for the nativist position at the time of the council and its primary institutional expression was Protestants and Other Americans United for the Separation of Church and State.[62] People who held this position were not disposed to be convinced by the changes made by the council or by the modern ecumenical movement. However, their influence and constituency has been vastly diminished by the experience of the Catholic Church in postconciliar years, so that their voice is seldom heard, outside of a choir of civil liberties lobbies on a range of predictable issues.[63]

### World Council of Churches

Second, there were the voices of the observers mentioned above and the representatives of the WCC who followed the council closely and commented on it analytically and critically. Immediately after the council, while showing some reservations about Catholic ecclesiology, the WCC person responsible for the issue of religious liberty was able to say:

> Nevertheless we think that the opinion which the Roman Catholic Church has of itself is far less important than its clear proclamation of full religious liberty for all men and for all religious confessions throughout the world.... This Roman Catholic Declaration on Religious Liberty creates a completely new fact after many centuries of Christian disagreement.[64]

Lukas Vischer, on the staff of the Faith and Order Commission, was one of the clearest voices.[65] He linked the declaration with the ecumenical discussions initiated in the Oxford Conference (1937) and the statements of the two World Council Assemblies, Amsterdam (1948) and New Delhi (1961). He noted three fields of application: (1) in church state relations, (2) as a principle of order within the state and in international life, and (3) as a principle of relationships of the churches among themselves.

Vischer identified points at which the positions of the WCC and the declaration converge, points that are not resolved, and points to be developed. It is his view that there is a convergence with regard to the juridical, constitutional, and social witness aspect where, he would claim, they share exactly the same conclusion. The church-state position remains unresolved because of the variety of ecclesial situations among the variety of members of the WCC and the variety of state contexts in which Catholicism is found. However, this issue continues to remain pertinent for joint ecumenical consideration, especially in local governmental situations where Christians minister side by side.

It is the third area that holds out the greatest hope: developing ways in which common witness to religious freedom can enhance the unity of Christians. Vischer's 1966 challenge has borne rich fruit in the dialogues surveyed in the following section. Vischer recommends common statements of the churches together on religious freedom both as witnesses to agreement between them and in advocacy before civil society. It is not surprising, then, that the Joint Working Group between the

WCC and the Catholic Church has returned to this issue three times and produced reports in 1971, 1982, and 1995.[66]

### Evangelicals

In addition to anti-Catholic Protestant voices and ecumenical Orthodox and Protestant partners, there is a vast and growing body of Christians who were not present, formally, at the council and who have only gradually found dialogue with the Catholic Church possible. For many of these Evangelical, Holiness, Pentecostal, and Peace church Christians, old prejudices lingered and points of contact were few in the aftermath of the council, so that evaluations were individual, tentative, and varied.

However, as the church moved into the 1970s and beyond, dialogue and the healing of memories became possible and issues of religious freedom and proselytism began to be discussed as a prelude to common witness.

## The Ecumenical Dialogues

In this section we will briefly survey some of the dialogues that have resulted with a view to highlighting the fruitful contribution the declaration has made to mutual understanding, convergence, and the opening up of new issues for Catholic exploration.

### Baptist

Baptist origins in the United States and England are intimately tied to the affirmation of religious freedom, long before it was a general American Protestant hallmark. Roger Williams (1603–1684) was exiled from Massachusetts colony to Rhode Island for his advocacy of religious freedom and adult baptism. At the time of the newly emerging United States, the Virginia Baptists were strong advocates of separation of church and state in the new nation. Therefore, the newly affirmed position of the Catholic Church at the Second Vatican Council was central to discussions initiated between American and Southern Baptists in this country and the Baptist World Alliance internationally. The declaration opened doors that had been previously shut tight.

The narrow, juridical understanding set forth in the declaration, however, is not the core of the issue as Baptists have traditionally confessed it. For Catholics and many other Christians, there is a tendency to see the issue of freedom in terms of the relationship of the church to secular society, and not as integral to Christology and soteriology. For Baptists it is the doctrine of grace, baptism, and salvation which evokes the deepest commitment to human freedom.[67] A Baptist does not baptize an infant because the child cannot freely enter into the covenant of grace to which he or she is called by the gospel. Therefore, in dialogue with Baptists, sacramental and evangelical questions must be rooted in discussions of the role of human freedom in God's saving will.[68]

For Catholics, on the other hand, the question of proselytism and what is perceived as unfair evangelism has a priority in this dialogue. The Baptist World Alliance dialogue in particular spells out some of the characteristics of unworthy evangelism and, in a repentant tone for both Catholics and Baptists, renounces these violations of religious freedom in the past.

An affirmation of religious freedom renounces every kind of physical violence, moral compulsion, and psychological pressure as well as the use of situations of distress, weakness, or lack of education to bring about conversion. It also rejects the use of political, social, and economic pressure as a means of obtaining conversion or hindering others, especially minorities; the casting of unjust and uncharitable suspicion on other denominations; and comparison of the strengths and ideals of one community with the weaknesses and practices of another community. The dialogue goes on to say that the term "proselytism" is often used inaccurately to characterize the free witnessing to the gospel as our churches understand it, without violating the religious rights of others.[69]

Certainly the Baptist link of religious freedom to evangelism, God's saving work operating in the human person, and the connection between sacramental reception and the freedom of the individual, will lead to a deepening of the understanding of religious freedom for Catholics.

### Evangelical

In the late 1970s, the Vatican Pontifical Council for Promoting Christian Unity (PCPCU) began sponsoring conversations with a group of Conservative Evangelical Christians. These conversations resulted in production of a text entitled *Evangelical, Roman Catholic Dialogue on Mission* in 1983.[70] The group included some members from churches with whom the Catholic Church has had regular dialogue and others from churches or movements that are not even open to the ecumenical movement. The result was that the text had a very unofficial and ad hoc character. However, since this body of Christians has an important international presence, especially in mission and evangelism, these talks constitute a particularly important historic contribution. Much of the historic anti-Catholicism has yet to be overcome in these churches and movements, for example. Likewise, it is from them that the more aggressive evangelism, sometimes proselytism, is likely to originate.

The World Evangelical Fellowship (now Alliance) (WEA) developed a somewhat negative statement on Catholicism in reaction to what its members in Spain and Latin America perceived to be compromises with Catholics. This statement provided the impulse for more formal dialogue, this time sponsored by both the WEA and the PCPCU. Both the informal dialogue and the 2002 text that resulted, *Church, Evangelization, and the Bonds of Koinonia*, touch on issues related to religious freedom. The discussions of "Gospel and Culture" and of "Unworthy Witness" lay the foundation for discussions on religious freedom. Both Catholics and Evangelicals express past difficulties of insensitivity to the freedom and autonomy of cultures into which the gospel is introduced, and different approaches they have had to one another, some of which infringe on the respect due to the religious freedom of the other.

The 2002 text takes up the question of evangelization in the context of different understandings of the church and agreements on biblical *koinonia*. It relies heavily on earlier texts and takes the line on unworthy witness discussed in the section on the Baptist dialogue above.[71]

### Pentecostal

For more than thirty years there has been an important dialogue between Pentecostals and the Catholic Church. The 1997 text *Evangelization, Proselytism and Common Witness* takes up religious freedom in the context of common witness and outlines some of the characteristics of un-Christian behavior that both communities hope to avoid.[72] Some Pentecostal groups target Catholics, even interrupting services with bull horns and loud preaching. Catholic communities have been known to vandalize and even burn down Pentecostal churches in Latin America. This text is particularly important for the U.S. Hispanic community and Latin America where the Pentecostal and Catholic communities are the largest Christian groups.

### Anabaptist

It has taken many years for a formal dialogue to develop with Mennonites, though Catholics and peace churches have talked together for years on the Faith and Order Commission.[73] The Anabaptist churches—Mennonite and Brethren—confess religious freedom, separation of church and state, and the relationship of personal freedom to sacramental life as central to the apostolic faith proclaimed in the gospel.

The 2003 text *Called Together to Be Peacemakers* is a significant marker in the reception of declaration for three reasons. (1) It begins with a healing of memories, confessing Catholic failures in the past; Mennonites and other Anabaptists have been persecuted by Catholics and Protestants since their emergence in the sixteenth century. (2) It affirms together the passing of the Constantinian era, when the churches, including the Catholic Church, excluded the right to religious freedom of others. Religious freedom was a central tenet of the sixteenth-century Mennonite reformation. (3) Finally, it begins to explore the gospel imperative for peacemaking with a community that confesses the biblical imperative for Christians to remain free of state-sponsored violence of any sort.[74] Catholics and Mennonites still disagree on the Christian calling to pacifism, but they are united in the call of the churches to witness to a nonviolent approach to conflict.

While not claiming agreement on the separation of religion from society or the Christian from violence, this text does begin a process of dialogue with the community that pioneered religious freedom in the West, even to the point of martyrdom.

### Methodist, Disciples, and Reformed

Dialogues with Methodists, Disciples, and Reformed on the international level and in the United States have made important contributions to Catholic ecumenical development on religious freedom. In international dialogues, the changed situation created by the declaration is noted and affirmed as a basis for moving forward toward full communion.[75]

In the United States, Presbyterian and Methodist communities have had a long history of investment in public education, even when it was basically Protestant education. Both churches can affirm with Catholics the freedom of parents to provide confessional schools for their children, which is a serious departure from the older nativist positions. However, neither of these churches is able to agree with Catholics on the state's role in support of parents in their free choice of schools, if the school is not the state-run public school.

The Disciples-Catholic *Receiving and Handing on the Faith* has given the most explicit attention to the American development of freedom, the individual, and culture in the context of authority.[76] The Christian Church/Disciples of Christ is a denomination that was born on the American frontier in the early nineteenth century and is steeped in the spirit of independence and individualism characteristic of that era of American church history. Therefore this text makes an important contribution to clarifying differences on Christian freedom and exploring common ground.

These dialogues demonstrate the importance of common Christian encounter on religious freedom issues in each culture and state where the context, demography, and constitutional provisions are so different.

### Orthodox[77]

The dialogues with the two Orthodox families, the Byzantine or Eastern and the Oriental or non-Chalcedonian Orthodox, present very different sets of questions and carry quite different histories.

In dialogues with both communities, the question of religious freedom is central in two dimensions. First, the role of the Eastern Catholic Churches, at one time as vehicles of proselytism and the primary mode of Catholic approach to the East, must be resolved. Second, the rights of Eastern Catholic to exist without Latinizing pressures within Roman Catholicism or denial of their very right to exist at all by the Orthodox must be affirmed. There are proposals for resolution of both of these difficulties. At a more official level than in the other dialogues, the Roman Catholic Church has renounced any proselytizing intent relative to the Orthodox (for example, policy toward the Coptic Church of Egypt, 1977). In the more recent tensions with the Eastern Orthodox after the dissolution of the Soviet Union and Marxist regimes in Eastern Europe, the Catholic Church has given authoritative directives relative to pastoral activity in this area. This has been necessary because in the post-1989 enthusiasm to "reconvert" Russia and other Eastern European countries, sometimes insensitive Catholic groups moved in and used unfair practices to lure Orthodox from their Christian faith to Catholicism, contrary to Catholic policy and principles.

By 1993 the international dialogue had moved on to treat the question of Eastern Catholic churches in communion with Rome. The council had revised the traditional understanding of these churches as "bridges" toward Orthodoxy or even as means of "converting" Orthodox churches to Roman Catholicism. Likewise, Orthodoxy's contention that these churches had no right to exist and that the individual members of these churches should be coerced into either membership in the Latin church or one of the Orthodox churches, has given way to a respect for the freedom of these Christians. The dialogue produced a proposal on unitiatism, proselytism and religious freedom, a proposal that acknowledges both the rejection of uniatism by the Catholic Church as a means of proselytism on the one hand and the freedom of the Eastern Catholic churches with their heritages to exist in communion with Rome on the other.[78] This text was controversial among the Orthodox and some of the Eastern Catholic churches, and dialogue ceased until recently.[79]

Lutheran, Anglican, and other dialogues have also touched on the theme of religious freedom. These few notes indicate the significance of ecumenical dialogue in enhancing the Catholic commitment to the declaration and how important it is that the results of these dialogues be integrated into Catholic formation for freedom. Parallel study of interreligious contexts will demonstrate both the contribution of the declaration to this ministry and the remaining challenges faced by the church in deepening its contacts with the world's religious communities.

A forty-year span is a short time in the long history of Christianity. These examples of some of the initial stages of reception, interpretation, and implementation demonstrate the irreversible contribution of the Declaration on Religious Freedom to Christianity and to the culture of the world as it moves into the twenty-first century.

# PART IV
# The State of the Questions

At the time of the promulgation of the Declaration on Religious Freedom in 1965, the North Atlantic region in particular was in the midst of major social transitions: the civil rights struggle in the United States, student rebellions in Europe and North America, polarization over the Vietnam War, the sexual revolution, military dictatorships in Latin America, and postcolonial developments in Asia and Africa. The so-called consensus of the 1950s in the Catholic Church and in North Atlantic society was gone. Debates over human freedom, racial and political liberation, and individual autonomy characterized many of these developments.

Such events inevitably affected the interpretation of the very specific Catholic teaching on religious freedom and even the implications of the council as an ecclesial development. In the United States, reception of the council coincided with the dissolution of the Catholic immigrant subculture and the cohesiveness and credibility of the intuitional forms of Catholicism that went with it.

Furthermore, the declaration itself intentionally did not treat certain issues: human rights and freedom within the Catholic Church, the theological evaluation of pluralism, the concordat system and the roles of the nuncios/ambassadors of the Holy See, the theological evaluation of the development of doctrine and historical consciousness. All of these were important areas opened by the declaration but left to the theological community and the local churches to discern and develop.

### THE MURRAY LEGACY

It is sometimes difficult to distinguish between evaluating the declaration and evaluating the work of one of its drafters, John Courtney Murray. The legacy of Murray serves several capacities:

1. John Courtney Murray was an icon of the American Catholic theologian, faithful when silenced, applying classical Catholic theology to a new context, and bringing American reflection into the universal Catholic community.

2. He was a servant of the council, as an advisor. However, his role as contributor to and interpreter of the Declaration on Religious Freedom needs to be clearly distinguished from his own personal contribution to the theological enterprise. He realized that the text itself did not resolve many of the theological questions. His line of argument was quite different, for example, from the positions proposed by French, German, and Polish experts.[1]

3. Interpretation of Murray's work as a private theologian needs to take into account its limited context, as brilliant as his contribution was. His work in the years immediately preceding the council suffered the lack of debate that silencing imposed on it. He did not benefit from the normal critical interchange with theological colleagues and the opening up of new sources such debate produces. In the words of William Portier, Murray "is, in many ways, a 1950's period piece."[2] Further, according to Michael Baxter, "as the nation veers further from that supposed founding philosophy, it must be asked whether or not Murray's compatibility [of American democracy with Catholicism] thesis continues to be plausible."[3] Finally, Murray died before the 1968 publication of the encyclical *Humanae Vitae*, which focused Catholic discussions of natural law, historical consciousness, the magisterium, and development of doctrine in entirely new ways.[4]

Therefore, Murray's work is a particular contribution, but not the unique focus for exploring the postconciliar development of questions raised by the declaration.

### REMAINING QUESTIONS

Among the questions left intentionally open by the council were those of the role of freedom and human dignity within the procedures of the Catholic Church, the value of pluralism, the implementation of the principles of the declaration through the diplomatic channels of the church and various states, the ecumenical program it implies, the means of implementing its educational initiatives, and the approaches the church should use in presenting its social witness. We have noted the tension within the text itself between a juridical (*DH*, 2–8) and a theological base (*DH*, 9–14). We have also seen different emphases both in interpreting the declaration in the papal teaching and in the subsequent development of Catholic social ethics.[5]

The development of new concordats entails debates on the relationship between church and state, the appropriate rights of the church in the context of a social teaching that advocates religious freedom, and the implied ecclesiology of such accords.[6] Ecclesiologists will want to study the evolution of the role of bishops' conferences and the Holy See as these new arrangements mature. Further questions inevitably emerge about the dignity of the human person within the church, and the importance of recognizing the freedom of the person and the protection of his or her rights. Many of the procedures used, for example by the Congregation for the Doctrine of the Faith, do not measure up, in the minds of some, with the understanding of the human person articulated by the council.[7] However, this is a matter pertaining more to ecclesiology than to the intent of the declaration, and therefore will not be treated here.

Finally, there are a host of social policy questions raised in applying the values of religious freedom to the church's role in society and history. For example, the insistence of the late Holy Father on adding recognition of the Christian roots of Europe to the constitution of the European Union has raised for some the question of how open church leadership is to allowing European society to develop independently of the historic shadow of Christendom.[8]

In this chapter we will treat the question of pluralism, especially (1) religious pluralism as it has developed since the council and (2) the issue of the universal character of the human right to religious freedom.

We will also address three educational issues: (1) parental rights, (2) educating for freedom, and (3) the pedagogical implications of the declaration's understanding of human dignity.


## Pluralism

### *Plurality of Religions*

For many Catholic thinkers, including Murray, pluralism of religions and the presence of unbelief in society is not a positive value, and not willed by God. The means for moving beyond pluralism for these thinkers varies, but restriction of the rights of the person is no longer an option for those affirming the Catholic understanding of religious freedom.

In Latin American society, for example, large segments of the Catholic population consider the presence of fellow Christians, unbelievers, and members of other religions as a "problem," rather than viewing these non-Catholics as fellow citizens or even dialogue partners in an ecumenical and interreligious spirit. Sometimes the language of "sect" is used to disparage groups in society that are not Catholic. This kind of language was common in pre–Vatican II magisterial documents and in Catholic social teaching.[9] Societies may have a nominal commitment to religious freedom, but they can also restrain the pluralism which it inevitably permits.

The declaration "unintentionally clarified the presuppositions for the dialogue among the religions of the modern world."[10] In facing the global encounter of the world religions, this issue of evaluating pluralism is quite pressing. It has also given rise to important debates and highlighted inconsistencies at the highest levels in the church.

On the one hand, Pope John Paul II in his 1990 encyclical *Redemptoris Missio* emphasizes the importance of spreading the gospel while taking account of the dignity of the human person. He cites the declaration explicitly. He then goes on to speak of elements of the Spirit in other religions.[11] This implies, without a hint of relativism or indifferentism, that pluralism is a given, providential reality disclosing something of God's will for the human community.

On the other hand, in attempting to reinforce the centrality and uniqueness of Christ, which is also a theme of the encyclical, the

Congregation for the Doctrine of the Faith a decade later, in 2000, issued *Dominus Iesus*, in which it declared other religions "*objectively speaking...gravely deficient.*"[12] This text is richly textured and carefully developed, and it also affirms elements of the Spirit in other religions quoting the 1990 encyclical. However, this summary judgment prior to dialogue and without verification of the assertion shows a different, negative emphasis in part of the church in approaching other religions in a pluralist society.

We can distinguish between (1) pluralism as a theological affirmation of the equal validity of a variety of truth claims, religious and otherwise and (2) pluralism as a given fact, grounded in the dignity and freedom of persons, providing an environment in which Christianity can flourish and proclaim its message freely through dialogue and evangelization.[13] Certainly the latter is now an option in Catholic theology. Even if one judges pluralism to be an evil in society, God is capable of bringing good out of this evil situation.

A second area of the Church's priority for dealing with pluralism and the world's religions is its dialogue with Islam. There are many Muslims with whom dialogue is possible, who read passages in the Koran disposed to tolerance and human dignity for all, and who understand historical development.[14] In the United Nations, for example, Muslims and Catholics have shown an ability to advocate together on important issues relating to the values of family and human life. However, on the global scene and in societies where Islam predominates, there is much to be done to find common ground for mutual understanding and possibilities for religious freedom or constitutional government.

In local contexts around the globe, dialogue with Muslims and members of other religions has developed well. Personal relationships and mutual engagement in promoting the common good are essential if a way to religious freedom is to be found. Such approaches to other religions are best pursued by Christians together ecumenically.

Whether one regrets pluralism as unfortunate or recognizes it as providential, it is a fact of life and of the global environment in which Catholicism witnesses today. "Our increasingly globalized world has at the same time become a pluralized world in which there are fewer and fewer monolithic cultures. This situation offers opportunities but is also fraught with dangers. Many people are fearful of a 'clash of cultures and religions.' We as Christians must resist this lethal danger with all our might. For as Christians we have respect for every religious conviction."[15]

## The Universality of Human Rights

In discussing the implementation of religious freedom in dialogue with civil society, we have noted that in the United Nations certain formulations have had to move away from the affirmations of the 1981 Universal Declaration, while not allowing this declaration itself to be rescinded. To some extent this has been due to the fact that several Muslim nations have objected to language allowing a change of religion as a right guaranteed by international consensus.

A number of other factors also have challenged the universal applicability of human rights in general and religious freedom in particular. One is the global economic force, largely emanating from the West, which is seen as a threat to non-Western societies, cultures, and religions.[16] Another is the resurgence of religious traditions, even Catholic communities, from the oppressive Communist regimes of Eastern Europe where the only experiences of society were of pre-Marxist Christian hegemony or Marxist repression. In some of these societies, for example in Russia or Poland, defense against new religious initiatives is seen as essential for the restoration of the churches and sometimes the preservation of national cultural identities.[17]

The major dialogue partners in the challenge to the universality of religious freedom as articulated in the council's declaration and those of the United Nations and the WCC are many of the Islamic nations. This is not the place to lay out the details of this conversation. However, the approach of the Catholic Church to these unresolved issues is dialogue built on truth and mutual respect.[18]

## Education

There are several elements of the declaration that touch on the education of Catholics. Only three will be explored here, all in the context of the Americas: the rights of parents, educating for responsible freedom, and pedagogy for evangelizing free Christians. A similar exploration of the issue in other contexts would help shed light on the open questions in other societies.

### Parents' Rights

The declaration does not spell out the state's responsibilities for Catholic schooling. It does, however, make very clear parents' rights to the religious instruction of their children. In the years following the council, two emphases have developed within United States Catholicism. It is obvious that these developments and debates take on a different character in countries where states exclude Catholic schools, where states support Catholic religion taught in public schools, or where church schools survive in Islamist or other difficult situations.[19]

On the one hand, the U.S. Conference of Catholics Bishops and the National Catholic Education Association have been strong supporters of the right of Catholic parents to educate their children in Catholic schools, and to benefit from government resources in pursuing this right.

On the other hand, the vast majority of American Catholic parents do not exercise their responsibility for the religious education of their children through Catholic schools. Therefore, in empowering the majority of Catholic parents to exercise their right and duty for the religious education of their children, the church finds other avenues for Catholic education. Some bishops invest more of their energy and the resources of their people in the adult faith formation of parents and in the training of Catholic educators for their parishes. They feel this will better enable the majority of Catholic parents to exercise their right and responsibility and provide parish communities with teachers who can help parents in this task.

The debate on the best strategy for enabling Catholic parents to provide for the religious education of their children is a difficult one as parishes determine how to use their dwindling resources, as dioceses attempt to meet the growing needs of all of the people, and as trained religious educators become more difficult to come by.[20] This debate is particularly challenging as a large sector of young people no longer take part in any Catholic educational program.

### Educating for Freedom[21]

The declaration is quite explicit on the importance of forming Catholic Christians to live in a society in which the church advocates the rights of all to their own conscientious convictions, but where Catholic truth claims and fidelity can no longer rely on external state or cultural support. During the third session of the council, Brazil's Cardinal Rossi praised the schema in the name of eighty-two Brazilian bishops. He also called for a section "that would explain the pastoral consequences of the assertion of the right of religious freedom, that is, what it meant for the education of the faithful."[22]

Yves Congar was sympathetic to the minority concerns during the council, and he recognized the danger of indifferentism as a possible result of the renunciation of Catholic social dominance. The Catholic Church has always been concerned that the truth claims to its uniqueness not be compromised by "indifference." Some Christian bodies, especially in the United States, have developed a "denominational" understanding of their churches, one which sees all the churches as equal under God. At the time of the council Congar talked about the specter of subjectivism and the pastoral responsibility of the church to fight false presuppositions in the new context created by the declaration.[23] During the last session of the council, as the vote on the Declaration on Religious Freedom drew near, Latin American bishops realized that a revolution would be necessary to prepare societies with a dominant Catholic population and centuries of isolation from other believers to live their faith responsibly in the context of religious freedom.

While the United States did not emerge from a state church situation, where the faith was the law of the land, certain sectors were just emerging from urban ethnic enclaves where the presence of the church, Catholic popular piety, and a Catholic presence in civil and political life were pervasive. As the immigrant church moved into the tolerant, pluralistic suburbs, a certain erosion of a type of Catholic culture was inevitable. Religious illiteracy, indifferentism, and neglect of Catholic practice have been on the rise in recent decades.[24] The Latin American church and immigrants who arrive in the United States are often unequipped to deal with the religious freedom and pluralism in which they find themselves. Because of the lack of education for freedom, for dialogue and for ecumenical and interreligious collaboration, many Catholics have moved into other churches and religious traditions.[25] In a pluralistic environment one must learn to resist unwanted evangelism and even proselytism in a free market of ideas.

In the postconciliar period, significant sectors of the Latin American Catholic Church began new initiatives to provide for needed catechetical renewal, pioneering family catechesis, Christian base communities, and lay ministry training.[26] However, these initiatives have not been uniform. The episcopal conferences in the variety of Latin American countries do not have the same mind as to the reality of pluralism, how to deal with it, and the priority to be given to lay Catholic education and catechesis.[27] There are still many sectors that wish to resist the inevitable pluralism of the globalized world and rely on popular piety as an adequate safeguard for Catholic identity in a culture presumed to be pervasively Catholic. Latin American reception of the council has been more effective in implementing its social teaching than in inculcating its teaching on religious freedom and ecumenism or in finding means of educating for pluralism.

In most sectors of the continent, Protestant theologians seem to give more attention to religious freedom than do Catholic scholars and bishops.[28] "It would appear that the Catholic Church is somewhat more inclined to accept political and ideological pluralism than religious."[29] A country like Colombia faces a major challenge when, for example, the 1991 constitution no longer requires state-supported Catholic religion classes in all public schools.

The church's concern for truth is implicit in much of the critique of liberal democracy in the papacies of Popes John Paul II and Benedict XVI and their concerns about pluralism in Latin America. In many instances, the church insists that its moral teaching become enacted in civil law. For those with different doctrines of Christian marriage and other ethical issues, or for non-Christians, this insistence on the church's role in pressing governments to implement its ethical values and morality appears to be a violation of religious freedom and the neutrality of the state.

Rather than attempting to protect Catholics in cultural isolation or blaming others who provide a welcoming gospel environment, educating for religious freedom challenges Catholics to develop a robust, self-confident, well-informed Catholic identity. Free believers need to know and be invited to affirm the truth claims of Catholicism and to be able to effectively enter into dialogue with ecumenical fellow Christians, assertive non-ecumenical Christians, and members of other religious traditions. In a pluralistic society that affirms religious freedom, comfortable reliance on popular Catholic piety will no longer suffice.

## Pedagogical Implications

In addition to affirming the rights of parents and calling for education for freedom in a pluralist society, the declaration also articulates principles about the human person that have implications for sharing the gospel. In the third session of the council, Melkite patriarch of Antioch Maximos IV made clear the need for a new approach to Catholic education for maturity and freedom.[30] In traditionally homogenous societies it was often presumed, rightly or wrongly, that Catholics coming to Catholic schools or requesting marriage or the baptism of their children were committed evangelized Christians. Even before the council, European Catholic educators were raising issues with the hierarchy's "endless refutations of modernity," as undermining the credibility of the faith among Catholics.[31] In the fourth session of the council, newly created Belgian Cardinal Cardijn reiterated the pedagogical and educational value of the declaration from his experience of specialized Catholic Action and engagement in lay formation.[32]

Today in America, attendance at a Catholic school by a baptized Catholic, a meeting to request a Catholic wedding, or the presentation of a child for baptism may be an occasion for primary evangelization. Even in cases of involvement with Catholic institutions or sacraments, the content and implications of the faith and the relationship of commitment to the truth cannot be presumed.

The declaration talks about taking account of human dignity in presenting the gospel to the person. This means that educational programs, textbooks, and teacher preparation need to be geared as much to touching hearts as to conveying information. Simple Christian data can be provided in secular religious studies classes, with no implications about free response, personal commitment, or truth claims. However, the transmission of the Christian faith in this environment of the free response of the Catholic has also stimulated wide-ranging debates on how Catholicism is to be presented in textbook, classroom, and parish.

Both the content of the tradition and the students' experience are important elements in Catholic education. Some emphasize the content, others the experience, but all are seeking a proper balance. It is the emphasis in that balance that causes the debates. There is also debate about whether it is best to use the common language of faith uniformly or language more suited to the recipient of catechesis.

The bishops at Vatican II, unlike those at Trent and Vatican I, decided not to produce a catechism. The Catechism of the Council of Trent had remained a standard resource for centuries. While another universal catechism was considered at Vatican I, it was never produced. After the Second Vatican Council a *General Catechetical Directory* was issued, with the understanding that it would be adapted to local needs as National Catechetical Directories. Originally Vatican II had opted for unity but not uniformity in the language, style, and method of catechesis. A National Directory was published in the United States in 1977 and in other parts of the world throughout the decade of the 1970s. These directories took account of psychological and cultural factors in approaches to Christian pedagogy.

The Roman Synod of Bishops in 1985 decided to produce the *Catechism of the Catholic Church* to ensure international and uniform distillation of the content of the faith. This catechism was completed in 1994.[33] The U.S. Conference of Catholic Bishops set up an ad hoc committee to supervise promotion for production of the *Catechism* in this country by overseeing published materials, ensuring their conformity to its content.

Some experienced religious educators and publishers, while adhering to the content of the *Catechism*, feel strongly that there is a need for a pedagogical approach that focuses less on the formulations of Catholic doctrine and more on the free receptivity of the students to the message, and that uses language adapted to the age and culture of the students.

Inherent in this debate are different evaluations of the culture from which young people come. Is Catholic doctrine a challenge to culture, correcting it? Or does the faith build on culture, affirming its goodness where possible and improving on it where deficient? Does one approach the student as a free individual responding to the gospel, or as a convinced believer who must be indoctrinated with important elements of its orthodox formulation? The bishops' committee can easily slip from the affirmation of Catholic orthodoxy to insisting on specific wording of doctrinal formulations, neglecting the Catholic understanding of the hierarchy of truths or espousing a propositional theory of divine revelation. Some educators can easily slip from an experiential approach to catechesis to an experiential theory of divine revelation.

Some bishops suspect that this experiential, student-centered approach can embody the relativism, subjectivism, and individualism which the declaration explicitly avoids in its definition of freedom.[34]

It is not clear how American Catholics will resolve this debate. However, it seems more important for the church to find competent educators fully sensitive to the freedom and dignity of the individual being evangelized and catechized, with a clear knowledge of the faith of the church and its truth claims. Books, theological theories, and conflict will not invite free persons to the richness of the Catholic tradition.

Questions having to do with the evaluation of freedom within the Catholic Church, how to live in a pluralistic global society, the appropriate strategies of inculturation in various societies worldwide, and the appropriate educational priorities for a church committed to freedom in society and unity among all Christians will continue to deepen and expand.

As the pilgrim people of God move toward their final goal, new challenges to the ordering of society and the freedom of the Christian will continue to call for development, renewal, reformulation, and return to the sources. In all of these developments and debates, the Holy Spirit provides confidence to a faithful people in their free and creative response to Christ's call.

# NOTES

## THE DOCUMENT

1. For an overview and bibliography of the historical, canonical, and legal issues in church and state, see *The New Catholic Encyclopedia*, vol. 3, ed. Berard Marthaler (Washington, DC: The Catholic University of America Press, 2003), 630–69.

2. Joseph Ratzinger, *Theological Highlights of Vatican II* (New York: Paulist Press, 1966), 95.

3. See Andrea Riccardi, *Ils Sont Morts pour leur Foi: La Persécution des Chrétiens au XXe Siècle* (Condé-sur-l'Escaut: Éditions Plon/Mame, 2002).

4. Max Stackhouse, "Church and State," in *Dictionary of the Ecumenical Movement*, ed. Nicholas Lossky et al. (Grand Rapids, MI: William B. Eerdmans, 2003), 186–90.

5. Bryan Hehir, "Catholicism and Democracy: Conflict, Change, and Collaboration," in *Change in Official Catholic Moral Teaching*, ed. Charles Curran (New York/Mahwah, NJ: Paulist Press, 2003), 21.

6. Walter Kasper, "Religious Freedom in Ecumenical Perspective," in *Building Bridges of Faith and Freedom*, ed. John Graz (Silver Spring, MD: General Conference of the Seventh-day Adventists, 2002), 27.

7. See John Turner, "Church and State," in Lossky et al., *Dictionary of the Ecumenical Movement*, 167–69. For analysis of "establishment" in the Irish constitution, see Enda McDonagh, *Freedom or Tolerance? The Declaration on Religious Freedom of Vatican Council II* (Albany, Magi Books Inc., 1967).

8. English-language theologians at the council preferred the language of "religious freedom" to "religious liberty," which in the minds of many evoked the secularist ideology of the French Revolution and laicist "liberty" laws. See Jérôme Hamer in *La Libertè Religieuse*, ed. Yves Congar, Jérôme Hamer, et al. (Paris: Les Éditions du Cerf, 1967), 103–5.

9. See <http://www.papalencyclicals.net/Pius09/p9syll.htm>.

10. Quoted by John Tracy Ellis in James Hennesey, *The First Council of the Vatican: The American Experience* (New York: Herder and Herder, 1963), 9.

11. Hennesey, *The First Council of the Vatican*, 329.

12. Quoted by John Tracy Ellis in Hennesey, *The First Council of the Vatican*, 12.

13. Philip Jenkins, *The Next Christendom: The Coming of Global Christianity* (Oxford: Oxford University Press, 2002), 142–62.

14. See <http://www.un.org/Overview/rights.html>.

15. Fredrick Pike, *The Conflict Between Church and State in Latin America* (New York: Alfred A. Knopf, 1964), 4.

16. See Mary Ann Glendon, *A World Made New: Eleanor Roosevelt and the Universal Declaration of Human Rights* (New York: Random House, 2001), 15; and John Nurser, *For All Peoples and All Nations: The Ecumenical Church and Human Rights* (Washington, DC: Georgetown University Press, 2005).

17. "The Declaration and the World Council of Churches," Appendix IV in Thomas Stransky, *Declaration on Religious Freedom of Vatican Council II* (New York: Paulist Press, 1967), 149–73.

18. For an explanation of this organization, see Thomas Stransky, "Catholic Conference for Ecumenical Questions," in Lossky et al., *Dictionary of the Ecumenical Movement*, 151.

19. John T. McGreevy, *Catholicism and American Freedom* (New York: W. W. Norton & Co., 2003), 193–208. See also Giuseppe Alberigo and Joseph A. Komonchak, eds., *History of Vatican II, Volume 4: Church as Communion, Third Period and Intersession, September 1964–September 1965* (Maryknoll, NY: Orbis Books/Leuven, Belgium: Peeters, 2003), 538. In his contribution to the United Nations discussions on the Universal Declaration on Human Rights, Maritain also counseled for a practical rather than a theoretical approach where agreement across cultures could be implicit without agreement on a common view of human nature or the world. Glendon, *A World Made New*, 77.

20. Josep Saranyana Closa, *Teología en América Latína* (Madrid: Iberoamericana, 2002), 26, 30.

21. Ibid., 111.

22. T. Stranksy, "Paul VI and the Delegated Observers/Guests to Vatican Council II," in *Paulo VI & Ecumenismo* (Brescia: Istituto Paolo VI, 2001), 127. "Blanshard conveyed fear of a total take-over of the nation by Catholics should they become a dominant plurality—part of the Vatican's orchestrated master plan to dominate the world, controlled by the Catholic bishops.... 'Watch out for the Pope's man' was a public slogan of many Protestant opponents of John F. Kennedy during his 1960 presidential campaign."

23. Vincent Yzermans, ed., *American Participation in the Second Vatican Council* (New York: Sheed and Ward, 1967), 630, 651.

24. There are two major commentaries written by drafters of the declaration: Pietro Pavan, "The Declaration on Religious Liberty," in *Commentary on the Documents of Vatican II*, vol. 4, ed. Herbert Vorgrimler (New York: Herder and Herder, 1968), 48–62, and Stransky, *Declaration*, which includes the reports of Bishop de Smedt and of the Secretariat, the commentary of John Courtney Murray, and the two WCC Declarations that were substantial contributions to the project. The most recent and detailed English account of the council and debates, utilizing available journals as well as published *Acta*, is Giuseppe Alberigo and Joseph A. Komonchak, eds., *History of Vatican II*, 5 vols. (Maryknoll, NY: Orbis Books/Leuven, Belgium: Peeters, 1995, 1997, 2000, 2003, 2006).

25. Stransky, *Declaration*, 17–18.

26. See <http://www.vatican.va/holy_father/john_xxiii/encyclicals/documents/hf_j-xxiii_enc_11041963_pacem_en.html> # 14; see also #158.

27. See <http://www.vatican.va/holy_father/paul_vi/speeches/1963/documents/hf_p-vi_spe_19630929_concilio-vaticano-ii_it.html>.

28. Although the American hierarchy was very committed to the issue of religious freedom, its reticence in ecclesiastical maneuvering is disclosed in a private interchange between two Chicagoans intimately involved in the conciliar processes: "Honestly I [don't] think that there is any power on earth that can make [Paul VI] again face up to the necessity for pushing chapters IV and V [of the draft on ecumenism, including religious freedom (IV) and on the Jews (V)], except the American bishops, and frankly George I [don't] think that they are able; they are congenitally (as bishops) unable to twist the papal elbow. And this is what is required." Private letter of Bishop Earnest Primeau of Manchester, NH, to Msgr. George Higgins, January 20, 1964, quoted in Silvia Scatena, *La fatica della libertà: L'elaborazione della dichiarazione "Dignitatis Humanae"* (Bologna: Il Mulino, 2002), 75n163.

29. Stransky, *Declaration*, Appendix I, 93–108.

30. See <http://www.vatican.va/holy_father/paul_vi/encyclicals/documents/hf_p-vi_enc_06081964_ecclesiam_en.html> # 42.

31. Stransky, *Declaration*, Appendix II, 109–30.

32. Ratzinger, *Theological Highlights*, 97.

33. Kenneth Himes in *The Catholic Church and the Nation-State*, ed. Paul Manuel, Lawrence Reardon, and Clyde Wilcox (Washington, DC: Georgetown University Press, 2006), 25.

34. Hamer, *La Libertè Religieuse*, 94–95.

35. Ratzinger, *Theological Highlights*, 103.

36. Alberigo and Komonchak, *History*, vol. 4, 385–406.

37. Yzermans, *American Participation*, 621.

38. See <http://www.vatican.va/holy_father/paul_vi/speeches/1965/documents/hf_p-vi_spe_19651004_united-nations_fr.html> # 6.

39. See John Courtney Murray, Appendix III in Stransky, *Declaration*, 135–48.

40. J. Grootaers, *Acts et Acterus à Vatican II* (Leuven: Leuven University Press, 1998), 332–36.

41. Stransky, *Declaration*, Appendix I, 99–108.

42. See, for example, "Religious Freedom, Democracy, and Human Rights," in Curran, *Change in Official Catholic Moral Teaching*, 64.

43. Curran, *Change in Official Catholic Moral Teaching*, 14.

MAJOR POINTS

1. See Norman Tanner, *The Church and the World: Gaudium et Spes, Inter Mirifica* (New York/Mahwah, NJ: Paulist Press, 2005), 38–49.

2. "For many Americans, the difference between these ideals [of separation of church and state, and the constitutional freedom from religious establishment] has become difficult to discern. The difference, however, was of profound importance to earlier Americans." Philip Hamburger, *Separation of Church and State* (Cambridge: Harvard University Press, 2002), 480–81.

3. The text is from the Vatican website, with minor modifications: <http://www.vatican.va/archive/hist_councils/ii_vatican_council/documents/vat-ii _decl_19651207_dignitatis-humanae_en.html>.

4. See "The Method and Principles of the Declaration," Appendix II in Thomas Stransky, *Declaration on Religious Freedom of Vatican Council II* (New York: Paulist Press, 1967).

5. Stransky, *Declaration*, Appendix I, Bishop Emil de Smedt, 100–108; Appendix III, John Courtney Murray, 141–48.

6. Joseph Ratzinger, *Theological Highlights of Vatican II* (New York: Paulist Press, 1966), 147.

7. "This paragraph is the key declaration: the *nature* of religious freedom (the right of the person); the *object* (immunity from coercion); the *basis* (dignity of the human person); the *subject* (the individual and the religious group)." Stransky, *Declaration*, 67n6.

8. Stransky, *Declaration*, Appendix II, 128–30.

9. J. Grootaers, *Acts et Acterus à Vatican II* (Leuven: Leuven University Press, 1998), 80.

## IMPLEMENTATION

1. James Burtchaell, "Religious Freedom," in *Modern Catholicism: Vatican II and After*, ed. Adrian Hastings (Oxford: Oxford University Press, 1991), 118.

2. See Ormond Rush, *Still Interpreting Vatican II: Some Hermeneutical Principles* (New York/Mahwah, NJ: Paulist Press, 2004).

3. Pietro Pavan, "Ecumenism and Vatican II's Declaration on Religious Freedom," in *Religious Freedom: 1965–1975*, ed. Walter Burghardt (New York: Paulist Press, 1977), 29.

4. D. Menozzi, "Opposition to the Council (1966–1984)," in *The Reception of Vatican II*, ed. G. Alberigo, J-P. Jossua, and J. Komonchak (Washington, DC: The Catholic University of America Press, 1987), 325–48. See also Yves Congar, *Challenge to the Church: The Case of Archbishop Lefebvre* (Huntington: Our Sunday Visitor, 1977) and Michael W. Cuneo, *The Smoke of Satan: Conservative and Traditionalist Dissent in Contemporary American Catholicism* (New York: Oxford University Press, 1997).

5. See, for example, Vladimir Feodorov, "Religious Freedom in Russia Today," *Ecumenical Review* 50, no. 4 (1998): 449–59. Paul Mojzes, *Religious Liberty in Eastern Europe and the USSR: Before and After the Great Transformation* (Boulder: Eastern European Monographs, 1992).

6. See Georg Evers, *Human Rights, Religious Freedom and the Catholic Church in the People's Republic of China* (London: Cultural Exchange with China, 2004); see also U.S. Catholic China Bureau, <www.usccb.net>.

7. See <http://www.mfa.gov.il/MFA/MFAArchive/1990_1999/1993/12/Fundamental+Agreement+-+Israel-Holy+See.htm>; "Fundamental Agreement between the Holy See and the State of Israel," in José T. Martín de Agar, *Raccolta di concordati 1950–1999* (Rome: Libreria Editrice Vaticana, 2000), 516–52; see also <http://members.ozemail.com.au/~adamgosp/popecov2.htm>; "Basic Agreement between the Holy See and the Palestine Liberation Organization," in Martín de Agar, *Raccolta*; and *I Concordati del 2000* (Rome: Libreria Editrice Vaticana, 2001), 53–56. See Rolando Minnerath, "Church/State Relations: Religious Freedom and 'Proselytism,'" *Ecumenical Review* 50, no. 4, (1998): 438–40.

8. For other contexts, see "Religious Freedom and Proselytism," *Ecumenical Review* 50, no. 4, (1998): 417–71, and Paul Manuel, Lawrence Reardon, and Clyde Wilcox, eds., *The Catholic Church and the Nation-State* (Washington, DC: Georgetown University Press, 2006).

9. See Conferencia Episcopal Española, *Los Acuerdos Entre la Santa Sede y el Estado Español* (Madrid: Editorial Edice, 2001); Olegario González de

Cardedal, *La Iglesia en España* (Madrid: Promoción Popular Cristiana, 2000); Paul Manuel and Margaret Mott, "The Latin European Church," in Manuel, Reardon, and Wilcox, *The Catholic Church and the Nation-State*, 53–68.

10. See Giuseppe Alberigo and Joseph A. Komonchak, eds. *History of Vatican II, Volume 2: Formation of the Council's Identity, First Period and Intersession, October 1962–September 1963* (Maryknoll, NY: Orbis Books/Leuven, Belgium: Peeters, 1997), 193; Giuseppe Alberigo and Joseph A. Komonchak, eds., *History of Vatican II, Volume 4: Church as Communion, Third Period and Intersession, September 1964–September 1965* (Maryknoll, NY: Orbis Books/Leuven, Belgium: Peeters, 2003), 110; see also Manuel, Reardon, and Wilcox, *The Catholic Church and the Nation-State*, 60–62.

11. T. Jiménez-Urresti, p. 232, quoted in Gustavo Gutiérrez, *Information Documentation on the Conciliar Church* (August 17, 1966), Doss. 66-13, 4.

12. Christopher Kauffman, "American Reactions to *Dignitatis Humanae*," in *Religious Liberty: Paul VI and Dignitatis Humanae*, ed. John Ford (Brecia: Pubblicazioni dell'Istituto Paolo VI, 1995), 71–88; Joseph Chinnici, "*Dignitatis Humanae Personae*: Surveying the Landscape for Its Reception in the United States," *U.S. Catholic Historian*, "*Dignitatis Humanae*, The Declaration of Religious Liberty, on its Fortieth Anniversary," 24, no. 1 (Winter 2006): 63–82.

13. Gerald Fogarty, "*Dignitatis Humanae Personae* and the American Experience," in *Vatican II and Its Legacy*, ed. M. Lamberigts and L. Kenis (Leuven: Leuven University Press, 2002), 285. This author does go on to say, however, that there was a widespread difference of understanding of the concept among United States Catholics.

14. Joseph Komonchak, "*Dignitatis Humanae*: American Echoes," presented at a conference in Brecia, Italy, sponsored by the Istituto Paolo VI, September 2004, "*Dignitatis Humane*: la libertà religiosa in Paolo VI." See also Kenneth L. Grasso and Robert P. Hunt, eds., *Dignitatis Humanae: Contemporary Reflections on Vatican II's Declaration on Religious Liberty* (Lanham: Rowman & Littlefield Publishers, 2006).

15. Richard Regan, "John Courtney Murray: The American Bishops and the *Declaration on Religious Liberty*," in Ford, *Religious Liberty*, 51–66.

16. Robert Kennedy, "Contributions of *Dignitatis Humanae* to Church-State Relations," in Ford, *Religious Liberty*, 93–113.

17. For example, Diana Henriques, "Religion Trumps Regulation as Legal Exemptions Grow," *New York Times* (October 8, 2006): 1, 22–23. Diana Henriques and Andrew Lehren, "Religion for Captive Audience, with Taxpayers Footing the Bill," *New York Times* (December 10, 2006): 1, 32–34.

18. Josep Saranyana Closa, *Teología en America Latina* (Madrid: Iberoamericana, 2002).

19. Marcos McGrath, CSC, *Cómo Vi y Vivi: El Concilio y el Postconcilio* (Bogotá: CELAM, 2000).

20. Giuseppe Alberigo and Joseph A. Komonchak, eds. *History of Vatican II, Volume 5: The Council and the Transition, The Fourth Period and the End of the Council, September 1965–December 1965* (Maryknoll, NY: Orbis Books/Leuven, Belgium: Peeters, 2006), 558.

21. Gutiérrez, *Information Documentation*, 10. This presentation, given at a theological congress in Rome, also analyzes the Spanish and World Council of Churches' responses to and interpretations of the declaration.

22. See Carlos Corral Salvador, *Acuerdos España-Santa Sede (1976–1994): Texto y Comentario* (Madrid: Biblioteca de Autores Cristianos, 1999), 636ff. Luigi Mistó, "Paul VI and *Dignitatis Humanae:* Theory and Practice," in Ford, *Religious Liberty*, 12–38.

23. For definition and cataloging of the agreements of the last half century, see Martín de Agar, *Raccolta*, 10.

24. Pavan, "Ecumenism," 25.

25. Mistó, "Paul VI and *Dignitatis Humanae,"* 24.

26. Archbishop Jean-Louis Turan, "Presentazione," in Martín de Agar, *Raccolta*, 5.

27. Martín de Agar, *Raccolta*; and *I Concordati*. Regions covered by the various types of accords included in these anthologies: 16 accords from Latin America, 7 from Africa, 3 from the Middle East, 16 from Eastern Europe, and 73 from Western Europe (including 30 from the various states now members of modern Germany).

28. Conferencia Episcopal Española, *Los Acuerdos*, 203.

29. Walter Kasper, "Religious Freedom in Ecumenical Perspective," in *Building Bridges of Faith and Freedom*, ed. John Graz (Silver Spring, MD: General Conference of the Seventh-day Adventists, 2002), 29.

30. Bryan Hehir, "Catholicism and Democracy: Conflict, Change, and Collaboration," in *Change in Official Catholic Moral Teaching*, ed. Charles Curran (New York/Mahwah, NJ: Paulist Press, 2003), 28–31; see also Samuel Huntington, "Religion and the Third Wave," *National Interest* 24 (Summer 1991): 30.

31. See <http://www.unhchr.ch/html/menu2/7/b/mrei.htm>.

32. For the 1981 text, see <http://www.ohchr.org/english/law/religion.htm>.

33. Timothy Shah, "Legislating International Religious Freedom," Monday, November 20, 2006. In the *Pew Forum on Religion & the Public Life*, <http://pewforum.org/events/index.php?EventID=133>.

34. Minnerath, "Church/State Relations," 436.

35. See <http://www.eni.ch/>. See also Reformed Ecumenical Council News Exchange, <http://community.gospelcom.net/Brix?pageID=18813>.

36. See <http://www.worldevangelicalalliance.com/textonly/3rlc.htm>.

37. See <http://ola.adventist.org/>. Public Affairs and Religious Liberty, *Religious Freedom World Report: 2004–2005* (Silver Spring: Seventh-day Adventist Church, 2005).

38. See <http://usinfo.state.gov/usa/infousa/laws/majorlaw/intlrel.htm>. For an academic discussion and update on the literature, see <http://pewforum.org/events/index.php?EventID=133>.

39. In 2006 Archbishop Charles Chaput of Denver and Bishop Ricardo Ramírez of Las Cruces were the prominent Catholics on the commission; <http://www.uscirf.gov/>. See Ricardo Ramírez, "U.S. Commission on International Religious Freedom," *Stirrings: A Basilian Social Justice Newsletter,* (Summer 2005).

40. See <http://www.religiousfreedom.com/ http://www.churchstate.org/>.

41. Mistó, "Paul VI and *Dignitatis Humanae.*" Angelo Maffeis, ed., *Dignitatis Humane: La libertà religiosa in Paolo VI* (Brecia: Istituto Paolo VI, 2004).

42. *Ecclesiam Suam,* <http://www.vatican.va/holy_father/paul_vi/encyclicals/documents/hf_p-vi_enc_06081964_ecclesiam_en.html>.

43. In Mistó, "Paul VI and *Dignitatis Humanae,*" 32.

44. Ford, *Liberty,* 18.

45. Ibid., 22.

46. Saranyana Closa, *Teología en America Latína,* 384.

47. Bryan Hehir, "*Dignitatis Humanae* in the Pontificate of John Paul II," in Ford, *Religious Liberty,* 169–83. See also Pope John Paul II, *Essays on Religious Freedom* (Milwaukee: Catholic League for Religious and Civil Rights, 1984).

48. Silvia Scatena, *La fatica della libertà: L'elaborazione della dichiarazione "Dignitatis Humanae"* (Bologna: Il Mulino, 2002), 190.

49. See <http://www.vatican.va/holy_father/john_paul_ii/messages/peace/documents/hf_jp-ii_mes_08121997_xxxi-world-day-for-peace_en.html>.

50. See Herminio Rico, *John Paul and the Legacy of Dignitatis Humanae* (Washington, DC: Georgetown University Press, 2002). For a treatment of Pope John Paul's understanding of ethical development, see Brian Johnstone, "Faithful Action, The Catholic Moral Tradition and *Veritatis Splendor,*" *Studia Moralia* 31 (1993): 283–305.

51. Hehir, "Catholicism and Democracy," 36.

52. *Evangelium Vitae,* 19, 20; <http://www.vatican.va/holy_father/john_paul_ii/encyclicals/documents/hf_jp-ii_enc_25031995_evangelium-vitae_en.html>.

53. Josep Saranyana Closa, *Cien Años de Teología en América Latína* (Bogotá: CELAM, 2005), 103–16, 154–71.

54. Mary Doak, "Resisting the Eclipse of *Dignitatis Humanae*," *Horizons* 33, no. 1 (Spring 2006): 50.

55. For his reflections at the time of the council, see Joseph Ratzinger, *Theological Highlights of Vatican II* (New York: Paulist Press, 1966), 95–100, 143–46. For more recent comments, see his 2006 Christmas Address to the Roman Curia: <http://www.vatican.va/holy_father/benedict_xvi/speeches/2006/december/documents/hf_ben_xvi_spe_20061222_curia-romana_ en.html>.

On the one hand, one must counter a dictatorship of positivist reason that excludes God from the life of the community and from public organizations, thereby depriving man of his specific criteria of judgment.

On the other, one must welcome the true conquests of the Enlightenment, human rights and especially the freedom of faith and its practice, and recognize these also as being essential elements for the authenticity of religion.

As in the Christian community, where there has been a long search to find the correct position of faith in relation to such beliefs—a search that will certainly never be concluded once and for all—so also the Islamic world with its own tradition faces the immense task of finding the appropriate solutions in this regard.

56. *Deus Caritas Est* (December 25, 2005); <http://www.vatican.va/holy_father/benedict_xvi/encyclicals/documents/hf_ben-xvi_enc_20051225_deus-caritas-est_en.html>.

57. Given at the Fourth Italian Ecclesial Congress on the theme: "Witnesses of the Risen Christ, Hope of the World," October 19, 2006, Verona, Italy. <http://www.vatican.va/holy_father/benedict_xvi/speeches/2006/october/documents/hf_ben-xvi_spe_20061019_convegno-verona_en.html>.

58. Jeffrey Gros, "*Dignitatis Humanae* and Ecumenism," in Ford, *Religious Liberty*, 117–48, and J. Robert Nelson, "The Ecumenical Reception of the *Declaration on Religious Liberty*," in Ford, *Religious Liberty*, 153–64.

59. Kauffman, "American Reactions to *Dignitatis Humanae*," 71–88.

60. Alberigo and Komonchak, *History of Vatican II, Volume 5*, 107. Outler explains the role of the declaration for the observers: "For us, the declarations on religious liberty and non-Christians are tests of the good faith of the Council as a whole—and the progressive majority in the Council understands this and agrees with it. But in the deepest logic of the Council these things are

consequences or presuppositions of the really fundamental developments in liturgy, episcopal collegiality and the apostolate of the laity." ("Vatican II—Between Acts," undated between sessions III and IV, p. 6 in Stransky archives, Box 11.)

61. For a synopsis of some of the debates from different religious perspectives, see Johan D. van der Vyver, "Religious Freedom and Proselytism," *Ecumenical Review* 50, no. 4 (1988): 419–29.

62. Paul Blanshard, *Paul Blanshard on Vatican II* (Boston: Beacon Press, 1966).

63. See <http://www.au.org/site/PageServer>.

64. A. F. Carrillo de Albornoz, *Religious Liberty in the World* (Geneva: World Council of Churches, 1966), 9.

65. "Religious Freedom and the World Council of Churches," in *Religious Freedom* (New York: Paulist Press, 1966), 53–63; also in Stransky, *Declaration*, 174–96; and World Council of Churches, *The Ecumenical Review* 13 (1966).

66. See <http://www.prounione.urbe.it/dia-int/jwg/doc/i_jwg-n3_06.html>; <http://www.prounione.urbe.it/dia-int/jwg/doc/i_jwg-n5_1.html>; <http://www.prounione.urbe.it/dia-int/jwg/doc/i_jwg_n7dc.html>.

67. See Glenn Hinson, *Soul Liberty: The Doctrine of Religious Liberty* (Nashville: Convention Press, 1975).

68. Gros, "*Dignitatis Humanae* and Ecumenism," 124–28.

69. *Summons to Witness to Christ in Today's World*, <http://www.prounione.urbe.it/dia-int/b-rc/doc/i_b-rc_report1988.html>.

70. See <http://www.prounione.urbe.it/dia-int/e-rc/doc/i_e-rc_ev-cath.html>.

71. *Church, Evangelization, and the Bonds of Koinonia*, <http://www.prounione.urbe.it/dia-int/e-rc/doc/i_e-rc_report2002.html>. See Kasper, "Religious Freedom in Ecumenical Perspective," 31–34.

72. See <http://www.prounione.urbe.it/dia-int/pe-rc/doc/i_pe-rc_pent04.html>. See Thomas Stransky, "*Evangelization, Proselytism and Common Witness:* Reflections on This Report," *Information Service* (1998), 97: I–II, 57–61.

73. See S. Mark Heim, ed., *Faith to Creed* (Grand Rapids, MI: W. B. Eerdmans, 1991); Marlin Miller and Barbara Nelson Gingrich, eds., *The Church's Peace Witness* (Grand Rapids, MI: W. B. Eerdmans, 1994); John Rempel and Jeffrey Gros, eds., *The Fragmentation of the Church and its Unity in Peace Making* (Grand Rapids, MI: W. B. Eerdmans), 2001.

74. See <http://www.prounione.urbe.it/dia-int/mn-rc/doc/i_mn-rc_fr2003.html>. See also Gros, "*Dignitatis Humanae* and Ecumenism," 141–42.

75. Gros, "*Dignitatis Humanae* and Ecumenism," 133–41.

76. See <http://www.prounione.urbe.it/dia-int/dc-rc/doc/i_dc-rc_2002.html>.

77. Gros, *"Dignitatis Humanae* and Ecumenism," 130–33.

78. *Uniatism, Method of Union of the Past, and the Present Search for Full Communion*; <http://www.prounione.urbe.it/dia-int/o-rc/doc/i_o-rc_07_balamand_eng.html>.

79. The question of "canonical territories" will also need to be addressed, in due course. "Catholics and traditional Protestant churches share a common claim freely to proclaim the gospel everywhere and to reject unfair methods of carrying out missionary work. It must be recognized that Orthodoxy has not shared the experience of the Catholic Church, which struggled for centuries to win its autonomy from the states." The claim of Russia and other Orthodox churches to responsibility for particular territories will need to be jointly examined to resolve tensions and articulate a common meaning for religious freedom. Minnerath, "Church/State Relations," 434–35. See also Edward Cassidy, *Ecumenism and Interreligious Dialogue: Unitatis Redintegratio, Nostra Aetate* (New York/Mahwah, NJ: Paulist Press, 2005), 112–17.

## THE STATE OF THE QUESTIONS

1. Herminio Rico, *John Paul and the Legacy of Dignitatis Humanae* (Washington, DC: Georgetown University Press, 2002), 106. See also Leslie Griffin, *"Dignitatis Humanae,"* in *Modern Catholic Social Teaching*, ed. Kenneth Himes (Washington, DC: Georgetown University Press, 2004), 257. Richard Regan, "John Courtney Murray, The American Bishops and the *Declaration on Religious Liberty,"* in *Religious Liberty: Paul VI and Dignitatis Humanae*, ed. John Ford (Brecia: Pubblicazioni dell'Istituto Paolo VI, 1995), 51–66. Richard Regan, *Conflict and Consensus: Religious Freedom and the Second Vatican Council* (New York: Macmillan, 1977). Giuseppe Alberigo and Joseph A. Komonchak, eds., *History of Vatican II, Volume 4: Church as Communion, Third Period and Intersession, September 1964–September 1965* (Maryknoll, NY: Orbis Books/Leuven, Belgium: Peeters, 2003) and *History of Vatican II, Volume 5: The Council and the Transition, The Fourth Period and the End of the Council, September 1965–December 1965* (Maryknoll, NY: Orbis Books/Leuven, Belgium: Peeters, 2006). Leon Hooper and Todd Whitmore, eds., *John Courtney Murray and the Growth of Tradition* (Kansas City: Sheed & Ward, 1996). Joseph Chinnici, *"Dignitatis Humanae Personae:* Surveying the Landscape for Its Reception in the United States," *U.S. Catholic Historian*, *"Dignitatis Humanae*, The Declaration of Religious Liberty, on its Fortieth Anniversary," 24, no. 1 (Winter 2006): 64. Joseph Komonchak, "The American Contribution to *Dignitatis Humanae:* The Role of John Courtney

Murray, SJ," in *U.S. Catholic Historian* 24, no. 1 (Winter 2006), 1–20. Donald Pelotte, *John Courtney Murray: Theologian in Conflict* (New York: Paulist Press, 1975).

2. William Portier, "Theology of Manners as Theology of Containment: John Courtney Murray and *Dignitatis Humanae* Forty Years After," *U.S. Catholic Historian* 24, no. 1 (Winter 2006): 105.

3. Michael Baxter, "John Courtney Murray," in *Blackwell Companion to Political Theology*, ed. Peter Scott and William Cavanaugh (Oxford: Blackwell Publishing, 2004), 154.

4. Correspondence and addresses given toward the end of his life offer some indication of how he might have responded to some of these developments; see John T. McGreevy, *Catholicism and American Freedom* (New York: W. W. Norton & Co., 2003), 245–47.

5. See Portier, "Theology of Manners," 102–5.

6. Martín de Agar, "Problimatiche recenti concordati," in *Raccolta di concordati 1950–1999* (Rome: Libreria Editrice Vaticana, 2000), 16–21.

7. See Pietro Pavan, "Repercussions of the Declaration 'Dignitatis Humanae' in the Life of the Church," *First World Conference on Religious Freedom* (March 21–23, 1977) cited in Griffin, *Dignitatis Humanae.* See also James Burtchaell, "Religious Freedom," in *Modern Catholicism: Vatican II and After*, ed. Adrian Hastings (Oxford: Oxford University Press, 1991), 120–25 for an analysis for developments within the Catholic Church that resonate with declaration principles.

8. Mary Doak, "Resisting the Eclipse of *Dignitatis Humanae*," *Horizons* 33, no. 1 (Spring 2006): 48; see also Paul Manuel, Lawrence Reardon, and Clyde Wilcox, eds., *The Catholic Church and the Nation-State* (Washington, DC: Georgetown University Press, 2006), 63–64.

9. John Courtney Murray, "The Declaration on Religious Freedom," in *Change in Official Catholic Moral Teaching*, ed. Charles Curran (New York/Mahwah, NJ: Paulist Press, 2003), 11.

10. Peter Hünermann, "The Final Weeks of the Council," in Alberigo and Komonchak, *History of Vatican II, Volume 5*, 475.

11. See <http://www.vatican.va/edocs/ENG0219/__P3.HTM>; see also Pope John Paul II's apostolic letter initiating the new millennium, *Novo Millennio Ineunte*, 55; <http://www.vatican.va/holy_father/john_paul_ii/apost_letters/documents/hf_jp-ii_apl_20010106_novo-millennio-ineunte_en.html>.

12. *Dominus Iesus*, 22; <http://www.vatican.va/roman_curia/congregations/cfaith/documents/rc_con_cfaith_doc_20000806_dominus-iesus_en.html>.

13. A third kind of pluralism has been suggested: "engaged religious diversity." See John Borelli, "Catholics and Interreligious Relations," *Monastic*

*Interreligious Dialogue Bulletin* 64 ( May 2000), <http://monasticdialog.com/a. php?id=301>.

14. See, for example, Tariq Ramadan, *Western Muslims and the Future of Islam* (New York: Oxford University Press, 2004); Abdulaziz Sachedina, *The Islamic Roots of Democratic Pluralism* (Oxford UniversityPress, 2001); Christian Troll, "Il Pensiero Progressista Nell'Islàm Contemporaneo," *La Civiltà Cattolíca* ( July 15, 2006), III:3746, 123–35.

15. Walter Kasper, "Religious Freedom in Ecumenical Perspective," in *Building Bridges of Faith and Freedom*, ed. John Graz (Silver Spring, MD: General Conference of the Seventh-day Adventists, 2002), 28.

16. John Nurser, *For All Peoples and All Nations: The Ecumenical Church and Human Rights* (Washington, DC: Georgetown University Press, 2005), 179–80; Mary Ann Glendon, *A World Made New: Eleanor Roosevelt and the Universal Declaration of Human Rights* (New York: Random House, 2001), 239; for the 1993 UN debate on human rights see Samuel Huntington, *The Clash of Civilizations and the Remaking of World Order* (New York: Simon & Schuster, 1996), 195–98. See also John L. Esposito, *Unholy War: Terror in the Name of Islam* (Oxford: Oxford University Press, 2002). For a recent statement of Pope Benedict XVI, see his address to the Roman Curia, December 22, 2006, <http://www.vatican.va/holy_father/benedict_xvi/speeches/2006/december/ documents/hf_ben_xvi_spe_20061222_curia-romana_en.html>.

17. See Vladimir Feodorov, "Religious Freedom in Russia Today," *Ecumenical Review* 50, no. 4 (1998): 449–59; and Paul Mojzes, *Religious Liberty in Eastern Europe and the USSR: Before and After the Great Transformation* (Boulder: Eastern European Monographs, 1992).

18. See, for example, Éric Benet and Roselyne Chenu, eds., *La Liberté Religieuse dans le Judaïsme, le Christianisme et L'Islam* (Paris: Les Éditions du Cerf, 1981).

19. James T. Burtchaell "Perspectives on Education, the State, and Religion: The State as an Established Religion," in *Partners in Peace and Education*, ed. Ronald White and Eugene Fisher (Grand Rapids, MI: William B. Eerdmans), 1988.

20. See Peter Steinfels, *A People Adrift: The Crisis of the Roman Catholic Church in America* (New York: Simon & Schuster, 2003), 203–52.

21. See É.-J. de Smedt, "Éducation a la Liberté Religieuse a L'Intérieur de L'Église Catholique," in *La Libertè Religieuse*, ed. Yves Congar, Jérôme Hamer, et al. (Paris: Les Éditions du Cerf, 1967), 216–35.

22. Alberigo and Komonchak, *History of Vatican II, Volume 5*, 92.

23. In this he seems more cautious than Murray. See Agnes de Dreuzy, "*Dignitatis Humanae* as an Encounter Between Two 'Towering Theologians,'

John Courtney Murray, SJ, and Yves Congar, OP," *U.S. Catholic Historian* 24, no. 1 (Winter 2006), 33–44.

24. See Christian Smith, et al., *Soul Searching: The Religious and Spiritual Lives of American Teenagers* (Oxford: Oxford University Press, 2005); Donald Wurel, "What a Catechist Is and Does," *Origins* 36, no. 23 (November 16, 2006), 362–367.

25. On some of the challenges among young U.S. Catholics, especially Hispanics, see Dean Hoge, et al., *Young Adult Catholics: Religion in the Culture of Choice* (Notre Dame, IN: University of Notre Dame Press, 2001), 146.

26. Enrique Garcia Ahumada, *Teología de la Educación* (Santiago: Fundación Tiberíades, 2003). For parallel developments in North America, see Chinnici, "*Dignitatis Humanae Personae*," 73–79.

27. For a discussion of the variety of national Latin American Catholic episcopates' responses on the eve of the 1992 CELAM (Council of Latin American Episcopal Conferences) meeting, see Jeffrey Gros, "Culture Wars: The Larger Picture," *New Theological Review* 6, no. 4 (November 1993), 79–87.

28. See Josep Saranyana Closa, *Teología en América Latína* (Madrid: Iberoamericana, 2002), 179–77.

29. Margaret Crahan, "Catholicism and Human Rights in Latin America," in *Religious Diversity and Human Rights*, ed. I. Bloom, J. P. Martin, and W. L. Proudfoot (New York: Columbia University Press, 1996), 274.

30. In Yves Congar, *Mon Journal du Councile*, vol. I (Paris: Les Éditions du Cerf, 2002), 228.

31. McGreevy, *Catholicism and American Freedom*, 194.

32. Pietro Pavan, "Fourth Draft or Fourth Schema," *Information Documentation on the Conciliar Church* (November 30, 1966), Doss. 66–67, 3.

33. See Bishop Elias Zoghby, "The Universal Catechism Proposed by the Extraordinary Synod of Bishops," 85–90; and Berard Marthaler, "The Synod and the Catechism," 91–98, in *Synod 1985—An Evaluation*, ed. Giuseppe Alberigo and James Provost (Edinburgh: T. & T. Clark Publishers, Ltd., 1986).

34. For the theological theories implicit in these debates, see Avery Dulles, *Models of Revelation*(Garden City: Doubleday & Company, Inc. 1982).

PART V

# FURTHER READING

RELIGIOUS FREEDOM

Carrillo de Albornoz, A. F. *Roman Catholicism and Religious Liberty*. Geneva: World Council of Churches, 1959.

Fogarty, Gerald P. *The Vatican and the American Hierarchy from 1870 to 1965*, Wilmington, DE: Michael Glazier, 1985.

Hooper, J. Leon, ed. *John Courtney Murray: Religious Liberty, Catholic Struggles with Pluralism*. Louisville: Westminster/John Knox, 1993.

———. *Bridging the Sacred and the Secular: Selected Writings of John Courtney Murray*, Washington, DC: Georgetown University Press, 1994.

Koshy, Ninan. "The Ecumenical Understanding of Religious Liberty: The Contribution of the World Council of Churches." *Journal of Church and State* 38 (1996): 137–54.

McGreevy, John T. *Catholicism and American Freedom*, New York: W. W. Norton & Co., 2003.

Mecham, J. Lloyd. *Church and State in Latin America*. Chapel Hill: The University of North Carolina Press, 1966.

Murray, John Courtney. *We Hold These Truths: Reflections on the American Proposition*. New York: Sheed & Ward, 1960.

Pelotte, Donald. *John Courtney Murray: Theologian in Conflict*. New York: Paulist Press, 1975.

Wogaman, Philip. *Protestant Faith and Religious Liberty*. Nashville: Abingdon Press, 1967.


THE COUNCIL

Congar, Yves, Jérôme Hamer, et al. *La Libertè Religieuse*. Paris: Les Éditions du Cerf, 1967.

Edelby, Neophytos, and Teodoro Jiménez-Urresti, eds. *Religious Freedom*. New York: Paulist Press, 1965.

Regan, Richard. *Conflict and Consensus: Religious Freedom and the Second Vatican Council.* New York: Macmillan, 1977.

Scatena, Silvia. *La fatica della libertà: L'elaborazione della dichiarazione "Dignitatis Humanae."* Bologna: Il Mulino, 2002.

Stransky, Thomas. *Declaration on Religious Freedom of Vatican Council II.* New York, Paulist Press, 1967.

### DEVELOPMENTS FROM THE COUNCIL

Burghardt, Walter, ed. *Religious Freedom: 1965–1975.* New York: Paulist Press, 1977.

Cair, W. Onclin. *Church and State: Changing Paradigms,* Leuven: Peeters, 1999.

Deiros, Pablo. "Religious Freedom in Latin America." *Transformation* 8, no. 2 (April/June 1991): 12–15.

Commission of the Churches on International Affairs. *Religious Liberty: Some Major Considerations in the Current Debate.* Geneva: World Council of Churches, 1987.

———. *Study Paper on Religious Liberty.* Geneva: World Council of Churches, 1981.

Coste, René. *Théologie de la Liberté Religieuse.* Gembloux: Éditions J. Duclot, 1969.

Ford, John, ed. *Religious Liberty: Paul VI and Dignitatis Humanae.* Brecia: Pubblicazioni dell'Istituto Paolo VI, 1995.

Grasso, Kenneth L., and Robert P. Hunt, eds. *Dignitatis Humanae: Contemporary Reflections on Vatican II's Declaration on Religious Liberty.* Lanham: Rowman & Littlefield Publishers, 2006.

Hooper, Leon, and Todd Whitmore, eds. *John Courtney Murray and the Growth of Tradition.* Kansas City: Sheed & Ward, 1996.

Koshy, Ninan. *Religious Freedom in a Changing World.* Geneva: World Council of Churches, 1992.

Murray, John Courtney, ed., *Religious Liberty: An End and a Beginning.* New York: The Macmillan Company, 1966.

Rico, Herminio. *John Paul and the Legacy of Dignitatis Humanae.* Washington, DC: Georgetown University Press, 2002.

Sigmund, Paul E. ed. *Religious Freedom and Evangelization in Latin America.* Maryknoll, NY: Orbis Books, 1999.

### ECUMENICAL DIALOGUES

"American Baptist–Catholic Dialogue." In *Building Unity,* edited by Jeffrey Gros and Joseph Burgess, 35–51. New York/Mahwah, NJ: Paulist Press, 1989.

*Growth in Agreement I: Reports and Agreed Statements of Ecumenical Conversations on a World Level.* Edited by Harding Meyer and Lukas Vischer, New York: Paulist Press, 1984.

*Growth in Agreement II: Reports and Agreed Statements of Ecumenical Conversations on a World Level, 1982–Mid 1998.* Edited by Jeffrey Gros, Harding Meyer, and William Rusch. Geneva: World Council of Churches, 2000.

*Growth in Agreement III: International Dialogue Texts and Agreed Statements, 1998–2005.* Edited by Jeffrey Gros, Thomas Best, and Lorelei Fuchs. Geneva: World Council of Churches, 2007.

Joint Working Group Between the Roman Catholic Church and the World Council of Churches. "The Challenge of Proselytism and the Calling to Common Witness." In *Growth in Agreement II*, 891–99.

Meeking, Basil, and John Stott. "Evangelical Roman Catholic Dialogue on Mission." in *Growth in Agreement II*, 399–437.

Mennonite World Conference–Catholic Dialogue. "Called Together to Be Peacemakers." In *Growth in Agreement III*, 206–67.

Orthodox-Catholic Dialogue. "Uniatism, Method of Union of the Past and the Present Search for Full Communion." In *Growth in Agreement II*, 680–85.

Pentecostal-Catholic Dialogue. "Evangelization, Proselytism and Common Witness." In *Growth in Agreement II*, 753–79.

"Religious Freedom and Proselytism." *Ecumenical Review* 50, no. 4 (1998): 417–71.

"Summons to Witness to Christ in Today's World: A Report on the Baptist-Roman Catholic International Conversation 1984–1988." In *Growth in Agreement II*, 373–85.

World Council of Churches' Central Committee. "Christian Witness, Proselytism, and Religious Liberty." In *A Documentary History of the Faith and Order Movement: 1927–1963*, edited by Lukas Vischer, 183–98. St. Louis: The Bethany Press, 1963.

World Evangelical Alliance–Pontifical Council for Promoting Christian Unity. "Church, Evangelization, and *Koinonia*." In *Growth in Agreement III*, 268–95.

# INDEX